PSYCHOANALYTIC PERSPECTIVES
ON A TURBULENT WORLD

In Memory of Laurence J. Gould

PSYCHOANALYTIC PERSPECTIVES ON A TURBULENT WORLD

Edited by

Halina Brunning and Mario Perini

KARNAC

First published in 2010 by
Karnac Books Ltd
118 Finchley Road
London NW3 5HT

British Library Cataloguing in Publication Data

A C.I.P. for this book is available from the British Library

ISBN-13: 978-1-85575-810-0

Typeset by Vikatan Publishing Solutions (P) Ltd., Chennai, India

www.karnacbooks.com

CONTENTS

v

This book is dedicated to
Szame, Adam and Basia
and to
Paola and Francisco

ACKNOWLEDGEMENTS

We wish to acknowledge and thank the following:

Sage Publications and NYUP for allowing us to reprint two original papers in this volume (details in relevant chapters).

The contributors to this book for their professionalism, high quality of collaboration and creativity.

Jim Krantz for his encouragement and positive response to the original ideas behind this volume.

Olya Khaleelee for her help with selecting appropriate images for the three acts and for offering us support throughout the editorial process.

Kristof Bien and Simon Brunning for their technical assistance.

THE CAST OF CHARACTERS

Halina Brunning is a chartered clinical psychologist, freelance organizational consultant and executive coach. She has published extensively on clinical and organizational issues and has co-edited several books, including *Executive Coaching: Systems Psychodynamic Perspective* (Karnac, 2006). She runs training events on coaching in Europe and the UK for the HEC, the Coach Academy, Il Nodo, Rasztow, BPS and other institutions. She is an associate fellow of the British Psychological Society, member of the International Society for the Psychoanalytic Study of Organizations (ISPSO), OPUS, Association of Coaching, founder member of the BPS Coaching Psychology Forum, and currently an associate with the Tavistock Consultancy Service, the Learning and Skills Improvement Service, and the National College for Leadership of Schools and Children's Services. She tries to integrate visual art and symbolic representation in all her professional work, including her clinical, consulting, and coaching practice.

Wesley Carr KCVO, MA, PhD is an ordained priest in the Church of England. Appointments include canon residentiary at Chelmsford Cathedral, for 10 years dean of Bristol and from 1997 dean of

Westminster. He holds honorary degrees from the University of the West of England and the University of Sheffield. Parkinson's disease forced his retirement in 2006. He had a long association with the Tavistock Institute group relations programme and its approach to organizations. He has had an international career in conferences (including directing "Leicester") and consultation. He is a prolific author with a number of books, including with Edward Shapiro *Lost in Familiar Places*, numerous reviews and articles. He has been honoured to give both the Margaret Rioch and the Eric Miller memorial lectures.

H. Shmuel Erlich is a training and supervising analyst, faculty member and past president of the Israel Psychoanalytic Society; associate professor emeritus at the Hebrew University of Jerusalem where he held the Sigmund Freud chair in psychoanalysis, and recipient of the Sigourney Award for distinguished contributions to psychoanalysis. He is co-founder of OFEK—The Israel Association for the Study of Group and Organizational Processes, has worked extensively in group relations conferences, and consults to individuals and organizations. He is one of the initiators of the German and Israeli "Nazareth" conferences, and founding member of PCCA—Partners in Confronting Collective Atrocities. He has published extensively on psychoanalytic and applied subjects, and is co-author of *Fed with Tears—Poisoned with Milk: Germans and Israelis—The Past in the Present*.

Laurence J. Gould PhD is the director of the Socio-Psychoanalytic Training Program, The Institute for Psychoanalytic Training and Research (IPTAR). He is also the founding co-director of the Program in Organizational Development and Consultation in Israel, and a founding member of the International Society for the Psychoanalytic Study of Organizations (ISPSO). Dr Gould is a co-editor of *The Systems Psychodynamics of Organizations* (Karnac, 2001), and *Experiential Learning in Organizations* (Karnac, 2004). In addition, he is the founding co-editor of Organizational and Social Dynamics. Dr Gould practises psychoanalysis and organizational consultation in New York City.

Olya Khaleelee is a psychoanalytic psychotherapist, corporate psychologist and organizational consultant, with a particular interest in organizational transition and transformation. She has worked with the Tavistock Institute for over 25 years in developing group relations both in the UK and abroad, has been on the staff of many conferences and was the first female director of the Leicester Conference, which explores authority, leadership and organization from a psychoanalytic and systemic perspective. She was for many years director of OPUS: an organisation for promoting understanding in society, and is also a past chairwoman of the council of the London Centre for Psychotherapy.

James Krantz is an organizational consultant and researcher from New York City. He is a principal of Worklab Consulting, which concentrates on strategy implementation, senior team development, and work process design. Dr Krantz has a PhD in systems sciences from the Wharton School and has taught on the faculties of Yale University and the Wharton School. He is past president of the International Society for the Psychoanalytic Study of Organizations, a fellow of the A.K. Rice Institute, and a member of OPUS. His writing has focused on the unconscious background of work life and on the socio-psychological challenges posed by emerging forms of organizations.

Susan Long, an organizational researcher and consultant, formerly professor of creative and sustainable organization, now an adjunct professor at RMIT University in Melbourne, Australia, where she supervises research students and conducts organizational research. As an organizational consultant she works with organizational change, executive coaching, role analysis, team development, and management training. She is currently president of the Psychoanalytic Studies Association of Australasia. Her research interests involve participatory action research projects in industry, government organizations, health, education, and correctional services. She has published five books, the latest being *The Perverse Organisation and its Deadly Sins* (Karnac, 2008).

Mario Perini MD chair of Il Nodo group and scientific advisor for Italian Group Relations Conferences Programme ("Seminari di Arona"), is a psychiatrist, psychoanalyst and organizational consultant, a member of the Italian Psychoanalytic Association, International Psycho-Analytic Association, and International Society for the Psychoanalytic Study of Organizations. He works as a consultant in the public, private, and voluntary sectors, a trainer for professional and management education, a group supervisor, and in private practice as a psychotherapist and personal coach. Professor of group dynamics at the Post-Graduate School of Health Psychology, Turin University, in 2007 he published the book *L'organizzazione nascosta* ("The hidden organization").

Howard S. Schwartz is a professor of organizational behaviour at Oakland University. He earned his PhD at Cornell University. He is the author of *Narcissistic Process and Corporate Decay: The Theory of the Organization Ideal* (New York University Press), from which the chapter in this book is taken. His current interest is in the psychodynamics underlying political correctness and the capacity of these psychodynamics to destroy organization. This investigation has resulted in two books: *The Revolt of the Primitive: An Inquiry into the Roots of Political Correctness*, published in 2003 by Transaction Publishers, and *Society against Itself: Political Correctness and Organizational Self-Destruction*, which will be published in 2010 by Karnac. Schwartz was one of the founding members of ISPSO.

Burkard Sievers Dipl Soz is professor emeritus of organization development in the Schumpeter School of Business and Economics at Bergische Universität, Wuppertal in Germany. In his research he focuses on unconscious dynamics in management and organization from a socio-analytic and systemic perspective. In 1995, he was awarded the prize for participation by HBK Bank in Antwerp, Belgium, for his book *Work, Death and Life Itself — Essays on Management and Organisation* (Berlin/New York: de Gruyter, 1994). He is past president (2007-2009) of the ISPSO and editor of *Psychoanalytic Studies of Organizations: Contributions from the International Society for the Psychoanalytic Study of Organizations (ISPSO) 1983-2008* (London: Karnac, 2009).

Lionel Stapley PhD is the director of OPUS, a world leader in providing a psycho-social understanding of societal dynamics that exists to promote "the reflective citizen". He is an organizational consultant working with individuals, groups, and organizations in the public and private sectors in the UK and other countries. He heads up the OPUS group processes programme and co-directs the advanced training workshops. He has a particular interest in organizational and societal culture and has written and presented papers and provided workshops on this topic over a 30 year period. He is the chair of the editorial management committee of the OPUS international journal *Organisational & Social Dynamics* and a member of ISPSO. His most recent publications are *Individuals, Groups and Organizations Beneath the Surface* and *Globalization and Terrorism: Death of a Way of Life* (Karnac, both 2006).

Mark Stein PhD is a senior lecturer in leadership and organizational behaviour at Imperial College Business School, Imperial College, London. He has a long-standing interest in the psychoanalytic study of leadership, groups, and organizations, and has undertaken many years of research, consultancy, coaching, and teaching using these ideas. His publications include two edited books and numerous journal articles. He received an Emerald Citation of Excellence for his paper on "Critical period of disasters" (published in *Human Relations* in 2004) and the Richard Normann Prize for an article on "Toxicity in organizations" (published in *Organization Studies* in 2007).

Vamik D. Volkan is an emeritus professor of psychiatry at the University of Virginia School of Medicine, an emeritus training and supervising analyst at the Washington Psychoanalytic Institute and the Senior Erik Erikson Scholar at the Austen Riggs Center in Stockbridge, Massachusetts. He holds honorary doctorate degrees from Kuopio University, Finland and from Ankara University, Turkey. He is the author or co-author of 40 books and the editor or co-editor of 10 more. He was a past president of the International Society of Political Psychology, the Virginia Psychoanalytic Society, the Turkish-American Neuropsychiatric Association, and the American College of Psychoanalysts. Dr Volkan received the Sigmund Freud Award given by the city of Vienna, Austria in collaboration with the World Council of Psychotherapy.

NOTES FROM THE EDITORS

Halina Brunning and Mario Perini

Although the initial idea of editing a book on this theme appeared separately in the mind of one of us (HB), this book actually originated from a couple of historical encounters between the two co-editors. The first occurred some years ago, when we met for the first time in Italy and agreed to run a workshop on executive coaching, which set the foundation for our enduring collaboration. The second happened in the summer of 2009 when we both attended the annual meeting of ISPSO (International Society for the Psychoanalytic Study of Organization), in Toledo, Spain, where we joined a broad community of colleagues to reflect on recent turbulent processes related to diversity, social complexity, and global political instability.

In a way our book is in itself a challenge of diversity and a trans-cultural enterprise: two genders, two nationalities, two professions, two different mother tongues, close collaboration with a wide and diverse group of colleagues from six countries in four continents. All are connected by one common idiom: a sort of merger, a cross-cultural fertilization and at the same time a complex migratory phenomenon between psychoanalysis, systems theory, sociology, politics, and economics. (Actually one of us

(Brunning, 1999) wrote a paper where merger is seen as a sort of migration process.)

As a matter of fact, migration is an inherent part of the history of psychoanalysis, from Freud's flight to London to escape from a Nazified Austria to the European analysts' mass movement to the United States, and the exodus of many analysts from Argentina during the military dictatorship. Several fruitful developments within analytic research and practice—among which we could also consider the Tavistock tradition—might be seen as a consequence of this worldwide migratory process of people and ideas.

A less dramatic migration involved Italy where one of the co-editors (MP) was born, lives and works. From the 18th century onwards Italy was a traditional destination for European artists, for their cultural and "inner" journeys. Freud himself often used to spend his summer holidays in Lavarone, near Trento, and many Italian analysts—like Musatti, Fachinelli, Fornari, and others—dared to leave their secure rooms and settings to "migrate" into the outer world and approach social institutions with their analytical lenses.

The central core of the book is psychoanalysis "leaning out of the consulting room window", so to speak, looking at the real external world. Firstly, we wanted to address a view that psychoanalysis and the analytic community had never been much interested in exploring the external reality, including issues concerned with social institutions, politics, work, money, and so on, or that psychoanalysis had nothing to say about these issues and should not venture into this domain of thought or praxis. Historically, Freud did not seem that attracted by the idea of building a "psychoanalytic sociology". Though personally he was interested in cultural issues like war, education, or religion, after his first, promising study of group processes and the dynamics of the leadership (1921), he did not develop these views further, turning his attention more to the origins of human civilization and the taming of instinctual drives by education.

It is an established fact that Freud's conviction that the early experiences of seduction reported by his patients were just mere fantasies paved the way for a growing loss of relevance of external reality and the role it played in psychoanalytic thinking. Although in Group Psychology and Analysis of the Ego Freud stated that "from the very first individual psychology ... is at the same time social psychology as well" (1921, p. 69), over time psychoanalysis would appear less and less engaged in questioning human institutions and "disturbing the universe". Social phenomena would often be read under the reductionist perspective of the individual's subjectivity and personal life story, with a prevailing emphasis on the perceived over the real. Some anecdotal stories, most likely fake, circulated: one was about analysts continuing to interpret fear of loss in their patients while thieves were breaking into their apartments; another, from the Second World War period, concerning a "controversial discussion" between Kleinians and Anna Freud's followers on the theme of death instinct. It was said that Donald Winnicott warned his esteemed colleagues that in the real world outside, real bombs were falling on London and they had better seek immediate and real cover! (As the legend goes according to Scarfone (2002), German bombs were pouring down on London while two of the three more or less formal groups of British psychoanalysts were fiercely battling each other in what were to be remembered in psychoanalytic history as the "Controversial Discussions". According to the same anecdote, while the discussions carried on, no less violent in a way than the bombing itself—which in the meantime grew more intense—a member of the third group, Winnicott, would raise a timid hand and, when finally given the right to speak, he would suggest that they postpone whatever urgent theoretical issue they were debating and all go for shelter.)

On the other hand the attempts made in the USA by Karen Horney, Eric Fromm, Harry Stack Sullivan, and the Williams Alanson White Institute to set the foundations for a "social psychoanalysis" were hastily knocked out by the International Psychoanalytic Association (IPA) as a "watered-down" psychoanalysis, and a more or less explicit judgmental stance on psychoanalysis as applied to social and political life.

In her chapter "Psychoanalysis and War" in Covington's volume *Terrorism and War* (2002) Diane Birkett notices that "psychoanalysis has curiously little to say about world events" and addresses them "almost exclusively in terms of the inner life of the individual". In the following chapter in the same volume Isabel Hunter-Brown replies to Birkett's argument, remarking that there is some evidence that psychoanalysis does take external world and actual traumatic experiences into account, and she quotes Freud's statement that "emphasis on an early experience does not imply underestimation of later ones".

Despite evidence that official psychoanalysis has had problems with resistance to addressing the question of *external reality* and to drawing a consistent theoretical and practical framework for a dynamic understanding of social processes and organizations, it is also true—as Hunter-Brown points out—that several IPA analysts did try to cope with this avoidant attitude and launched brave explorations beyond the traditional borders.

Let us name a few important developments pointing to this trend, to begin with social experiments of Vera Schmidt and her Psycho-analytic Nursery in Moscow, the so-called "Freudian left" (Fenichel, Reich, and others), the developments originated within and around the Frankfurt School. A longer list of examples would include:

- Bion, Sutherland, Rickman, Jaques, Menzies, Turquet, and others working at the Tavistock on the frontier of groups, work, and organizations;
- Balint on family medicine;
- Winnicott on child upbringing and the mothering environment;
- Kris on war propaganda;
- Erikson on the impact of social structure on the development of the individual;
- Segal and Fornari on war and nuclear threat;
- Mitscherlich and the psycho-social research at the Sigmund-Freud-Institut in Frankfurt;
- Money-Kyrle on politics;
- Musatti and the industrial anthropology at Olivetti;
- Foulkes and Kaës on group analysis and institutions;
- Benedetti, Cremerius, Morgenthaler and others on psychotherapy and human sciences;
- Main and Hinshelwood on therapeutic community;
- Paumelle, Lebovici, Woodbury, Racamier, and the pioneering community psychiatry experiences of the French "Secteur" and the "institutional psychotherapy";
- Moses, Erlich, and other Jewish and German analysts on the Holocaust and the Israeli-Palestinian conflict in the light of the Nazareth/Cyprus Group Relations Conferences;
- Volkan on ethnic conflicts and international relationships;

- Viderman, Tuckett, and others on money, economics, and financial markets;
- Amati Sas on torture and refugees;
- Bauleo, Langer, and other Argentinean analysts involved in the fight against dictatorship;
- Kets de Vries, Obholzer, Shapiro, and others on leadership, power, and authority;

and many others, more or less renowned, within or outside the IPA, which space prevents us from mentioning.

On the threshold of the 21st century, in a world increasingly traumatized and pressured by political and economic turbulence, the IPA decided to create an "Outreach Committee" with many local committees established by its regional societies, all given a specific mandate of building an interface with society at large. (Outreach activities are aimed "to interchange with and learn more about the surrounding culture; to develop interventions derived from psychoanalysis; to increase involvement with universities and mental health disciplines, social sciences, and humanities; to establish international networks of analysts working in these settings; and to respond to negative views about psychoanalysis" (Holder, 2005)).

The aim was to address the "problems of decreasing analytic practice" as well as to explore the border territories of psychoanalysis. The idea was to include attempts at understanding and making thinkable catastrophic processes like post-9/11 terrorism, globalization, the ethnic, religious and commercial wars, the growing risks for the environment, etc.

Two psychoanalytically-inspired organizations that have felt comfortable with this discourse for over a quarter of century are in our view OPUS ("an organisation for promoting understanding of society") and ISPSO (International Society for Psychoanalytic Study of Organizations). We are both members of ISPSO and one of us is also a member of OPUS. It should therefore be of no surprise that, in planning this volume, we have invited colleagues associated with both organizations to contribute their thinking to this book.

Let us end by saying that in this turbulent world of ours, where recently we have all had to confront a number of exploding myths (like self-regulation of the free market, the West exporting democracy all over the world but with the help of tanks, the overall "well-being and safety" ensured by technology, etc., etc., to mention but a few), has the time now come for psychoanalysis to renew its mission? Against this background, what might the mission of psychoanalysis and psychoanalytic thinking be?

Not an easy one, really, nor a popular one: to bring "the plague" of uncomfortable truths in a world confused and terrified by reality, where feelings are uncontained, people abandoned to their own anxieties by uncertain or unreliable leaders, and disappearing institutions. Against this background can psychoanalytic thinking help people to begin to trust their own minds, to encourage thinking beyond slogans, beyond sound bites and beyond the politically correct, to look for some solutions to the turbulence?

If this is too lofty an expectation, can the psychoanalytic framework at least offer an alternative explanation of persistent troubling and turbulent phenomena and help us all, at least to contain the paralysing anxiety, to bring a fresh perspective to old troubles, and to offer some realistic hope?

With this in mind we are offering this volume to the reader.

References

Birkett, D. (1992). Psychoanalysis and War. *British Journal of Psychotherapy, 8*; and in: C. Covington et al. (Eds.), *Terrorism and War: Unconscious Dynamics of Political Violence*. London: Karnac, 2002.

Brunning, H. (1999). Merger as an emigration –towards the Psychology of organisational mergers. *Organisations and People* (Journal of the AMED), *6*(4): 38-42.

Eizirik, C. L. (2005). "Psychoanalysis and the IPA: the future is not an illusion" (The new President's column - from President-elect Cláudio Laks Eizirik). *International Psychoanalysis*, June 2005, *14*(1): 16–17. www.ipa.org.uk/Files/media/PrevSite/Docs/NewsMagazines/IPA_ENG_14.1.pdf

Freud, S. (1921). Group Psychology and the Analysis of the Ego. *S. E.*, *23*: 65-144. London: Hogarth.

Holder, A. (Ed.) (2005). *International Psychoanalysis, 14*(1): 17.

Hunter-Brown, I. (1992). Psychoanalysis and War—Response to Diana Birkett. *British Journal of Psychotherapy*, 8; and in C. Covington et al. (Eds.), *Terrorism and War: Unconscious Dynamics of Political Violence*. London: Karnac, 2002.

Scarfone, D. (2002). Controversial discussions, the issue of differences in method. *International Journal of Psychoanalysis*, 83: 453-456.

INVITATION TO THE DRAMA

Olya Khaleelee

'I come no more to make you laugh; things now
That bear a weighty and a serious brow,
Sad, high, and working, full of state and woe,
Such noble scenes as draw the eye to flow,
We now present. Those that can pity, here
May, if they think it well, let fall a tear:
The subject will deserve it.....'

Prologue, *Henry VIII*, by William Shakespeare

Psychoanalytic Perspectives on a Turbulent World was conceived as a drama that is happening around us and one in which we play our part. The vision of three independent yet interconnected dramatic Acts appeared to Halina Brunning, one of the two editors, in a dream. Each Act depicts three Scenes and the whole is introduced via an introductory Prologue and completed with an Epilogue. Act I illuminates with scenes from war and conflict. Act II focuses on the dramatic disappearance of psychological "containers" for dependency needs such as banks, financial institutions, and large employing organizations. Act III poses the question whether a different style of leadership—perhaps one embodying hope and spiritual renewal—might consciously or at the level of the collective unconscious generate some form of resolution for all of us as citizens at a global level.

The themes encompassed by this book are part of our experience in the world today, being offered to the reader at the moment when we have just managed to avert an economic calamity, so bad that it generated for many people fantasies of the complete global collapse of capitalism. Events have left several countries bankrupt including the United Kingdom, with a national debt of £800 billion (BBC News, April 22, 2009) and with unemployment expected possibly to reach three million, including up to one million young people. Apart from the economic realities, the psychological cost and sorrow is equally high, with a dramatic loss of confidence and trust in institutions and in the government, which have previously been important psychological containers for dependency needs.

Financial institutions, some having been bailed out at enormous cost by the taxpayer, are, a year later, reaping huge profits and are once more putting aside millions in bonuses for their traders and other staff. "Greed is good" as Gordon Gecko (played by the actor Michael Douglas) stated in the 1987 film, *Wall Street*. I wonder why it is that the same behaviour that gave rise to the recent economic crisis is still being manifested now, when we as citizens have already paid such a high price for the same mistakes. Might it be to do with unconscious rage?

Looked at from a psychoanalytic perspective, greed is "a form of introjection carried out in anger. The violence of the oral incorporation, involving biting, leads in phantasy to the destruction of the object. The end state is that there has been no oral satisfaction, since the introjected object is worthless ... it gives rise to a greater and greater hunger for 'good' objects to alleviate the internal state of dominance by anxiety and destructive introjections. ... Hunger giving rise to more hunger is greed" (Hinshelwood, 1989, p. 309 and p. 350).

This definition of greed makes clear that it is underpinned by destructive aggression, resulting in inner emptiness and a yearning for existential meaning. Such aggression, particularly heightened at present, can also be seen globally in the violent activities of al-Qaeda and the Taliban. The almost biblical wrath that we see and have evoked in the world today can be described as inordinate and uncontrolled feelings of hatred, manifest as vehement denial of the truth (Wikipedia).

Denial may both be expressed to others and take the form of self-denial. For example, President Ahmadinejad of Iran, a man of Jewish origin, denies the Holocaust and openly wishes to destroy the Jewish state which represents his inner world. This rage is also associated with impatience with the procedure of law, the desire to seek revenge outside the workings of the justice system, and with the wish generally to harm others. Transgressions born of wrath and vengeance include assault, murder, and in extreme cases, genocide. Recent examples of each, whether in Iraq, Afghanistan, Rwanda, Somalia, or elsewhere on the globe can easily spring to mind. Rage and vengeance manifested through war, conflict, terror, kidnap, and suicide bombings abound.

This is one side of the equation. On the other side it is important to register that al-Qaeda and the Taliban represent—through Sharia law, which refers to the wide body of Islamic religious law—an alternative, even a pure ideology which is extremely attractive to the many who feel alienated from Western society's values, those who feel spiritually empty and in need of fulfilment. Pascal, Hegel, Rousseau, and Kant explored in different ways how "man needs religion to give him a sense of place in the world, a sense of his own identity, an idea of himself that satisfies him; for, without it, he, who differs from other animals in being self-conscious, is intolerable to, and seeks to escape from, himself…." They go on to describe how, if man can see no other reason for existence than just being there, then "since he knows that he is ephemeral, inconstant and frail, he feels himself to be a lost being, a finite mind in a mindless universe, a feeble light in a dark wilderness" (Plamenatz, 1970, p. 86). Religion has many functions, providing a structure for behaviour, bringing people close to each other through faith, and offering consolation at times of suffering and grief. But, most importantly, "it also provides them with a conception of a man's place in the world which makes life worth living" (Plamenatz, p. 87).

So it is useful to remember that, alongside our self-made experiences of economic crisis, greed, denial, rage, violence, and emptiness, are yearnings for a different order of experience which also needs to find expression. These, often forced into the shadows, may be seen as the virtues of chastity, temperance, charity, diligence, patience, kindness, and humility. Qualities such as these, whilst articulated within the Christian tradition, are also common to the other main religions as a template for the desired behaviour of the citizen.

Some of these qualities are also embodied in the reflective stance offered by a psychoanalytic way of thinking about and trying to understand these events in the world, as evidenced by the authors of the excellent papers you are about to read. Others can be seen in the shifts in leadership being exercised in the world today. Moving from the leadership of George Bush to that of Barack Obama represents a shift from a *fight* leader, shooting from the hip so to speak, to a thoughtful leader who represents *hope*. Obama is evidently the recipient of many projections from individuals seeking meaning in their lives. He follows Martin Luther King in not just having a dream but realizing it. "Yes, we can!" he said. More broadly, he represents the unconscious hope for resolution and peace, to such an extent that, to the surprise of many, he has already won the Nobel Peace Prize despite being heavily involved in a war. This may tell us about that aspect of our collective psyche that he represents in the world.

> "Make war breed peace, make peace stint war, make each
> Prescribe to other, as each other's leech.
> Let our drums strike"

> (final words from *Timon of Athens* by William Shakespeare).

Let the Drama begin!

References

Hinshelwood, R. D. (1989). *A Dictionary of Kleinian Thought*. London: Free Association.

Plamenatz, J. (1970). *Ideology*. London: Pall Mall Press.

Shakespeare, W. *Henry VIII*. P. Alexander, William Shakespeare The Complete Works (p. 748). London: Collins, 1951.

Shakespeare, W. *Timon of Athens*. P. Alexander, William Shakespeare The Complete Works (p. 968). London: Collins, 1951.

PROLOGUE

The Myth that Binds: The past and present as prologue to the future

James Krantz

The prologue was the invention of Greek playwrights. On an empty stage, before the play begins, a character appears to provide the context that enables the audience to understand the ensuing drama. The play itself often recounted a calamity that emerged— inevitably—from the facts provided during the prologue.

In one sense a prologue for this volume is entirely superfluous because each author provides a rich and compelling context of understanding for their presentation. Yet, a prologue also makes sense because although each presentation stands on its own, there are connecting themes that underlay, and give added meaning to, these chapters which make up the scenes and acts of the upcoming play.

One theme is calamity. Stories of disaster and disruption provide the ground of understanding. They are clustered into three groups— the acts of this play: war and conflict; the financial meltdown; and finally issues of leadership and the illusion of containment.

What sets the stage for them is the persistent and dominating myth of rationality which functions as the "blind eye", opening the way for the destructive enactments and catastrophes explored herein. This myth, which persists in spite of overwhelming evidence, is itself rooted in the Enlightenment project that has held sway over Western thought since the 17th century. Armed with ultimate faith in reason and science, Enlightenment thinkers took aim at dogma. Through the application of reason to orthodoxies, tradition, and unquestioned convention, the Enlightenment aspired to emancipate people from barriers to free thought.

Our presentations illustrate how belief in rationality becomes its own dogma, one that can itself inhibit thought and obscure any understanding of forces that reside in the primitive register of the psyche. It becomes an essential calcifying ingredient of the defensive posture that holds awareness of the impact of irrationality at bay. These nine scenes illustrate how flight from underlying emotional realities is both a manifestation of suffering and a source of further suffering.

Psychoanalysis provides another connecting strand. Each scene examines social and organizational life through the lens of psychoanalytic thinking. Freud was, himself, firmly rooted in the Enlightenment. His unwavering faith in science and reason, as famously expressed in his critique of religion, saw the unquestioning mind as imprisoned by infantile forms of thought and feeling. Ironically, while Freud's work was an expression of Enlightenment thinking, it also exposes the limits of its deepest moorings—the ideals of pure rationality and objectivity.

Psychoanalysis exposes the precariousness of reason and demonstrates its vulnerability to all sorts of regression. The unconscious residue of infancy and childhood creates an inevitable, ever-present influence on adult states of mind. At the cultural level, regression is always an imminent danger, evidenced by how often common bonds are affirmed by finding a victim or culprit on whom to displace communal hostility and anxiety.

Act I uses a wide aperture to explore questions of war and conflict. Each scene surfaces the curious, paradoxical "dance" of hope and despair contained in psychoanalytic thinking. Only through integrating awareness of our vulnerability, our primitive states, and our "darker sides", it tells us, can we hope to avoid or mitigate calamity. Conversely, certainty in the objectivity and truth of one's own viewpoint predisposes us to tragedy. The projective dynamics stimulated by self-idealization enforce cycles of denigration and destructiveness.

Mario Perini invites us to consider that although psychoanalytic approaches to addressing peacemaking can arouse omnipotent fantasies of transformation and righteousness, its authentic realization leads to more modest and grounded aspirations. Einstein and Freud echo this point in two cameo appearances, recalling their famous exchange about whether psychoanalysis contained the seeds of world peace. Invoked by both Perini and Volkan, Freud answers Einstein's hopeful question starkly: "Violence is inevitable." Efforts to replace brute force by the "might of an ideal" were doomed. Yet he also offers hope that some measure of our dark forces might be diverted into other channels when he says that "Whatever makes for cultural development is working also against war" (Nathan & Nordon, 1960).

Each scene in this Act is aimed at just such refinement by offering ways in which psychoanalytic perspectives can help people attain deeper understanding of, and hence empathy for, the other. Shmuel Erlich looks beyond the typically pejorative accounts of terrorist mentality to appreciate how it is rooted in the struggle to find a meaningful self in today's world through identification with an ideology. He puts the dynamic into a broader cultural context by linking their struggles with widespread threats to selfhood, social fragmentation, and dislocation. Vamik Volkan reviews many years of work with large scale conflict by focusing on the violent re-emergence of old (sometimes ancient) trauma in the fragile relationships between large groups. He offers an intriguing account of diplomats, psychoanalysts, and policy makers working together to develop a deeper appreciation of the underlying emotional underpinnings of large, seemingly intractable, conflict situations.

Act II considers several financial crises, where the myth of rationality returns in new guises. Siren songs of vast wealth have consistently clouded awareness of the toxic and corrosive processes operating in modern organizations. It is difficult to imagine a sequence of events that more vividly demonstrates the dangers of over-reliance on the rationality of markets or economic actors than the most recent economic implosion.

Burkard Sievers explores primitive states of mind that underlay our economic crisis and describes how rationalistic approaches to solving it may, paradoxically, prolong the dreamy disconnection from reality that led to the crisis in the first place. As Sievers' analysis would anticipate, the siren song breeds short memory. Even now controversial practices of the credit-bubble are returning to financial institutions, encouraging companies and consumers to assume crippling levels of debt by offering credit with few conditions and allowing repayment of debt with more debt (Henny Sender in the *Financial Times*, December 1, 2009).

Efforts to understand the context of the financial crisis inevitably raise questions about the capacity of our organizations to contain anxiety. Practitioners of psychodynamic consulting often encounter images of rational managers and rational management practice. In spite of rigorous methods and quantitative models that guide decision making, the workplace is profoundly shaped by emotional reality. Howard Schwartz describes the downward spiral of General Motors in terms of unconscious self-idealization through which it lost touch with reality; a prophetic article that was written well ahead of GM's final collapse into bankruptcy. Mark Stein introduces a different perspective on psychoanalytic understanding of organizations. By considering the impact of Oedipal dynamics on Enron's leaders he offers an invaluable new dimension of understanding of what was the largest corporate failure in history to that point.

Act II underscores how organizations and communities, like individuals, develop defensive routines and patterns in order to manage frightening emotion. These patterns can undermine the capacity for adaptation and change. The success and viability of our social institutions is deeply connected to the methods used to contain the deep, and often painful, anxieties that are stimulated in the workplace.

As our play nears conclusion the focus narrows to spotlight the leader. Act III explores the meaning of leadership and how leaders are used to contain and symbolize the shared hopes and fears of community life. Building on Freud's original insights about how group life is shaped through identification between leader and follower, Susan Long reviews various images of leadership that have emerged from psychoanalytic thinkers.

The psychological space between leader and follower is saturated with symbolic meaning and deep emotional currents. Wesley Carr, who was at the centre of the unfolding drama of Princess Diana's death, provides a moving description of how shared images of the "institution in the mind" functioned to link people to one another around shared purpose. His reflections on the event demonstrate that the unconscious negotiation of shared reality often occurs through the collective meaning conferred upon leaders.

The final scene brings us up to the current moment of Barack Obama's leadership and asks what it augurs for the future. Larry Gould discusses the interplay of psychological dynamics underlying the behaviour of leaders, cross-currents that arise from oscillation between differing states of mind. In contrast to the massive idealization and colossal expectation that propelled his ascendency, the reality of Obama's leadership is the focus of Gould's presentation. It serves as a reminder of the inevitable fallibility of leaders, the consequences of human vulnerability in the exercise of authority, and the need for followers and leaders alike to recognize their common humanity rather than revert to primitive expectations and embittered disappointment.

Psychoanalytic thought contains the insight that we participate, often unknowingly, in creating our own misfortune. Clinging to the myth of rationality, and thus enforcing denial of the unconscious, irrational strata of human life, sets the stage for the often catastrophic events discussed in this play and in countless other situations.

I conclude by turning to how this volume itself serves as a kind of prologue—how past and present, as presented by our authors, is a prologue to the future. The challenges of managing emotional states in social institutions are great; vastly more so with accelerating rates of social, organizational, and economic change. The authors underscore the importance of being able to think about, and integrate an understanding of, unconscious and irrational forces into our policies and decisions. Although there seems to be widespread yearning for meaningful work and relationships, there are worrisome signs that the capacity to symbolize, to reflect, to analyse, and to interpret experience is diminishing in the cultural sphere. How we ultimately relate to the darker sides of experience will play a major role in the extent to which our futures will rhyme with the past.

Now, it is time for the play. The stage is set for the drama to begin. A solitary dark beam illuminates it ...

References

Nathan, O. & Nordon, H. (Eds.) (1960). *Einstein on Peace* (pp. 186–203). New York: Schocken.

Sender, H. (2009). "Fears grow about overheated US debt market", *Financial Times*, FT.com, December 1.

ACT I

ON WAR AND CONFLICT

In Act I the stage is set for bloody conflict and war that rages continuously across the Ages both within and between the communities.

Is there a way of understanding and managing conflict that can offer some new hope and salvation?

A beam of darkness—understanding the terrorist mind[1]

H. Shmuel Erlich

> Nowadays not even a suicide kills himself in desperation. Before taking the step he deliberates so long and so carefully that he literally chokes with thought. It is even questionable whether he ought to be called a suicide, since it is really thought which takes his life. He does not die with deliberation but from deliberation.
>
> —Søren Kierkegaard (1846)

Terrorist violence has increasingly become part and parcel of our everyday life. Different world areas feature daily in the news and have become associated in our mind with terrorism—to mention Iraq, Afghanistan, and the Middle East—but the phenomenon is undoubtedly much more widespread and no one anywhere is immune to it. Recent terrorist attacks in India and Indonesia followed on the heels of those in the West: Great Britain had its share with Sinn Féin in Ireland and London, Germany coped with the Baader-Meinhof

---

[1] This chapter has been developed from Shmuel Erlich's earlier work (2003a).

3

gang, Italy with the Red Brigades, Spain with ETA, and the United States was catapulted to the top of this list by the attack on the World Trade Center twin towers, which came only a few years after the Oklahoma City bombing. World-wide security precautions, personal searches, and careful baggage scrutiny are constant reminders of the prevalence of terror and the fear it inspires. In many ways, terrorism has succeeded in changing—perhaps forever—our feeling of personal and social security and our accustomed mode of life. The fact that we have become blasé about it and willingly submit to intrusive scrutiny is testimony to the extent to which terrorism has become an integral global component of our daily lives and cultural experience.

One may argue that such a perspective on terrorism is misleading in that it singles out one kind of violence from the widespread trend of greatly increased brutality and bloodshed, which is perhaps indicative of a more pervasive underlying social dynamic that is plaguing us at this historic juncture. There may well be such an underlying connection between these different kinds of aggression. But I would object to lumping together gang attacks, high seas piracy, and violent crimes with terrorist activity, even though they all contribute to the overall sense of insecurity. My objection requires, however, that I define what is unique and essential about the violence of terrorism. I believe that my own definition of terrorism, which I would like to offer here, can account for this differentiation: *terrorism is always ideologically inspired, and the ideology in question is used to exonerate and justify the violence perpetrated.* The significance of this definition is that it eschews some of the motives frequently attributed to terrorist violence, such as poor social and economic conditions or psychological disturbance. Not that these are not sometimes present; yet in and of themselves they do not offer a sufficient cause for the phenomenon, indeed not even a necessary one.

Appreciating the fact that ideology is an intrinsic component of terrorism should considerably advance our understanding of terrorism as a social phenomenon and movement. But we are still faced with a mystery: how is this *social* dynamic explicable in terms of *individual* motivation and action, and even more so—how can it be integrated with our understanding of the workings of the minds of the individuals who engage in terrorism? Can our well-worn theories of the mind account for and explain how and why a given individual becomes a willing participant and activist in what most people would consider outright anti-social behaviour? Is it madness, psychopathology, some form of newly emerged sickness of the mind and deviance of the soul? In order to attempt to answer these questions we clearly need to delve more deeply into the mind of the terrorist.

That the subject of the terrorist's mind rivets psychoanalytic attention is understandable: as psychoanalysts, we are torn between our social indignation with atrocities of whatever sort and scope, and our clinical and therapeutic stance, which generally deeply imbues our social posture. A patient of mine who is far removed from the therapeutic field, but is married to an analyst, put it well. Expressing his anger at what he considers to be his wife's overly lenient, permissive and "understanding" attitude towards their children, he said, "If she met Hitler, she would express her sympathy for his difficult childhood and life circumstances, whereas I would probably kill him." Much of contemporary psychoanalytic understanding of violent behaviour in general and of terror in particular seems biased by a form of "understanding" that tends to regard people as victims of their life circumstances. This view also permeates and colours various facets of the social attitude towards crime and deviation and consequently its treatment.

Ever since Freud, the psychoanalytic stance has been marked by the recognition of a psychic continuum. This groundbreaking recognition, however, has inadvertently contributed to blurring the boundaries between conscious and unconscious life, between reality and fantasy, between murderous wishes and their actualization, between normality and its aberration. Psychoanalysts thus have a share in the factors that undermine more spontaneous, perhaps "naïve", moral distinctions and judgments that allow one to totally repudiate and dissociate oneself from violent and murderous acts. Like most people, we may prefer to regard terrorists as a social aberration or a kind of cultural freak show. But many factors make it difficult for the psychoanalyst (and anyone who is psychoanalytically informed and influenced) to dissociate himself from what is evil or aggressive. A major contributor to this difficulty is the awareness of ubiquitous dissociative psychic mechanisms such as projective identification. This awareness makes it difficult to condemn the terrorist as an individual (as distinct from condemning "terrorism") because we might be accused (internally as well as externally) of projecting our own aggression and violence on him. The ubiquitous nature of projective identification underscores the dangerous tendency to dissociate oneself from evil and madness, while unconsciously maintaining strong links and investment in their continued presence.

And yet the terrorist's mind greatly fascinates us because it poses two essential challenges and dilemmas. The first is a sort of Occam's razor: can we delineate the factors that make a person capable of committing the kind of heinous acts that took place on September 11? The second stems from the first and evokes an issue of identity: if we cannot identify what makes a person a terrorist, can we be certain that *we* will never become that person? This last is reminiscent of the anxious question I have encountered among adolescents in the wake of a classmate's suicide: "Could I be next?" These are serious issues for the psychoanalyst: we feel called upon to provide answers that would explain, predict, and allay such anxieties. I must caution, therefore, that as far as I can see, the straight or simple answer to this quest is not to be found. The sigh of relief we wish to heave after defining "the difference that makes all the difference" must, regrettably, be postponed.

It is instructive in this connection to note very briefly some of the landmarks in the psychoanalytic attempt to understand terrorism. Perhaps the earliest entry of the term is in Ferenczi's (1949) phrase, "The terrorism of suffering", in a paper presented to the International Psychoanalytic Congress in 1932 and first published in 1933. Ferenczi described a relationship in which the adult (parent) is emotionally unavailable to the child, yet controls him by adopting a narcissistic, self-indulging, masochistic, complaining, and suffering stance. One possible outcome is the child's precocious assumption of an adult carer's role, spawned by identification with the aggressor. "Terrorism" here refers to the obliteration of and disregard for the real needs and existence of the other. The traumatogenic childhood of such a sadomasochistic parent is clearly implied by Ferenczi as the root cause for terrorizing the child, thus suggesting an endless chain of "exogenous" environmental mistreatment. Winnicott similarly linked delinquency with early deprivation. As Ana-Maria Rizzuto observed, "Present-day violence and systematic terrorism from nations and individual groups make Winnicott's observations about the connection between emotional deprivation and delinquency an important source of reflection for those who may be interested in working preventively with children who are at risk" (1990, p. 812). The current widely held psychoanalytic stance is clearly expressed in these formulations: mistreatment, delinquency, and disregard for others stem from faulty or traumatogenic early object relations. While this formulation may apply to many delinquents and to certain terrorists, it is neither sufficient nor even relevant to all terrorists.

The anarchism associated with the students' revolt of the late 1960s and the spate of terrorist activities (notably in Germany and the Middle East) that followed in the 1970s gave rise to several psychoanalytic papers. A new understanding of terrorism was advanced which in addition to an object relations perspective re-emphasized an intrapsychic need for a total experience of paradisiacal bliss and perfection. Greenacre related this wish to the youthful yearning for a Utopian state: "Except when the contagious fury of destruction takes over and becomes a blind end in itself, the rationalization seems to be—to get rid of everything that is, and something good will take its place. This appears essentially as a death and rebirth fantasy, which is externalized and put upon society. But back of it is the eternal Utopian dream of a perfect world" (1970, p. 358). Her thoughts were echoed by Ostow (1986), who described the powerful social tendency for an apocalyptic experience, marked by an initial phase of savage destruction that is followed by a phase of messianic rebirth. This dimension is exceedingly important, to my mind, yet it still exhibits the Procrustean constraint of casting such tendencies in a regressive and psychotic mould.

What can we say today about the mind of the terrorist? Certainly not that it is marked by gross deviance. I believe that the attempt to depict "The Terrorist" as a deranged, emotionally deprived and impoverished, mentally ill person is misleading and basically wrong. I must confess, however, that my assertions are stronger than my evidence. I cannot base my claims on the analysis or treatment of terrorists—unlike Hacker, who wrote a pioneering book on the subject (1976), having interviewed a pair of Arab terrorists who had held hostage a train with Jewish refugees near Vienna. To my knowledge, such treatments are extremely rare. What I say must therefore be viewed as tentative. Nonetheless, it is supported by a number of sources: frequent exposure and glimpses into the Jewish and Palestinian extremists who dot our TV news and newspapers; research reports of Palestinian psychologists; known histories of Jewish resistance fighters (considered terrorists by the British), their deeds and deaths; disturbed adolescents in treatment; several discussions in the Israel Psychoanalytic Society; and my own and others' psychoanalytic understanding.

Many (though not all) suicide bombers are youths, ranging in age from the late teens to the late twenties. One sometimes gets a glimpse of their families as they mourn their deaths. Difficult and precarious as this is to assess and judge, the impression one gets is not of depriving or unloving families, or of deprived, unloved children. Real grief and sorrow are usually evident, yet they are often tinged with pride, acceptance, and support for the son's or daughter's self-sacrifice. A significant corollary of this attitude is the social and financial support these families receive. They put up the traditional "mourners' hut" in which they receive visitors, family, and friends who come to pay their respects and to support and share in their bereavement. Their son's or daughter's heroic death is regarded as a noble sacrifice, the achievement of martyrdom, and has the open support and endorsement of the community in which they live.

In order to understand these typically young, unmarried men and women (the occasional older person, married and with family, is no exception to the trends I will describe), several factors must be taken into account. First and central among these is *the need for an existence rooted and submerged in something greater than one's self*. This need may have been echoed in Turquet's proposed fourth Basic Assumption of Oneness in groups (1974). I have further expanded this notion through concepts that span and integrate the individual and group levels, as I will elaborate below (Erlich, 2003b). This "greater than self" entity can be provided by a cause, an ideology, a religion, or an idea that promises an idealized state. Western thinking typically maintains that the well circumscribed and autonomous "Self" chooses and adopts an idea, and this choice is then often vicariously or externally rationalized along utilitarian lines. However, the mind of youths in general, and of these youths in particular, works differently. An *idea* becomes the focus and vehicle for the actualization of the self. Selfhood, life, and mere existence are meaningless if not suffused with this life-giving force. An endless array of possibilities (ideologies, religious beliefs, philanthropic causes, etc.) offered by the dominant culture or counter-culture beckon to be taken up in this way and to form the nucleus around which one's ego-ideal (or idealized self image) and identity may coalesce. Moreover, it is where such ideological identification fails, usually because of some individual and familial psychopathology, that there will be recourse to alternative means to satisfy this need, ranging from drugs to sex, from suicide to self-mutilation. The motivating force behind these manifestations is always the same: the need to submerge oneself in a larger and greater cause in order to regain oneself in a "new" form, in which one is merged and connected with this greater entity. This is not a regressive stance or need. It is a progressive, developmental, typically adolescent need which may well linger on beyond the normal period of youth.

The forms this need takes vary enormously, not so much along individual psychopathological lines (though these may play a role) as along pre-existing cultural patterns. What we meet in this juncture is the crucial dovetailing of intrapsychic development with culturally provided and expected aims, transmitted and made available in the form of values and ideals. Freud referred to this when he said, "The ego-ideal is of great importance for the understanding of group psychology. Besides its individual side, this ideal has a social side; it is also the common ideal of a family, a class, or a nation" (1914, p. 101). And again: "Mankind never lives completely in the present. The ideologies of the super-ego perpetuate the past, the traditions of the race and the people" (1933, pp. 95–96). These "ideologies" are the "glue" of the bonding and connectedness that normally takes place—to one's family, social group, and history; but also to one's self, one's bodily experience, and identity. Without them one shrivels up, feels empty and is experientially adrift; and equally so, deprived of its mooring in such an ideological substratum, society itself becomes alienated and fragmented.

What are the ideologies that provide the breeding ground and fertile soil for terror? It should come as no surprise that the ideologies underscoring politically-based terrorism are too numerous to be listed. They cover socio-political visions stemming from the entire political gamut, from Left to Right, usually representing the extreme positions at either end of the spectrum or going beyond it. Anarchism, utopianism, anti-authoritarianism, and sexual liberation movements are but a few salient examples. Clearly, however, religion plays a major role in this array, if by religion we understand not merely a code of injunctions, prohibitions, and precepts, but the embodiment and expression of the values governing social related-ness and purity of the self (I will have more to say about this later on). All religions offer the appealing prospect of "joining" through one's merger with a greater-than-self entity, whether it is the com-munity of believers, a Supreme Being, or a coherent system of ideals and beliefs that can introduce order and make sense of existence and reality. It is indeed the promise of such a merger that is the source of their attractiveness. The ways to achieve this merger and its expression differ considerably from one religion to another, as well as within a given religion, subject to specific interpretation. Thus, for example, the Catholic Church offers merger with Christ through the sacraments; in certain Eastern religions it is practised and some-times achieved through meditation and reaching out-of-self states; in Chassidic Judaism, joyous dancing and singing serves as a means for ecstatic merger with God. In all religions, however, these quests underlie and are poignantly expressed in their fundamentalist or extreme forms. (For a searching review of the role currently played by religious fundamentalism in general and in Islam in particular see Bohleber (2002).)

Of the several factors affecting this particular form of merger, the most crucial is the attitude taken towards death. It forms the view of the afterlife, which in turn shapes and affects the attitude towards reality that is maintained and shared by the co-religionists. A commonly supported view in the Moslem religion, for example, regards the afterlife of a martyr as an eternal pleasure-filled paradi-siacal existence, in which 70 virgins attend every "*Shaheed*" (martyr or self-sacrificing hero). It is not merely the promise of everlasting pleasure that is so attractive; it is rather the *idea* of merging with and becoming part of such eternal bliss, the Utopian state described by Greenacre. Yet it is not a psychotic regression that enables the youth to give up his life for such a vision. It is the immense power and blissful peace that comes from being merged with the larger cause— this *is* paradise. It is a state of mind that no longer needs to make calculations or instrumental choices. It may even be characterized by calmness and serenity, as if one has been transposed to another realm of existence. It is the point at which one's self becomes part of something greater—venerated and supported by one's ego-ideal as well as one's family and community. This does not mean that the families of these young men necessarily actively encourage them to undertake suicide missions. The same bonds of love and the fears of loss and bereavement operate in them as in all human beings. The support comes afterwards, but the youth knows that it will come, and that along with the pain of his loss there will also be acceptance, approval, and even pride. It must be appreciated that, contrary to the Western view, these deaths are not considered "suicides" (which are forbidden by the Moslem religion as by almost all other religions). They represent martyrdom, through which one's individual and personal existence becomes forever fused and welded with the historical path of the community, past, present, and future.

An article published in one of Israel's leading newspapers (*Haaretz*, July 16, 2002) seems to confirm my thesis. Its title reads: *"The Suicide Bomber, the Doctoral Student Is Convinced, Is a Happy Person Who Loves Life"*. The claim that suicide bombers are driven by personal despair or poverty is totally rejected by the Hamas activists interviewed. One of them says, "When I saw children who threw stones at tanks get killed, when my friends at the university were killed...I decided to join up. I did not know how to hold a weapon or use it. I was moved by a feeling of revenge to defend the Motherland.... What drives a person like me are emotion and the faith that God will protect you and help you achieve victory." Osama Mazini, who is completing his doctorate in psychology at the Islamic University in Gaza, says, "Psychologically speaking, a distinction has to be made between a person who ends his life because of mental suffering, and the *Shaheed*, who is a happy, life-loving person, one with inner strength."

What are the psychological mechanisms that enable and support these dispositions and actions? A model of intrapsychic functioning that I have developed may be of help in understanding these phenomena. The model refers to the internal processing of sense data that gives rise to *what* we experience but mainly to *how* we experience it, with special emphasis on the experienced relationship of self and other. The model assumes that the psychological processing of our experience takes place along dual (rather than a single) parallel and independent tracks, dimensions, or modalities. In one, self and other are clearly demarcated, differentiated, and separate from each other. Consequently, this modality is one in which objectivity predominates, together with instrumental, goal-directed mental activity, best exemplified by realistic, logical, and scientific thinking. The separation and demarcation of self and other (object) also makes for the appearance of desire in the form of wishing and longing for the object, and hence for experiencing drive impulses and conflicts. In the second modality, self and other are experienced as fused, merged, and inseparable (for as long as the experience lasts). This modality makes no use of separateness and boundaries, and the focus is subjective and purely existential—on the experience of "ongoing-ness", existing, being alive, and being connected and fused with essential "others", such as a lover, the universe, a group, or a set of ideas. This modality is what makes us feel alive and part of whatever we experience ourselves as merged with. It should not be surprising that for shorthand reference I named the first modality *Doing* and the second one *Being*. It must be borne in mind, however, that these modalities are not synonymous with "doing" and "being" as descriptive acts or contents, but rather that the underlying processes described give rise to such experiential contents. Finally, it appears that the integration of these modalities presents a crucial developmental task in adolescence (Erlich, 1998, 2003b).

The youthful quest for a Utopian state reflects the quest, poignantly experienced during adolescence and young adulthood, for the integration of the two modalities I described. Youth is deeply concerned with this integration and is quite anxious lest what was dearly cherished in childhood might be relinquished without sufficient "compensation". The struggle centres on the formation of the ego-ideal and its socially incorporated ideals and values, which provide the basis for an *identity* that spans one's innermost experience of "ongoing being" and one's sense of belonging to a group, community, nation, or history, even to humanity itself. This is the fertile ground from which youths (and adults) need to proceed in order to experience their existence as merged with a larger cause, represented by ideals and values, whether these are made available by an organized religion or its secular equivalents. This is the background that makes intelligible the renunciation of one's mortal life and existence in lieu of the merger with a larger and eternal existence.

An additional component in understanding the mind of the terrorist, which connects it to the issue of prejudice, has to do with *purity*. I hypothesize a fundamental sense of *"purity-of-self"* that must be maintained and protected from threats of contamination. This "purity" cannot be understood or approached in logical, functional, or instrumental ways. It is *not* an aspect of a power struggle or of territorial ambitions (though the "sanctity" of a territory is a manifestation of the need for purity) and all attempts to study it along such utilitarian lines are doomed. It is rather an aspect of the *Being* dimension of mind, mental life, and existence that I have just described (Erlich, 2003b). This concern with purity is readily found in the sphere of ideas and ideologies, rather than in pragmatic and realistic motives. Ideologies are the breeding grounds for notions of purity/impurity. Religions are concerned with the purity of soul and living and can therefore be major contributors to the formation of prejudice.

Prejudice becomes a social issue when it leads to enactment. The need to enact a prejudice stems from the "impure" aspects of the self that cannot be contained, metabolized, and tolerated, and are externalized (projected) into an other as a way of preserving the purity of one's self. Hence prejudice is always an intersubjective, interpersonal, and interactive phenomenon, involving self and other. The other becomes the repository and depository for the impure aspects of oneself. Particular or specific others are selected as targets of prejudice and projection by virtue of the actual or fantasized characteristics they possess, as in Bion's notion of valence (1961).

The quest for purity and the need to defend it are motivating forces behind attacks on infidels, people of different colour, and political enemies. In a study of what makes for discourse with an enemy or blocks it (Erlich, 1997), I distinguished between an enemy experienced at the Oedipal level of development, with whom there is a commonly shared cultural "third" that enables and facilitates discourse, and enemies experienced at a pre-Oedipal level. In the latter, more extreme cases, splitting and projective identification demand the enemy's actual and utter physical annihilation. Once again, this leads directly to the sanctification of giving up one's life in the cause of obliterating the impurity that threatens one's pure existence. In so many ways, this need is also what drives terrorist acts.

In closing, I suggest that what we see in terrorist actions and in the terrorist mind is not so much a function of overwhelming rage, hatred, and destructiveness, though these may indeed be encountered. More importantly, we see a need to "re-find" the self by losing it, by allowing it to obliterate its boundaries and to merge with a greater entity by immersing oneself in an idea or ideology. This need is driven by an underlying quest for preserving the "purity" of the self (met in notions like Winnicott's True Self or Modell's Private Self) from the contaminating impurity attributed to an other who becomes "The Enemy" (Erlich, 1997). As a progressive, developmentally significant stage, it may enjoy the full support and endorsement of one's community, and thus provide the link by which the individual joins and merges himself with it.

What I have described may well, and rightly so, be regarded as a pessimistic point of view, for it implies that so long as one's own purity requires the annihilation of the "impure" other, acts of violence and terror will not cease. Regrettably, the attribution of terrorism to circumstantial or empirical causes only serves to deny its inherently human roots in the nature of things, or in Virgil's immemorial phrase, *Lacrimae rerum*.

References

Bion, W.R. (1961). *Experiences in Groups*. London: Tavistock.

Bohleber, W. (2002). Collective Preconceptions, Destructiveness and Terrorism (*Kollektive Phantasmen, Destruktivität und Terrorismus*). [Paper delivered at Conference of European Psychoanalytic Federation, Prague, April 2002.]

Erlich, H.S. (1997). On discourse with an enemy. In: E.R. Shapiro (Ed.), *The Inner World in the Outer World* (pp. 123–142). New Haven, CT: Yale University Press.

Erlich, H.S. (1998). On loneliness, narcissism, and intimacy. *American Journal of Psychoanalysis, 58*: 135–162.

Erlich, H.S. (2003a). Reflections on the terrorist mind. In: S. Varvin & V.D. Volkan (Eds.), *Violence or Dialogue? Psychoanalytic Insights on Terror and Terrorism*. London: International Psychoanalytical Association.

Erlich, H.S. (2003b). Experience—what is it? *International Journal of Psychoanalysis, 84*: 1125–1147.

Ferenczi, S. (1949). Confusion of the tongues between the adults and the child—(the language of tenderness and of passion). *International Journal of Psychoanalysis, 30*: 225–230.

Freud, S. (1914). On narcissism: An introduction. *S.E., 14*: 73–102.

Freud, S. (1933). Lecture XXXI, New Introductory Lectures. *S.E., 22*: 57–80.

Greenacre, P. (1970). Youth, growth, and violence. *Psychoanalytic Study of the Child, 25*: 340–359.

Hacker, F.J. (1976). *Crusaders, Criminals, Crazies: Terror and Terrorism in Our Time*. New York: Norton.

Kierkegaard, S. (1846). *The Present Age and of the Difference between a Genius and an Apostle*. New York: Harper Torchbooks, 1962.

Ostow, M. (1986). The psychodynamics of apocalyptic: discussion of papers on identification and the Nazi phenomenon. *International Journal of Psychoanalysis, 67*: 277–285.

Rizzuto, A-M. (1990). Deprivation and delinquency. *Journal of the American Psychoanalytical Association, 38*: 811–815.

Turquet, P. (1974). Leadership: The individual and the group. In: E. Gibbard, J. Hartman & R. Mann (Eds.), *The Analysis of Groups* (pp. 75–91). San Francisco: Jossey-Bass.

Virgil. *The Aeneid*, Book I, line 462.

SCENE TWO

"Si vis pacem para bellum" Psychoanalysis, peace education and conflict literacy[1]

Mario Perini

> You cannot expect to be able to solve a complex problem using the same manner of thinking that caused the problem.
>
> —Albert Einstein (*Essays in Science*, 1933)

Si vis pacem, para bellum—"If you want peace prepare for war". (At the beginning of the 20th century this sentence inspired the name of a firearm given to German officers and actually called "parabellum".) the Latin motto comes from Vegetius, a Roman functionary living under emperor Theodosius (4th–5th century AD), who wrote a treatise on warfare, *Epitoma rei militaris*, while oddly enough he was not actually a general nor an expert in military matters. Since then this sentence has been repeatedly used in political studies (e.g., in Machiavelli's *Prince*) and in international affairs, especially to legitimate the *principle of deterrence*, a policy based on the creation of a military power comparable to that of an actual or potential enemy, as a system to equilibrate the relationships between nations and to

---

[1] From a paper presented at the Associazione Freudiana's Workshop "Educating to the (im)possible" (Turin, March 31, 2007).

avoid conflicts. The term "conflict" is used here as a synonym of "war". We will see later how this equivalence may be psychologically inappropriate.

Peace and deterrence

The Cold War experience seems to have demonstrated that a peace negotiation and a decent coexistence, or at least a non-aggression pact, may be held more easily when there is an equality of offensive weapons and their use can be limited as a deterrent. In other words, when diplomacy's tools fail or are exhausted, the last chance remains to prepare to fight: if the other party realizes you are serious, some agreement probably becomes inevitable. The psycho-political basis of deterrence would therefore imply persuading a potential enemy that the costs he might have to pay after launching an attack will be higher than the benefits he hopes to gain from it.

So, if a substantial component of people's inner experience of peace is seemingly a feeling of safety, then we should try to understand what implicit element of instability might be lying behind a "terror equilibrium". If this kind of peace is only maintained through fear, then the very feelings of insecurity will end up to undermine it and stir war up again.

Certainly, Cold War warded off the danger of a clash between the two blocks and that of a nuclear holocaust, but could not quite avoid the multitude of small and extraordinarily cruel local carnages, which covered the planet with blood during the second half of the 20th century. The keystone of current international, and even internal politics, seems to be a strategic use of fear for such purposes as managing hegemonies, forcing insecure people, blackmailing governments or electorates, making business, healing humiliations, and exporting or imposing one's own culture, values, or just interests.

However, at certain levels of intensity and duration fear no longer acts as a source of moderation and prudence, and may go out of control also for its strategists; continuing terrors cannot evolve into a steady state of mind, nor be depotentiated or transformed into habits or a lifestyle, even in the Middle East where it permeates people's everyday life. On the contrary, a persistent menace may generate two specific monsters: the first is *denial*, based upon omnipotence and the unthinkability of extreme dangers, like the nuclear holocaust or the global terror; the second is a *counter-phobic impulse* to get rid of fear by acting out the feared risk itself, which once it become real, stops being a threat. To put it in another way, war may occur just out of fear of war—as happens in preventive attacks— with a defence mechanism very similar to that used by some adolescents, who are so scared of death that they run against it by engaging in dangerous pursuits.

Similarly, governments and public opinions may escape all awareness of danger, while centres for strategic studies develop nonsense theories about "limited wars" or "sustainable losses", and websites give instructions on how to build a nuclear bomb or to set off an effective terrorist attack. We must accept the reality: fear no longer works as a simple deterrent, nor for those who manipulate others' fears and refuse to listen to theirs, and even less so for those who every day celebrate a wedding with martyrdom.

And what about peace, then? Shall we surrender to pessimists' or militarists' views of peace as "just a parenthesis between two wars" or as "negative peace", not so much a parenthesis but rather a quasi-war, a warfare-organization not actually fighting, while engaged in building new enemies and finding reasons and funds for increasingly more sophisticated weapons.

A paradox is that, unlike war, the opposite condition—peace—is not so easy to define, whether it is a specific individual, social, and political state of mind oriented to friendly and co-operative relations, or simply the "absence of war". Likewise, it is hard to decide to what extent it may be a sensible choice to use force to preserve it—as in *peace-keeping* and *peace-restoring* operations—and what does it actually mean to have peace policed by soldiers.

Most pacifists however do not seem to have many doubts about the nature of peace: it is a principle, namely, a way of life that naturally leads to peace. Of course among pacifists there are also tormented and doubtful people, besides the "pure and tough" militants who are against war always and everywhere, using a somehow pre-political (pre-Oedipal?) thinking which disregards real societies and their evolution. Their idea of peace recalls what Spinoza said: "Peace is not absence of war; is a virtue, a mood, a disposition to benevolence, trust, and justice" (*Tractatus theologico-politicus*, 1670).

Well, who would disagree with him in principle? We are all against war, for heaven's sake!

Peace is, unfortunately, a "politically correct" matter par excellence. Reaffirming its sacrosanct values makes us feel that we are on the right side, but this does not allow us to take one single step towards a real achievement of true and durable peace, or help to explain why such destructive conflicts permeate the fabric of all human experience, from Iraqi carnage to child-killing mothers, from street feuds to Saturday night casualties.

Yes, indeed, at a global level several macro-systemic factors play a primary role: energy policies, global market dynamics, ethnic and cultural diversity, poverty, migrations, etc. But what about ordinary people? Why are so many individuals or groups, within families or workplaces, in the wine bars or in Parliament halls, inclined to come to blows and to war against one another?

Such a paradox, constantly mixing war and peace, friendship and enmity, collaboration and conflict, is probably an anthropological fact linking together the fate of individuals, groups, organizations, and nations, with inner conscious and unconscious vicissitudes of the mind, in an uncanny *continuum* which does not allow simplistic solutions or comfortable explanations. Working effectively for promoting peace is not as easy as just thinking about it: the political cultures which are genuinely preoccupied with peaceful coexistence do not pursue abstract, noble or fashionable Utopias of a Universal Peace, but try to build the concrete, fragile, and provisional peace, woven with compromises and counterbalances, that human wisdom is sometimes able to conceive.

However, if we think more in terms of the educational tasks, bearing in mind our own children—and in a broader sense the next generations—and hoping they will not be called up for military operations in Afghanistan or involved in a group rape at the college, then we cannot escape from facing a series of hard questions:

- What does "educating for peace" mean?
- In what way shall we consider the conflict, from its various social, political, moral, and psychological perspectives?
- Is war and conflict the same thing or different forms of the same phenomenon?
- Should we try to extinguish, resolve or minimize conflict, or is it more reasonable to try to manage it in some non-destructive way?

There is a view that an increase in urban violence in Western societies—in schools, colleges, streets, stadiums, and even in family life, which is becoming an increasingly unsafe place—is the result of the absence of war. This is predicated on the assumption that aggressive drive, particularly in young people, has no legitimate channel for expression.

Apart from the disquieting idea of ascribing to war a kind of "regulatory function" in the area of human relations, we all know that there are a number of more or less sublimated ways of using aggression as alternatives to violence and war: political fight, competitive sports, some dangerous or physically demanding jobs, like stuntmen, fireguards, policemen, chess, surgery, literature or film critique, martial arts, trade unions, video-games, break dance, stock exchange, rap music, etc.

On the other hand, is it possible to say that wars are absent? Certainly neither in the Third World, where they are endemic, nor in Europe or in Western countries, still deeply engaged in military "peace-keeping" operations all over the world; not to mention today's global terrorism which has spread around as far as our doorstep.

Well, then, why war?

Why war?

This question was the title to a short, intense correspondence between Einstein and Freud (*Warum Krieg?* 1933), which prophetically occurred on the threshold of the Nazi conquest of Germany. Since 1915, just after the outbreak of WWI, in "Thoughts for the Times on War and Death", Freud exposed his reflections on this subject, developing two intertwined arguments: the impossibility to eradicate mankind's primitive evil impulses; and the incapacity to effectively contrast them by means of reason (Freud, 1915a).

Albert Einstein wrote to Freud on the invitation of the League of Nations to choose a person of his liking for "a frank exchange of views on any problem". In his letter he asked Freud whether he could imagine "any way of delivering mankind from the menace of war". Einstein hoped the League would be able to set up "a legislative and judicial body to settle every conflict arising between nations", a sort of international court "competent to render verdicts of incontestable authority and enforce absolute submission to the execution of its verdicts". Although he was a sincere pacifist,

Einstein felt that "law and might inevitably go hand in hand" (Einstein, quoted in Freud, 1933, pp. 199–200).

The main point of his discourse however is the insight that failure of all attempts at regulating social conflicts without turning to war does not only depend on a thirst for power or the pursuit of some political and economic interests by the dominant classes, but also on the evidence that "strong psychological factors are at work, which paralyse these efforts" (ibid., p. 200). In wondering how it may be possible for the masses to let oligarchic governments and their propaganda carry them away "to such wild enthusiasm, even to sacrifice their lives", Einstein supposes the existence of "a lust for hatred and destruction", a sort of collective psychosis. That is why he asks Freud as an expert of human mind, if it might be possible "to control man's mental evolution so as to make him proof against the psychoses of hate and destructiveness", entrusting therefore psychoanalysis with a mission of educating mankind about worldwide peace (ibid., p. 201).

In his reply Freud totally agrees with Einstein's assumptions about aggressive drives and the relationship between law and power, acknowledging that in general "conflicts of interest between men are settled by the use of violence", whether it is a matter of muscular strength, weapons, or intellectual superiority. The final purpose of the fight is that "one side or the other was to be compelled to abandon his claim or his objection by the damage inflicted on him and by the crippling of his strength" (Freud, 1933, pp. 203–204).

If victory is achieved by physically eliminating or killing the adversary, the victor gains the practical advantage of liquidating the opponent and deterring others from following his example; but also it satisfies "an instinctual inclination" to hatred and destruction, which Freud calls Thanatos, or *death instinct*, and believes is at work in every human being, although counterbalanced by Eros, the libido or *life instinct* (ibid., pp. 211–212).

In what follows of his letter Freud summarizes the basic elements of his drive theory and his views about the development of civilization through education. His stance however is bitterly pessimistic and not at all consoling. In exploring the path of human evolution from brute primitive violence to the modern law-based state, he suggests that right emerges from "the union of several weak ones" which restrains and contrasts the violent might of the single individual. As Freud states:

>...right is the might of a community. It is still violence, ready
to be directed against any individual who resists it; it works
by the same methods and follows the same purposes. The only
real difference lies in the fact that what prevails is no longer the
violence of an individual but that of a community. (Freud, 1933,
p. 205)

In order to prevent the return of the individual's violence the community has to be stable, permanent and organized, and "must institute authorities to see that ... the laws ... are respected and to superintend the execution of legal acts of violence" (ibid., p. 205).

But even this organization does not ensure a full protection from violence or the suppression of conflicts: as inequalities are unavoidable, "the justice of the community then becomes an expression of the unequal degrees of power obtaining within it; the laws are made by and for the ruling members and find little room for the rights of those in subjection" (ibid., p. 206). Tensions and disparities not only feed internal fights within a community—which anyway can often be resolved through negotiation—but also external conflicts among communities, towns, tribes, peoples, religions, or nations, which tend to be nearly always resolved by a proof of force, namely, by war.

Einstein's view of a possibility to avoid war by creating a strong central authority, to which resolution of international conflicts could be delegated, is discarded by Freud as a generous but unrealistic dream. Freud nevertheless tries to bring some hope by pointing out the importance of the effort to achieve truth—which is a genuinely psycho-analytic process—by unmasking the aggressive tensions hiding behind declared ideals, or, even better, showing how noble values and motives can be used to conceal or justify unconscious destructive impulses and intentions.

To hope to achieve some sort of governance on destructive forces must therefore imply that firstly we do not deny, disown or minimize our common human subordination to their influence, and secondly give up the comfortable but dangerous illusion of becoming able to suppress them once and for all. In Freud's words:

>...there is no question of getting rid entirely of human aggressive impulses; it is enough to try to divert them to such

an extent that they need not find expression in war. [...] If willingness to engage in war is an effect of the destructive instinct, the most obvious plan will be to bring Eros, its antagonist, into play against it. Anything that encourages the growth of emotional ties between men must operate against war. (ibid., p. 212)

Another way that Freud suggests to contrast the propensity to war involves the development of mature leadership. Even so his conclusions seem rather disheartened. Freud maintains a pessimistic and problematic vision when peace is faced with war, a phenomenon which might appear "as another of the many painful calamities of life" and "seems to be quite a natural thing, to have a good biological basis and in practice to be scarcely avoidable", at least "so long as there exist countries and nations that are prepared for the ruthless destruction of others" (ibid., pp. 213–214).

What stands out from this exchange of ideas is an abhorrence—which Freud and Einstein share—against an event which "puts an end to human lives that are full of hope, because it brings individual men into humiliating situations, because it compels them against their will to murder other men, and because it destroys precious material objects which have been produced by the labours of humanity" (ibid., p. 213). What also remains is Freud's strong statement on war as the opposite of civilization, as why "we are bound to rebel against it; we simply cannot any longer put up with it. This is not merely an intellectual and emotional repudiation; we pacifists have a *constitutional* intolerance of war" (ibid., p. 215).

In conclusion, Freud's reply does not seem to leave much hope. Aggression and destructiveness are instinctual processes intrinsic to the human mind, and innate, unsuppressible expressions of what since 1919, after the First World War, the loss of his nephew killed on the front, and the death of his daughter Sophie, he had come to call the "death instinct", building an extraordinary psycho-social construct connecting war, death, the mourning process, hatred, loss, conflict, and melancholy.

And yet his considerations, however brutally realistic, do open some hopes and further perspectives to both sociologic and psychoanalytic reflections that would come after him.

Conflict and psychoanalysis: From Freud's Vienna to the world after 9/11

Psychologists give different definitions of conflict, but a prevailing emphasis is put on the individual as subjected to inner strains or interpersonal disagreements as a result of contrasting circumstances, motivations, goals, impulses, behaviours, ideas, values, interests, or feelings, which are reciprocally antagonistic or incompatible, but generally of equal intensity.

Psychoanalysis made the *conflict* a cornerstone of its theoretic system and the core target of its therapeutic method for the care of psychic disorders. As an inevitable human dimension, Freud sees it substantially as a clash between different conscious but mainly unconscious psychic "forces" operating inside the individual mind. It is above all a matter of intra-personal, or intra-psychic, conflicts, which if unresolved may lead to the rising of anxiety and the creation of neurotic symptoms.

Such a conflict, involving drives, affects, and desires, but also memories, fantasies, and thoughts, may be described in more abstract terms and from an inner world perspective as a contrast between different psychic agencies (id, ego, super-ego) or between drives and the defences against the anxieties aroused by these drives, or, in more "relational" terms, it might be conceptualized as a clash between pleasure principle and reality testing, or even an opposition between self and object, and their respective emotional investments. Psychoanalytic work, while helping the patient to get a fuller awareness and a deeper understanding of conflicts emerging during the sessions, may enable him/her to face these conflicts with less pain and in a more constructive way.

The appearance of psychoanalysis, with its emphasis on subjectivity and the "discovery" of unconscious, within the 20th century cultural landscape, helped to shift the reflection about conflict from a mainly historical, political, ethical, and social perspective, to the inner psychic scenario, and issues of personality and mental functioning. However, despite the apparent prevalence of an intra-psychic point of observation, the "individual" emerging from this conceptualization is far from a lone or isolated entity, but necessarily involved in identifications with his peers and in social connections to a number of bodies and institutions existing in the external world.

These identifications and connections not only serve as a matrix for identity and development, but are also a source of those libidinal "emotional ties" that Freud (1933) hoped would be able to mitigate and counterbalance human natural destructiveness. In this sense, one could say that peace has to be built essentially in the individual mind.

A relevant aspect, already implicitly present in Freud's formulations, but fully developed mainly by his followers, is the emphasis that should be put on conflict's potential for fostering development, creativity, and growth. The progressive shift of the psychoanalytic paradigm from its original deterministic, drive-centred, and radically intra-personal roots towards the recent, more relational, and inter-subjective approaches, has also brought about significant changes of perspective in the theory of conflict, leading it to oscillate between internal world, interpersonal, and group contexts, social reality and ecological environment.

On the other hand, such sway between inner and outer world is already clearly visible in Freud's conception of the *Oedipal conflict*. A crossroads of both individuals' and communities' stories, myths and biological fates, Oedipus' vicissitudes do not only concern the internal fight among drives; they also represent the social scenario for a wide range of conflicts opposing each other: parent and child, individual and group, tradition and innovation, family loyalty and exogamy, leadership and followership, nature and nurture, awareness and denial, competition and collaboration, and—logically also—war and peace. (See Scene 9 by Susan Long in this volume.)

With the rise of ego psychology and later on of Kohut and the so-called "self psychoanalysis" we can see a clear turning point from a traditional conflict-based psychopathological frame to a new "defective" model of mental disorders, more centred on self deficiencies and developmental stops. As Eagle argues:

> As is exemplified by the self psychology of Kohut (1971, 1977, 1984) and his followers, recent psychoanalytic developments can be characterized as a move away from a psychology of conflicts and wishes to a psychology of defects and needs. […] Conflicts are replaced by defects, wishes are replaced by needs, and resolution of conflict is replaced by repairing self-defects and building up of psychic structures. (Eagle, 1990)

A by-product of the diminished role of conflict in individual psychology has been that some analysts became more interested in its psychosocial and relational dimension. The subsequent line of socio-psychoanalytic research on conflict, destructiveness, and war—from Money-Kyrle, Rickman, and Bion to Segal, Moses, Volkan, Kernberg, Hinshelwood, Erlich, Eisold and, in Italy, Fornari and Pagliarani—would pay a growing attention to how *working through conflicts* may enrich experience and creativity in individuals, groups, and organizations, while on the contrary avoided or unmanaged conflicts end up by developing a destructive potential. (See Scene 1 by Shmuel Erlich and Scene 2 by Vamik Volkan in this volume.)

Since 1948 Wilfred Bion, writing on "psychiatry in a time of crisis" and referring to Toynbee's definition of our society as a "suffering civilization", pointed out how an extraordinary technological progress did not go with an equivalent emotional development, which might relieve the civilization's inherent pain (Bion, 1948). Human beings, competent enough when engaging in external relationships, often fail in dealing with emotional unconscious tensions, which represent the deepest and most complex aspect of sociality, and at the same time a source of conflicts and a threat to civilization.

"Sociality" is defined (Random House Dictionary, 2009):

a. social nature or tendencies as shown in the assembling of individuals in communities.
b. the action on the part of individuals of associating together in communities.
c. the state or quality of being social.

In his last creative period, a short time before dying, Bion was interested in questions like the exercise of authority and leadership, and the subject of power. He was persuaded of the need to combine the psychological and sociological perspectives, in order to integrate individual, group, and institutional dimensions, and as an attempt at facing the emotional underdevelopment which afflicts the suffering society. Thus he had come to identify two forms of power management: a good form, characterized by the triad "globality, integration and consistence", and a bad one where monopoly and exclusion instead prevail (Trist, 1985).

Bion approaches human destructiveness just from these emotional unconscious elements; that is why he addresses psychologists and psychiatrists as professionals experienced in mental life. Their contributions could be to provide an appropriate psychological education to community leaders, whose lack of emotional competence might not only impair their creativity, but also transform them into the destructive "oppressive minority" described by Toynbee (1946). This might also give individuals and groups opportunities for a suitable emotional development.

With his studies on groups Bion makes a further step forward exploring social conflict "from within". He remarks how a group tends to become an external "enacted" representation of its members' psychic processes, and parts of their personalities conflicting with the compromises required by interpersonal (couple, family, group) and social relationships. According to Bion the individual/society conflict is therefore primarily intra-psychic, and as such may be unfolded, faced and resolved by group work.

Drawing on Kleinian theories and Money-Kyrle's studies on psychoanalysis of war and politics (1934, 1951), Franco Fornari was among the first analysts who applied psychoanalytic understanding to the wider society and in particular to war. In 1964 he presented a paper entitled "Psychoanalysis of War", which stirred up a great interest among European analysts, setting the basis for a wider work published two years later (Fornari, 1966).

In his book Fornari wonders how the "rational", political, economic, demographic motives for war may turn into pure senseless destructivity. His hypothesis is that war's primary task may be to express and at the same time evacuate depressive or persecutory psychotic anxieties, which are innate in mankind as a sort of original madness; war would thus paradoxically act as a defence for individuals and groups, allowing them to disown and project unconscious guilt or loss on the "enemy" by means of a paranoid working-through of mourning, and to live the criminal madness of war killing as an ordinary ethical necessity or the safeguard of a threatened common love object.

Relying upon his clinical experience Fornari comes to the conclusion that "war is a safety 'organization', not in that it enables us to defend ourselves from real enemies, but rather as it can find or even invent real enemies to be killed, otherwise our society would risk to leave its members defenceless in face of the emerging 'Terror', their deep anxieties, the 'internal enemy'" (Fornari, 1966).

Well, if from the clinical evidences brought by psychoanalysis war could be defined as "an individual crime fantasized individually and carried out collectively" (ibid.), then the responsibility for its origins and its consequences can be traced back to the individual and also to groups and institutions. The problem is that while individual anxieties can be dealt with by a therapy, would it be possible to have institutions that may cure collective psychotic anxieties without resorting to war?

Fornari's ambitious design was to create the scientific and cultural bases for promoting a deep transformation in social and political institutions that regulate the relationships between the individual and the state, and also to sow the seeds of a new culture of peace, which should be founded on personal assumption of guilt and responsibility and on refraining from using institutions as a depository for paranoid projections.

Starting from Bion's lessons and Fornari's studies, Gino Pagliarani (1997) shed light in particular on the relationship between individual and institution and put a special emphasis on the need to develop an "emotional education", trying to foster in people—and mainly in their leaders—an emotional competence that may enable them to cope with complex realities and to elaborate conflicts in a creative way.

Concerning the conflicts, he stresses the importance to "be skilled, be capable, be up to" in order to manage the conflict with intelligence (Pagliarani, 1993), and replaces the pair "peace-war" with the triad "peace-war-conflict", pointing out how *"war" is a synonym of "conflict", but at the same time its negation,* and how *peace actually is not a peaceful state but a highly conflictual one.*

If peace is not peaceful, but actually an ambiguous and complex reality, then we should see conflicts as an unavoidable component of everyday life, or, better, potential sources of creativity and enrichment for individuals, groups, and institutions, while war is regarded as a sick, insane form of conflict, "a paranoid working through of conflict" (Pagliarani, 1997).

To be capable of elaborating conflict in an "intelligent" way means above all to accept the complexity of reality; the main skill required is creativity, necessary to allow the opposites to coexist without denying them. "We need much more courage"—says Pagliarani—"to face peace day by day confronting its complexity and its conflicts than to make war" (ibid.).

Although it produces intense sufferings, human beings continue to prefer using war to deal with societal conflicts, apparently as a mode of conflict resolution, but deeply as a denial process because only one position eventually prevails, and all differences and dilemmas are buried under stacks of dead and ruins. Peace is a costly and complex practice indeed, and not exempt from pain, as finding agreements and solutions implies compromises, painful sacrifices, losses, and an effort of understanding others' points of view.

Among the few contemporary psychoanalysts who studied social conflicts, I would mention two of them who explored these issues in more depth, and whose last contributions are included in this volume (see Scene 1 by Shmuel Erlich and chapter 2 by Vamik Volkan in this volume).

Shmuel Erlich, living and working in Israel, currently the middle of one of the most turbulent parts of the planet, made significant reflections on the question of enmity, with a crucial distinction between enemies within and without (and also enemies in the past and in the present), emphasizing paranoid and regressive processes in groups, as well as the need to find "ways of talking, communicating and discoursing with an enemy".

> The question is: does psychoanalysis have anything of importance to contribute to the understanding of what an enemy is and how to deal with him? Can it tell us anything that is unique and pertinent about this problem? And does it have any course or solution to offer? (Erlich, 1994)

Although well aware that "the answers to these questions are not easily forthcoming", Erlich brought forward (in association with Rafael Moses and Eric Miller) a particular model of dialogue based on the Tavistock "group relations" tradition, which in 1992 resulted in a series of conferences aiming to explore the German-Israeli relatedness in the post-Holocaust era (Erlich, Erlich-Ginor & Beland, 2009). (These conferences, known as "Nazareth Conferences" from their original venue, since 2004 are held in Cyprus.)

Another psychoanalyst deeply engaged in exploring war and conflict is Vamik Volkan, a renowned scholar not only in the field of clinical psychoanalysis and large group dynamics, but particularly for his interdisciplinary contributions matching psychoanalytic thinking with history, politics, and sociology, with special reference to international relationships, diplomacy, war, ethnic conflicts, and terrorism (Volkan, 1988, 1997, 2004; Volkan, Julius & Montville, 1990–91; Varvin & Volkan, 2003).

According to Volkan the need for *recognition*, so firmly rooted in individuals, groups and even nations, is crucial to understand most of the conflicts. In practice the demand for recognition turns into a necessity to find friends and allies, but also a need to "cultivate" hostile relationships (Volkan, 1988). His work in the domain of "psycho-politics" led to a development of new theories on large group behaviour in times of both peace and war.

Volkan however is not just a theoretician: during many years he has been leading several interdisciplinary teams in turbulent places all over the world and working successfully to put together some high-profile enemies—like Greek and Turkish Cypriots, factions among Bosnians, Israelis and Palestinians—in unofficial long-lasting dialogues.

From a different perspective Eisold (1991) points out to what extent war may serve the conscious and unconscious needs to be distracted from one's own "domestic conflicts", like unemployment, economic decline, homelessness, educational failures, environmental disasters, etc.:

> ...the cognitive and emotional simplification that pervades the psychological system at war splits everything. In the world of "good" and "evil" established by the war [...] not only do the extremes of splitting lead to the polarizing of issues, but they create a vacuum in the center; things disappear. War is a good time to raise prices and renegotiate contracts, a good time to silence minority complaints.... Much of this is done craftily, consciously. But much more occurs out of awareness, including the complicity of those who fail to notice or who fail to object to the injustices they do perceive as they turn their attention elsewhere. *War is a seductive invitation to renounce our hard won achievements of complexity and responsibility* [my italics]. (Eisold, 1991)

With the 9/11 Twin Towers attack the planet's face changed and new visions of the conflict were also outlined: a sharp almost religious dualism between Good and Evil confronted international policies for a widespread terrorism, which had become "apolitical", techno-logical, boundary-less, and moving from the traditional turbulent scenarios (Balkans, Middle East, Africa) into the Western societies' ordinary daily life.

What was the psychoanalytic community's reaction?

Contemporary Psychoanalysis, in its first issue of 2002 on trauma in adulthood included a large collective article ("Voices from New York: September 11th 2001") reporting in a free, conversational form the reflections of six analysts who had some meetings together after 9/11 events.

> The accounts made by these colleagues touch on many differ-ent subjects: how 9/11 tragedy affected their patients' dreams and behaviour, how their own lives changed since that day, how therapists and patients concretely behaved in the session, [...] was it possible to analyze transference implications, and so on. It is a moving document, among the many produced at that time in New York, and an attempt, say, to provide self-help for profes-sionals particularly exposed to the risk of post-traumatic stress disorder, and therefore more in need for a therapeutic working through. (Gensler et al., 2002, reviewed in *Psychomedia*, 2006)

In Italy in 2002 a book was published under the title *Psyche and War: Images from within*, where a group of Jungian analysts, discussing how global war seemed to mirror the world inside us, after what happened in New York felt that "the internal boundary which ena-bles the differentiation between imagination and reality has been broken down" (various authors, 2002).

The same year Karnac published *Terrorism and War: Unconscious Dynamics of Political Violence*, edited by Coline Covington and others, a volume which Anton Obholzer in his foreword not only recom-mends to psychologists and analysts, but particularly to politicians, journalists, and opinion makers (Covington et al., 2002). In this vol-ume, besides many relevant contributions (by Eissler, Segal, Brit-ton, Hinshelwood, Fonagy, and others), Diana Birkett and Isobel Hunter-Brown's dialogue on "Psychoanalysis and War" stands out for its brave exploration on how difficult it appears for psychoanalytic practice and research to appropriately address social reality and current traumatic events.

After the Twin Towers attack, in most psychoanalytic organizations world-wide a variety of study meetings, workshops, and congresses were held on war, terrorism, fundamentalism, and destructiveness, all more or less explicitly focused on the crucial question, "whether and how psychoanalysis might contribute to peace".

As shown in the above-mentioned examples, by no means a comprehensive list, during the last decades psychoanalytic thought actually shifted its focus on conflict from an exclusive intra-psychic perspective to a greater concern for conflicts involving individuals, groups, and nations, exploring the vicissitudes of aggression and its relation to personal and collective destructiveness. Unfortunately, its crucial contribution to understanding the problem has not generated so far significant learning and cultural changes in practical applications to education, social life, and international relationships, thus adding further arguments to Freud's view of psychoanalysis as an "impossible profession".

While a real education for peace seems a still distant target, we nevertheless could wonder whether the psychoanalytic paradigm might have something helpful to teach concerning strategies and techniques of *conflict management* which are nowadays widely recommended in areas like social/ethnic conflicts, school life, marital problems, international affairs, business negotiations, etc.

Although it is not exactly a true specialization, this "applied psychoanalysis" might aim towards a more realistic and sustainable project of peace education, based upon fostering awareness and in-depth exploration of the shadow sides of human nature rather than on principles, good intentions, and wishful thinking. In short, embracing a "culture of conflict".

A culture of conflict

Conflict is a basic feature in all relationships and knowledge processes. It is in the last analysis a mode of encounter between human beings or between their organizations, and the way it evolves towards co-operation instead of competition, antagonism, enmity, and war will depend above all on the nature and the development of the relatedness within the involved systems.

There are different ways to classify social conflicts, but for our purpose most important is the distinction between destructive and constructive conflicts. While commonly conflict is viewed as a negative phenomenon, psycho-social approaches acknowledge that, besides the risks of a violent or destructive evolution, conflicts also have constructive potentials, for example the conflict between powers—legislative, executive, and judicial—on which modern democracies are based, or the Oedipal conflict as a driver for psycho-sexual and social development.

It is also due to the above-mentioned risks that in ordinary culture conflict is viewed in a deeply ambivalent way. On the one hand one can acknowledge conflict is a vital source of differentiation, maturity, tension to an aim, divergent, and non-conformist thinking, thus contributing to the construction of identity and of personal and social responsibility. In Bion's terms we could say that accepting conflict is intrinsically part of a "depressive" state of mind, where all choices have their emotional costs, and desires are always confronted with laws, restrictions, inner limits, and sometimes impossibility.

On the other hand contemporary attitudes generally tend to escape from conflict through making it unspoken or unapproachable by experience. Amplified by the concomitant incapacity of modern institutions to act as mediators, this leads to social repression of diversity, weakening of differentiation processes, and a denial of asymmetric role responsibilities in educational, managerial, and caring tasks (Weber, 2006).

In organizational life to work with teams or hold talks or negotiate with other systems or sub-systems or groups one needs to be prepared to properly manage the unavoidable conflicts. What is required are essentially a culture of conflict and an institutional device for conflict management.

A *culture of conflict*, by accepting conflict as a natural process inherent in human relations, does not deny it but does not demonize it either, rather makes it sustainable, manageable and as far as possible creative. An *institutional device for conflict management*, by acting from within (negotiation) or from without (third-party mediation, arbitration) pursues whenever possible a "*win-win*" compromise solution. This attitude also implies a "depressive" stance, as all involved parts have to give up the idea of a full conflict resolution and need fulfilment, accepting an albeit partial gain.

When in a culture a denial of conflicts prevails they tend to hide under the surface and end up in chronic quarrelling or sudden destructive outbursts. On an emotional level the conflict will probably be dealt with in a completely unconscious and "do-it-yourself" way, which would activate within the organization a number of social defences such as scapegoating, paranoiagenesis, bureaucratization, delegation upwards, etc. (Jaques, 1955, 1976; Menzies, 1961).

The lack of a conflict management system leaves substantially unresolved apparent and hidden conflicts, which are to be evacuated and exported whether horizontally to other groups (like in inter-department struggles) or vertically upwards (idealization of the leadership followed by its denigration) or more frequently downwards, thus leading to frontline endemic micro-conflicts. In particular, unconfronted conflicts at the top, or at the level of mission, values, or inter-organizational relationships, tend to discharge on lower operating levels, which may unconsciously enact them in different ways: as "wars of religion" between practices or ideologies, inter-professional or inter-group rivalries, interpersonal clashes or even intra-psychic conflicts, namely resulting in neurotic symptoms.

The fate of a conflict—whether it will turn to antagonism or co-operation, to peace or war—depends therefore on how it is managed, and what structures enable it to be worked through.

"Conflict management", "working through conflict" is, indeed, preferable over and above "conflict resolution". These are the key words of the whole issue and I shall now turn to them.

Conflict management and conflict literacy

Over the times many different approaches and theories on how to deal with conflicts have followed one another. At the beginning a prevailing model was that of *conflict resolution*: this method, still very popular, is focused on the assumption that a conflict may be ended or at least weakened once and for all by using various communicational tactics or behavioural techniques.

During the last two decades an alternative school of thought emerged, and was also successfully applied to business and negotiations: the model of *conflict management*, based on such concepts as power, controls, and values, and on a growing awareness of the interpersonal and systems dynamics involved in driving the conflict towards an end in a more reflective and controlled way.

Finally, a more recent approach pursues a *"non-violent transformation of the conflict"*, with an emphasis on the relational, dynamic, provisional, and changing nature of conflict rather than on ultimate and static solutions (Galtung, 2006). Its applications—which should not be confused with "naïve" pacifism—seem particularly suitable to political and social conflicts, provided they are able to integrate the different implied perspectives, rational, perceptual, and emotional.

Conflicts could be managed in constructive and non-coercive ways by means of some well-known techniques, which are essentially negotiation, mediation, arbitration, and lawsuit. At an international level the looseness of social ties between nations and the lack of a legitimate monopoly authorized to use force get conflicts to blow up in the most violent form: war. During the last decades, however, an intense development of constructive methods of conflict management took place also in international affairs: short- and long-term negotiations, strategic mediation, multitrack diplomacy are only some of the tools employed to try to transform ethno-political fighting into non-violent controversies. But besides appropriate techniques and tactics an effective conflict management requires above all an acceptance of a "science of conflicts", that is a strong theoretical basis on which to rely. Among the emerging approaches an operational model is gaining ground which integrates three conceptual roots:

- the psychoanalytic method
- the systemic approach
- a sociology of complexity.

Such a science should, first of all, include a realistic *menschanschauung*, a vision of humanity well aware of what men really *are* and how their minds actually work, acknowledging that communality and group work, apart from their complex and non-linear dimensions, do not peacefully coexist with individual personality, but can arouse in people irreducible conflictual states, for instance the dynamics of collaboration *vs.* competition, so common in the workplace.

Here the psychoanalytical lens may prove helpful in clearing the ground of some comforting but risky illusions. Peace, after all, is not an ordinary state of mind: human beings are not easily inclined to harmony and coexistence, and co-operation and trust in interpersonal relations do not look so "natural" or spontaneous. Violence as a means for dealing with conflicts appears ubiquitous and unavoidable, men have destroyed and killed all the time, and yet we could interpret this not quite as a natural fate, but rather as a culturally learned and established ritual. If this is true, then we could hope to make it evolve towards less destructive or even creative forms, on condition that

a. we resist the temptation to demonize conflict or otherwise to submerge it under a flood of good feelings
b. we learn how to use conflict appropriately, creatively, and with full awareness.

This means, in effect, promoting in the current culture a kind of "literacy" of conflict, which may help people as well as leaders and groups to tolerate, contain, and make conflict thinkable, in a sense carrying on what Winnicott describes as one crucial task of a good enough mother: educating the child to hate as a way to detoxify his/her mind of hatred (Winnicott, 1947). (In an African centre for the rehabilitation of child-soldiers a relevant part of treatment implied making the children "play war" with wooden weapons to help them to re-symbolize and work through their destructive traumatic experiences).

From this perspective looking towards psychoanalysis as a hope to *resolve* human conflicts is a risky idealization, which may lead to the vain hope that conflicts can always be "healed" if only one finds the appropriate mix of technical competence and goodwill. As ever the best weapons of psychoanalysis are the struggle for knowledge and the courage of awareness. If we wish to avoid omnipotence, magic thinking, and impossible missions, we could simply conclude that a psychoanalytic approach might make conflict more readable, more tolerable, and somewhat more manageable, while giving up all expectations to extinguish it and being humble enough to know that sooner or later conflict will flare again.

References

Bion, W.R. (1948). Psychiatry in a time of crisis. *British Journal of Medical Psychology, 21*(2): 81–89.

Birkett, D. (2002). Psychoanalysis and war. In: C. Covington et al. (Eds.). *Terrorism and War: Unconscious Dynamics of Political Violence*. London: Karnac.

Covington, C., Williams, P., Arundale, J. & Knox, G. (Eds.) (2002). *Terrorism and War. Unconscious Dynamics of Political Violence*. London: Karnac.

Eagle, M. (1990). The Concepts of Need and Wish in Self Psychology. *Psychoanalytic Psychology, 7*(Supplement): 71–88.

Einstein, A. (1933). *Essays in Science*. New York: Wisdom Library.

Eisold, K. (1991). On war: a group relations perspective. *Psychologist-Psychoanalyst, XI*(Supplement): 32–35.

Erlich, S. (1994). On discourse with an enemy: a psychoanalytical perspective. *Palestine-Israel Journal, 1*(4).

Erlich, S., Erlich-Ginor, M. & Beland, H. (2009). *"Fed with Tears—Poisoned with Milk": The Nazareth Group Relations Conferences*. Giessen, Germany: Psychosozial-Verlag.

Fornari, F. (1966). *The Psychoanalysis of War*. Bloomington, IN: Indiana University Press, 1975.

Freud, S. (1915a). Thoughts for the Times on War and Death. *S.E., 14*. London: Hogarth. pp. 273–302.

Freud, S. (1933). Why War? *S.E., 22*. London: Hogarth, pp. 197–215.

Freud, S. (1937c). Analysis Terminable and Interminable. *International Journal of Psychoanalysis, 18*: 373–405.

Galtung, J. (1996). *Peace By Peaceful Means: Peace and Conflict, Development and Civilization*. Oslo: International Peace Research Institute.

Gensler, D., Goldman, D.S., Goldman, D., Gordon, R.M., Prince, R. & Rosenbach, N. (2002). Voices from New York: September 11, 2001. *Contemporary Psychoanalysis, 38*: 77–99.

Hunter-Brown, I. (2002). Psychoanalysis and war: response to Diana Birkett. In: C. Covington et al. (Eds.), *Terrorism and War: Unconscious Dynamics of Political Violence*. London: Karnac.

Jaques, E. (1955). Social systems as defence against persecutory and depressive anxiety. In: P. Heimann, M. Klein & R. Money-Kyrle (Eds.), *New Directions in Psychoanalysis*. London: Tavistock.

Jaques, E. (1976). *A General Theory of Bureaucracy*. New York: Halsted.

Menzies, I.E.P. (1961). The functioning of social systems as a defence against anxiety: A report on a study of the Nursing Service of a

General Hospital. In: *Containing Anxiety in Institutions: Selected Essays*. London: Free Association, 1988.

Money-Kyrle, R. (1934). A psychological analysis of the causes of war. In *The Collected Papers*. Perth: Clunie Press, 1978.

Money-Kyrle, R. (1951). *Psycho-Analysis and Politics*. London: Duckworth.

Pagliarani, L. (1993). *Violenza e bellezza. Il conflitto negli individui e nella società*. Milano: Guerini e Associati.

Pagliarani, L. (1997). La sfida di Bion, oggi più che ieri. Psicosocio-analisi del potere e dei conflitti. In: B. Castiglione, G. Harrison & L. Pagliarani, *Identità in formazione*. Padova: Cleup, 1999.

Psychomedia (2002). Review of "Voices from New York", *Contemporary Psychoanalysis*, 1, 2002. (www.psychomedia.it/pm-revs/journrev/contpsy/contpsy-2002-38-1-b.htm).

Spinoza, B. (1670). *Tractatus theologico-politicus* (Theological-political treatise). Cambridge University Press, 2007.

Toynbee, A.J. (1946). *A Study of History, Vol. 1*. Oxford University Press, 1987.

Trist, E.L. (1985). Working with Bion in the 1940s: The group decade. In: M. Pines (Ed.), *Bion and Group Psychotherapy*. London: Routledge & Kegan Paul.

Various authors (2002). *Psiche e guerra: immagini dall'interno*. Roma: Manifestolibri.

Varvin, S. & Volkan, V.D. (2003). *Violence or Dialogue*. London: International Psychoanalytical Association.

Volkan, V.D. (1988). *The Need to have Enemies and Allies: From Clinical Practice to International Relationships*. Northvale, NJ: Jason Aronson.

Volkan, V.D. (1997). *Bloodlines: From Ethnic Pride to Ethnic Terrorism*. New York: Farrar, Straus & Giroux.

Volkan, V.D. (2004). *Blind Trust: Large Groups and Their Leaders in Times of Crises and Terror*. Charlottesville, VA: Pitchstone Publishing.

Volkan, V.D., Julius, D.A. & Montville, J.V. (Eds.). (1990–1). *The Psychodynamics of International Relationships, 2 Vols*. Lexington, MA: Lexington Books.

Weber, C. (2006). Conflitti generativi. Istituzioni e crisi della capacità di mediazione. Relazione tenuta al Convegno Internazionale "Il Bambino Ir-Reale" (Castiglioncello, 5–7 maggio 2006) (www.polemos.it/paper/cwilbambino.doc).

Winnicott, D.W. (1947). Hate in counter-transference. In: *Through Paediatrics to Psychoanalysis*. London: Hogarth.

Psychoanalysis and international relationships: Large-group identity, traumas at the hand of the "other," and transgenerational transmission of trauma

Vamik D. Volkan

During her presidency of the European Union in 2006, Austria declared the same year to be the Year of Freud as well as the Year of Mozart. Freud's and Mozart's pictures were everywhere in Vienna. At the same time, I had the pleasure of being the Fulbright/Sigmund Freud Privatstiftung Visiting Scholar of Psychoanalysis, living in Vienna for four months, with an office at Berggasse 19. In celebration of Freud's 150th birthday the Sigmund Freud Foundation in collaboration with the Bruno Kreisky Forum for International Dialogue brought together psychoanalysts and diplomats from various countries such as Austria, Norway, Turkey, and United States to expand Freud's theory of group psychology.

When large groups (i.e., ethnic, national, religious, and political ideological groups) are in conflict, psychological issues also contaminate most of their political, economic, legal, or military concerns. People assigned to deal with these conflicts on an official level usually establish short- and long-term strategies and mobilize resources to implement them. In so doing they develop assumptions that support psychological advantages for their own group over that of the "other". At this meeting our focus was on another type of psychology, more hidden, mostly unconscious, addressing obstacles

41

42   PSYCHOANALYTIC PERSPECTIVES ON A TURBULENT WORLD

that thwart peaceful, adaptive solutions to large-group conflicts. We noted that at the core of this psychology lies the concept of large-group identity, which is articulated in terms of commonality such as "we are Polish; we are Arab; we are Muslim; we are communist". Large-group identities are the end-result of myths and realities of common beginnings, historical continuities, geographical realities, and other shared historical, linguistic, societal, and cultural factors. Large-group identity can be defined as a subjective feeling of sameness shared among thousands or millions of people, most of whom will never know or see each other. Yet, a simple definition of this abstract concept is not sufficient to explain the power it has to influence political, economic, legal, and military initiatives and to induce seemingly irrational resistances to change.

This chapter examines the concept of large-group identity, its relationship with massive traumas at the hand of the "other", its role in international affairs, and how it raises substantial barriers to peaceful co-existence between former enemies. This chapter also raises questions of whether or not collaborations between psychoanalysts and diplomats provide new ways to develop strategies for dealing with current world affairs.

Noticing the influence of historical external events

In their professional lives, the psychoanalysts who participated in the meeting celebrating Freud's 150th birthday did fieldwork outside their offices, and the diplomats present were interested in the role of both conscious and unconscious psychodynamics in politics and world affairs. In 2006, as at the present time, all of us were daily subjected, at least on television screens, to examples of human beings injuring or killing other human beings "in the name of identity" (Volkan, 2006). This meeting attempted to examine how certain elements of large-group identity converge to create prejudices, diplomatic difficulties, and/or massive violence. We noted that when there is shared anxiety and regression after a massive trauma at the hand of "others" who belong to another identity, the members of the attacked large group become preoccupied with maintaining, repairing, and redefining their large-group identity, even if this means tolerating shared masochism or sadism. The perpetrators do the same.

During this meeting, I recalled how in 1932 Albert Einstein wrote a letter to Sigmund Freud asking if psychoanalysis could offer insights that might deliver humankind from the menace of war. In his response to Einstein, Freud (1932) expressed little hope for an end to massive violence and war, or the role of psychoanalysis in changing human behaviour beyond the individual level. I wondered about Freud's pessimism. Having an office in Freud's house at that time was a deeply emotional experience for me. Sometimes I would sit silently looking out of a window as I imagined Freud had done years earlier, and wonder about his life, especially when the Nazis rose to power in Germany and during the Nazi period in Vienna. I remembered seeing an exhibit at the Freud Museum during a 2003 visit to 19 Berggasse, titled Freud's "*verschwundene Nachbarn*" ("lost neighbours"). At that time I noticed a letter written by the Nazi authorities to Freud's sisters ordering them to vacate their apartments. The story of Freud and his immediate family's departure from Vienna under Nazi rule is well known. He was spared a more malign fate while his sisters and Jewish neighbours were not, but nevertheless, in the name of his Jewish large-group identity, he was subjected to suffering, humiliation and, I believe, extreme "survival guilt" (Niederland, 1961, 1968). Although Jacob Arlow (1973) later suggested some optimism in certain of Freud's writings on the psychoanalytic influence on large-group conflicts, Freud's personal psychology, I believe, played a role in inhibiting psychoanalytic contributions to the realm of international relationships.

In post-World War II Germany there has been both German and German-Jewish analyst-supported resistance to exploring the intertwining of the internal and external wars and the influence of the Nazi era traumas on analysands' psyches (Grubrich-Simitis, 1979; Eckstaedt, 1989; Jokl, 1997; Streeck-Fischer, 1999). During 1997 and 1998 I was asked to work with a small group of ethnic German and Jewish-German analysts and therapists in Germany when they formed an organization to end "the silence" about the Holocaust-related issues that come up during clinical practice. I realized that such a "silence" was still real and that it was difficult to deal with (for details see Volkan, Ast & Greer, 2001).

In Great Britain Melanie Klein also provided an example of ignoring influences of a war while treating one of her patients. In 1961, she reported the analysis of a ten-year-old boy named Richard, which had taken place in England during World War II. It appears that throughout Richard's analysis, the terror of the war was never examined. Was Melanie Klein's neglecting to include the dangerous external circumstances simply due to her theoretical stance? Was she denying her own fear of the external danger? We will, of course, never know for sure why she did not explore the intertwining of an external war with Richard's internal wars.

In the United States, Harold Blum's (1985) description of a Jewish patient who came to him for re-analysis illustrates the extent to which mutual resistances against being fully analysed may prevail when both analyst and the analysand belong to the same large group which was massively traumatized by an external historical event, in this case the Holocaust. Blum's patient's first analyst, who was also Jewish, failed to "hear" their large group's shared trauma at the hands of the Nazis in his analysand's material. As a consequence, mutually sanctioned silence and denial pervaded the entire analytic experience, leaving unanalysed residues of the Holocaust in the analysand's personality characteristics and symptoms.

I surmise that after World War II many analysts in Germany, England, the United States, and elsewhere were like Melanie Klein or Harold Blum's patient's former analyst. Without being aware of it, they influenced the application of psychoanalytic treatment in a way that tended to ignore Holocaust-related external reality. Some of them who were influential in our field exaggerated their bias towards a theoretical position that focused only on the analysand's internal wishes and fantasies and defences against them during the analytic treatment and left out the influence of external wars and other large-group conflicts. This, I think, has played a key role in limiting the contributions psychoanalysis has made to international relations in general. There were, of course, exceptions (Glower, 1947; Fornari, 1966), but they followed Freud's lead in another area, and this too blocked the potential influence of psychoanalysis on politics and diplomacy: these writers, like Freud, primarily focused on what individuals' unconscious perceptions of the mental representations of a large group and its political leader symbolically stand for instead of on large-group psychology and leader-follower relations in their own right. Another factor also played a role in limiting such contributions. Psychoanalysts followed the tradition that originated with Freud's giving up the idea of the sexual seduction of children coming from the external world in favour of the stimuli coming from the child's own wishes and fantasies for the formation psychopathology. This tradition was generalized to de-emphasize external historical events during analytic treatment.

Psychoanalysis remained primarily an investigative tool of an individual's internal world, and massive human movements were examined according to individual psychology that brings people together, not according to the psychology of large-group rituals and interactions. Psychoanalysis largely failed to consider how mental representations of existing historical/societal/political processes influence the personality development of individuals belonging to the same large group including the political leaders, how they change group members' narcissistic investment to large-group identity and initiate new historical or political movements (Volkan & Fowler, 2009). Only a handful of psychoanalysts and historians with psychoanalytic training have focused on such phenomena. For example, Peter Loewenberg (1995) described the history of the Weimar Republic and emphasized its humiliation and economic collapse as a major factor in creating shared personality characteristics among the German youth and their embrace of Nazi ideology. Alexander Mitscherlich and Margarete Mitscherlich (1975) focused on post-World War II German's inability to mourn, and Sudhir Kakar (1996) explored the effects of religious conflict in Hyderabad, India.

Meanwhile, many authors who were interested in human affairs and who were not themselves practising psychoanalysts have referred to psychoanalysis in their attempt to understand world affairs and large-group psychology in general. They often referred to Freud's writings such as *Totem and Taboo* (1913), *Group Psychology and the Analysis of the Ego* (1921), *The Future of an Illusion* (1927), *Civilization and its Discontents* (1930), and Freud's correspondence with Einstein mentioned above. As Ives Hendrick (1958) noticed long ago, these writers argued the validity of psychoanalysis "as if it were a philosophy, an ethical system, a set of theories; such discussion … seems alien and unproductive to the analyst himself, whose primary convictions originate in what his patients have told him" (p. 4). On the other hand, with few exceptions, practising psychoanalysts have tended to treat patients without much interest in or attention to international relations and large-group psychology. They have usually applied theories of individual or small therapy group psychology to large-group processes without taking into consideration that once ethnic, national, religious, or ideological processes begin they take on their own specific directions and initiate large-group movements shared by thousands or millions of persons.

At the present time, especially since September 11, 2001, this situation is changing. Psychoanalysts in various countries, belonging to different "schools" and organizations, have seriously turned their attention to an in-depth understanding of the influence historical events, especially massive traumas, have on individuals and even on large groups themselves. The events of September 11 led psychoanalytic organizations, including the International Psychoanalytic Association, to pay attention to terrorism, religious and ethnic identity issues, large-group regression, and mourning over shared losses. References to such studies are too numerous to list here.

My own involvement in studying large-group psychology in its own right started decades before September 11, 2001. I studied the Cypriot Turks' shared response to 11 years (1963–1974) of living in enclaves restricted geographically to only 3 per cent of the island and surrounded by their enemies, and their response to the island's 1974 war which *de facto* divided Cyprus into north/ Turkish and south/Greek sections (Volkan, 1979, 2009b). Another event—Egyptian president Anwar el-Sadat's remarkable visit to Israel in 1977—crystallized my efforts to understand the psychology of international relations. When Sadat addressed the Israeli Knesset he spoke about a psychological wall between Arabs and Israelis and stated that psychological barriers constituted 70 per cent of all problems existing between the two sides. With the blessings of the Egyptian, Israeli, and American governments, the American Psychiatric Association's (APA) Committee on Psychiatry and Foreign Affairs followed up on Sadat's statements by bringing together influential Israelis, Egyptians, and later Palestinians for a series of unofficial negotiations that took place between 1979 and 1986. My membership in this committee and my chairing it initiated my study of enemy relationships, interactions between political leaders and their followers, and their special focus on large-group identity.

Later I observed other "enemy" representatives—such as Russians and Estonians, Georgians and South Ossetians, Serbs and Croats, or Turks and Greeks—in various multi-year unofficial negotiation series. For the past two years, politician and psychoanalyst Lord

(John) Alderdice of Northern Ireland and I have co-chaired a series of gatherings where informed individuals from the USA, Europe, Israel, and Russia have met in unofficial diplomatic dialogues with counterparts from locations such as Iran, Arab Emirates, Jordan, and Turkey. Our purpose is to look at present world affairs from a psychopolitical angle and search for "entry points" for peaceful co-existence. In my work I have also interviewed traumatized people in various refugee or internally displaced persons camps where "we-ness" becomes palpable. Furthermore, I spent time with political leaders such as the former US president Jimmy Carter, former Soviet leader Mikhail Gorbachev, the late Yasser Arafat, the former Estonian president Arnold Rüütel, the former Northern Cyprus president Rauf Denkta , and many other high-level diplomats and observed aspects of leader-follower psychology through these leaders' verbalized thought processes and actions. Eventually, I was able to note that the notion of "large-group identity" is a key concept and its contamination of world affairs, consciously and unconsciously, needs to be understood by utilizing clinical psychoanalytic techniques and insights (Volkan, 1988, 1997, 2004, 2006).

In this chapter I will explore *only* a few aspects of large-group identity, namely the role of massive traumas at the hand of the "other" in threatening and modifying it, and political and destructive consequences of threats against the shared sense of belonging to one large group. First, I will define the concept of large-group identity further. Then I will describe shared psychological responses to massive traumas in the name of identity, transgenerational transmissions of trauma, establishment of "chosen traumas", evolution of entitlement ideologies and their manipulations, and "time collapse", which create obstacles to peaceful co-existence among former enemies. Lastly, and very briefly, I will suggest a need to include insights from psychoanalytically informed large-group psychology as we explore new strategies for peaceful solutions of certain, especially chronic, international conflicts.

Large-group identity

When I think of the classical Freudian theory (1921) of large groups I visualize people arranged around a gigantic maypole, which represents the group leader. Individuals in the large group dance around the pole/leader, identifying with each other and idealizing the leader or attempting to identify with the leader. I have expanded this maypole metaphor by imagining a canvas extending from the pole out over the people, forming a huge tent. This canvas represents the *large-group identity*. I have come to the conclusion that essential large-group psychodynamics centre around maintaining the integrity of the large-group identity, and leader-follower interactions are just one element of this effort.

Continuing the analogy to explain large-group identity, think in terms of how we learn to wear two layers, like fabric, from the time we are children. The first layer, the individual layer, fits each of us snugly, like clothing. It is one's core personal identity that provides an inner sense of persistent sameness for the individual (Erikson, 1956). The second layer is the canvas of the tent, which is loose fitting, but allows us to share a sense of sameness with others under the same large-group tent. Some common threads, such as identifications with intimate others in one's childhood environment, are used in the construction of the two layers, the individual garment as well as the canvas of the tent. Thus, the core individual identity and the core large-group identity, psychologically speaking, are interconnected. While it is the tent pole—the political leader—that holds the tent erect, the tent's canvas psychologically protects both the leader and the group. From an individual psychology point of view, the canvas may be perceived as a nurturing mother by a person (Rice, 1965; Turquet, 1975; Kernberg, 2003a, 2003b). From a large-group psychology point of view it represents the large-group identity that is shared by thousands or millions of people.

Under a huge large-group tent there are subgroups and subgroup identities, such as professional identities. A person can change a subgroup identity without much anxiety, unless such a change unconsciously becomes connected with a personal psychic danger such as losing an internalized mother image. For practical purposes, an individual cannot change his or her core individual and large-group identities, especially after the adolescence passage (Blos, 1979), since by then both identities are intertwined and crystallized (Volkan, 1988). Think of a man—let us say he is Italian—who is an amateur photographer. If he decides to stop practising photography and take up carpentry, he may call himself a carpenter instead of a photographer, but he cannot stop being an

Italian and become an Englishman. His Italian-ness is part of his core large-group identity, which is interconnected with his core individual identity.

In our routine lives we are not keenly aware of our large-group identity, the canvas of the tent, just as we are not usually aware of our constant breathing. If we develop pneumonia or if we are in a burning building, we quickly notice each breath we take. Likewise, if our huge tent's canvas shakes or parts of it are torn apart, we become preoccupied with the canvas of our huge tent and will do anything to stabilize, repair, maintain, and protect it, and when we do, we are willing to tolerate extreme sadism or masochism if we think that what we are doing will help to maintain and protect our large-group identity. What I described here is easily observable in refugee or internally displaced persons' camps or settlements.

Before going any further I must explain that here I am speaking of large-group processes shared by the majority of persons under the metaphorical tent, leaving out certain people such as immigrants or those who may be products of parents from more than one ethnic group. Furthermore, dissenters in a large group do not modify the basic elements of a large-group identity unless they have huge followers and thus they start an influential subgroup and become involved in a new large-group identity. History tells us that very seldom does a large group evolve a new large-group identity only through the influence of some centuries-long historical events. For example, a large group of South Slavs became Bosniaks (Bosnian Muslims) while under the rule of the Ottoman Empire.

Each large-group identity includes "identity markers" that only belong to its members. Let us go to the huge tent analogy and look closely at the canvas. Each canvas has its own specific designs. On occasion, a design on a canvas, such as certain religious or linguistic elements, may appear to be similar to a design on another huge tent's canvas. However, even under these circumstances we note "minor differences" in such elements. When conflicts arise between the two large groups, such minor differences become major concerns. What is crucial is the existence of certain markers that are very specific for a particular large-group identity. Among such markers are the shared mental representations of the large group's real and fantasized historical events.

Historical events of the past: chosen glories and chosen traumas

Large groups consist of individuals and therefore large-group processes reflect individual psychology, but a large group is not a living organism that has one brain. Therefore, once members of a large
group start utilizing the same mental mechanism, it establishes a
life of its own and appears as a societal, and often a political, process. When thousands or millions of persons share anxiety caused by
threats to large-group identity, a large-group regression takes place.
I borrow the word "regression" from individual psychology since
I have not yet found a good term that describes a large group's
"going back" to the earlier levels of its psychic development. First of
all, it is difficult to imagine that large groups have their own psychic
developments. The closest thing to the concept of a psychic development in a large group is its usually mythologized story and the
history of how the group was "born." In fact, when large groups
regress, they reactivate certain, sometimes centuries-old, shared historical mental representations, which I named "chosen glories" and
"chosen traumas" (Volkan, 1991, 2004, 2006).

Large groups celebrate independence days or have ritualistic recollections of events and heroes whose mental representations include a shared feeling of success and triumph among
large-group members. Such events and heroic persons attached
to them are heavily mythologized over time. These mental representations become large-group amplifiers called *chosen glories*.
Chosen glories are passed on to succeeding generations through
transgenerational transmissions made in parent/teacher-child
interactions and through participation in ritualistic ceremonies
recalling past successful events. Chosen glories link children of
a large group with each other and with their large group, and
the children experience increased self-esteem by being associated with such glories. It is not difficult to understand why parents and other important adults pass the mental representation
of chosen glories to their children; this is a pleasurable activity.
Past victories in battle and great accomplishments of a religious
or political ideological nature frequently appear as chosen glories. In stressful situations political leaders reactivate the mental representation of chosen glories and heroes associated with

them to bolster their large-group identity. While no complicated psychological processes are involved when chosen glories increase collective narcissism, the role of a related concept, "chosen traumas", in supporting large-group identity and its cohesiveness, is more complex. *Chosen traumas*—shared mental representations of ancestors' traumas *at the hands of "others"*—are more complicated, and stronger, large-group amplifiers.

After a massive trauma at the hands of others, members of a large group experience the following (Volkan, 2006, 2009a):

1. Shared sense of shame, humiliation, and victimization,
2. Shared sense of guilt for surviving while others perished,
3. Shared inability to be assertive,
4. Shared (defensive) identification with the oppressor,
5. Shared difficulty or often inability to mourn losses.

When such experiences continue and the people cannot find adaptive solutions for them, they become involved in a sixth shared experience:

6. Shared transgenerational transmission of trauma.

Attempts to complete unfinished psychological tasks associated with the ancestor's trauma are handed down from generation to generation. All these tasks are associated with the shared mental representation of the same event and eventually this mental representation evolves as a most significant large-group identity marker, a chosen trauma. Not all past massive tragedies at the hands of "others" evolve as chosen traumas. We see the mythologizing of victimized heroes and moving stories associated with a trauma popularized in songs and poetry, and we see political leaders of later times create a preoccupation with a past trauma and related events and turn this historic event into a chosen trauma. Sentiments about chosen glories and chosen traumas are often mixed.

More than a child's identification with traumatized adults, the concept of "depositing" self- and object images into the self-representation of a child explains how *transgenerational transmission of trauma* occurs (Volkan, 1987; Volkan, Ast & Greer, 2001). Depositing is closely related to "identification" in childhood, but it is in some ways significantly different from identification. In identification, the child is the primary active partner in taking in and assimilating object images and related ego and superego functions from another person. In depositing, the other, the adult person, more actively pushes his or her specific self- and internalized object images into the developing self-representation of the child. In other words, the other person uses the child (mostly unconsciously) as a *permanent* reservoir for certain self- and object images belonging to that adult. The experiences that created these mental images in the adult are not "accessible" to the child; yet, those mental images are pushed into the child, without the experiential/contextual "framework" which created them. Memories belonging to one person cannot be transmitted to another person, but an adult can deposit traumatized self- and object images—as well as others, such as realistic or imagined object images that are formed in the depositor's mind as a response to trauma—into a child's self-representation. Judith Kestenberg's term (1982) *transgenerational transportation*, I believe, refers to "depositing" traumatized images. It is related to a well-known concept in individual psychology called "projective identification" (Klein, 1946). Depositing in the large-group psychology, however, refers to a process shared by thousands or millions, starts in childhood and becomes like a "psychological DNA", creating a sense of belonging. The term "chosen trauma" accurately reflects a large group's *unconscious* "choice" to add a past generation's mental representation of a shared event to its own identity.

In open or in dormant fashion, or in both alternatively, chosen traumas can continue to exist for centuries. In "normal" times the chosen traumas can be ritualistically recalled at the anniversary of the original event. Greeks link themselves when they share the "memory" of the fall of Constantinople (Istanbul) to the Turks in 1453; Russians recall the "memory" of the Tatar invasion centuries ago; Czechs commemorate the battle of Bila Hora in 1620, which led to their subjugation under the Hapsburg Empire for nearly 300 years; Scots keep alive the story of the battle of Culloden in 1746 and the failure of Bonnie Prince Charlie to restore a Stuart to the British throne; the Dakota people of the United States recall the anniversary of their decimation at Wounded Knee in 1890; and Crimean Tatars define themselves by the collective suffering of their deportation from Crimea in 1944. Israelis and Jews around the globe, including those not personally affected by the Holocaust, all to some degree define their large-group identity by direct or indirect reference to the Holocaust. The Holocaust is still too "hot" to be considered a truly established chosen trauma, but it already has become an ethnic marker, even though Orthodox Jews still refer to the 586 BC destruction of the Jewish temple in Jerusalem by Nebuchadnezzar II of Babylonia as *the* chosen trauma of the Jews. Some chosen traumas are difficult to detect because they are not simply connected to one well-recognized historical event. For example, the Estonians' chosen trauma is not related to one specific event, but to the fact that they had lived under almost constant dominance (Swedes, Germans, Russians) for thousands of years.

Entitlement ideologies, re-activation of chosen traumas and time collapse

Chosen traumas fuel entitlement ideologies. Not unlike the exaggerated entitlement we notice in a person with a narcissistic personality organization, an *entitlement ideology* provides a shared belief system for the members of a large group in that they have a right to possess whatever they desire. Entitlement ideologies reflect a large-group's attempt towards a narcissistic reorganization following a regression and are connected with the large group's difficulty mourning losses, people, land, or prestige at the hands of an enemy in the name of large-group identity. In individual psychology, mourning is an obligatory human psychobiological response to a meaningful loss. When a loved one dies, the mourner has to go through predictable and definable phases. The individual mourning processes can be "infected" due to various causes (Volkan, 1981; Volkan and Zintl, 1993) just as "infected" large-group mourning for losses caused by the actions of another large group will appear on societal/political levels.

Irredentism is a political entitlement ideology. It became a political term after the Italian nationalist movement sought annexation of lands referred to as *Italia irredenta* (unredeemed Italy), areas inhabited by an ethnic Italian majority but under Austrian jurisdiction after 1866. Many authors (Herzfeld, 1986; Koliopoulos, 1990; Markides, 1977; Volkan and Itzkowitz, 1994; Volkan, 1979, 2009b) extensively studied another well-known entitlement ideology and its sometimes deadly consequences known as *Megali Idea* (*Great Idea*) among Greeks. It refers to a specific political entitlement ideology that demanded the reunification of all Greeks of the former Byzantine Empire. Megali Idea played a significant role in Greeks' political, social, and especially religious lives since the Greek Orthodox Church was instrumental in keeping the Megali Idea alive and active. Since Greece's membership of the European Union, its investment in this ideology has waned.

Even when chosen traumas are recalled ritualistically, emotionally speaking they may lie dormant for a long time, like effectively repressed unconscious conflicts in an individual; yet, like individual conflicts, the chosen trauma with associated entitlement ideologies can be reactivated and emotionally inflamed to exert a powerful psychological force in the lives of the group members. Chosen traumas act like fuel to maintain large-group conflicts, even if the conflicts have their origins in economic, legal, political, or military controversy. When a large group regresses due to present threats against its identity and suffers from shared narcissistic hurt, its members do not simply recall their chosen traumas in ritualistic ways. They reactivate the chosen trauma in an effort to repair and maintain the large-group identity and the narcissistic investment in it. Indeed, some political leaders seem intuitively to know how to inflame a chosen trauma, especially when their large group is in conflict or has gone through a radical change and needs to reconfirm or enhance its identity. Elsewhere (Volkan, 1997) I described in detail how Slobodan Miloševi and his associates re-reactivated the 600-year-old Serbian chosen trauma, the 1389 battle of Kosovo, and the tragic consequences of this reactivation.

When a chosen trauma is reactivated, a *time collapse* occurs and affects, expectations, and defences concerning the present threats become psychologically combined with responses to the chosen trauma. This magnifies the present danger. In the unofficial diplomatic negotiations I have taken part in during the last 30 years, when one side feels shame or humiliation, the representatives of this large group often focus on their chosen traumas in order to patch up their large-group identity and differentiate themselves from participants who belong to an opposing large-group identity. This obstructs realistic negotiations (Volkan, 1999, 2006). In other words, a time collapse presents itself at the negotiation table as a resistance to finding peaceful solutions. Psychoanalytically informed diplomatic strategies are best suited to deal with such a difficulty.

Psychoanalytically informed diplomatic strategies

Attempting to understand large groups is a daunting task, and one that may be "a defense against the experience of despair about the world, a grandiose effort to manage the unmanageable" (Shapiro & Carr 2006, p. 256). As I have learned more and more about various aspects of large-group psychology during the last three decades, I have come to a conclusion that the above statement is correct. Nonetheless, I also realize that some seemingly very difficult large-group conflicts can be managed in a peaceful way if we apply psychoanalytically informed diplomatic strategies to them. My colleagues and I from the University of Virginia's Center for the Study of Mind and Human Interaction (CSMHI) (closed in 2005) developed such strategies, among them an unofficial diplomatic methodology that we named the Tree Model. The root, trunk, and branches of a tree represent the three phases of this model.

During the first phase, which includes in-depth psychoanalytically informed interviews with a wide range of the large group's members, the interdisciplinary facilitating team of psychoanalysts, historians, political scientists, and others from different disciplines begins to understand the main conscious as well as unconscious aspects of the relationship between the two opposing large groups and the surrounding situation to be addressed.

During the psychopolitical dialogues under the direction of the psychoanalytically informed facilitating team—which consist of a series of multi-day meetings over several years—psychological obstacles are brought to the surface, articulated, and interpreted so that more realistic communication can take place. For practical purposes, psychopolitical dialogues are a series of intensive workshops during which the facilitating team brings into the open previously unrecognized thoughts and feelings and helps the participants work through them. The goal is to prevent these disturbing thoughts and feelings from remaining in the shadows and interfering with a realistic evaluation of and relationship with the "enemy". In this sense, the workshops are therapeutic, but not at the level of personal problems.

Since they deal with conflicts pertaining to participants' large-group identity, images of the enemy group, and historical grievances, they are primarily in the service of removing psychopolitical obstacles experienced by participants from opposing large groups.

Psychopolitical dialogues become a process where historical grievances are aired; perceptions, fears, and attitudes are articulated; and previously hidden psychological obstacles to reconciliation or change rise to the surface. Their aim is not to erase the images of past historical events and differences in large-group identity and culture, but rather to detoxify the relationship so that differences do not lead to renewed violence. When two large groups are in conflict, the enemy is obviously real, but it is also fantasized. If participants can differentiate their fantasized dangers from the current issues, then negotiations and steps towards peace can become more realistic.

To be effective on a long-term basis, the series of psychopolitical workshops calls for the same 30 to 40 influential participants (legislators, ambassadors, government officials, well-known scholars, or other public figures) to meet two to three times per year for three to four days each time. During the workshops, there are plenary sessions, but most of the work is done in small groups led by members of the facilitating interdisciplinary team. The participants from the opposing large groups become spokespersons for their ethnic or national groups, and the facilitating team seeks to spread the insights gained to the broader population through concrete programmes that promote peaceful strategies and co-existence.

If psychopolitical dialogues are to succeed and have any impact on a society, the facilitating team must earn the trust of the participants from both sides. In order for the gained insights to have an impact on social and political policy as well as on the populace at large, the final phase requires the collaborative development of concrete actions, programmes, and institutions. What is learned is operationalized so that more peaceful co-existence can be achieved.

In this brief chapter I will not provide details of the Tree Model. The reader can find such details elsewhere (Volkan, 1999, 2006). It will be sufficient to state that this methodology, especially during the psychopolitical dialogues, pays full attention to large-group psychology topics described in this chapter. It takes into consideration the importance of threats against large-group identity, it notices the importance of the shared mental representation of the large-groups' histories, and includes the impact of transgenerational transmission of trauma, chosen glories, chosen traumas, as well as the time collapse. One crucial aim of the psychopolitical dialogues is to establish a "time expansion" between the more recent problems and the past ones belonging to the ancestors so that more realistic negotiations about current issues can take place. This is done by not forgetting or denying ancestors' traumas but by understanding and feeling how the mental representations of such traumas have become large-group identity markers.

Political and diplomatic efforts to find peaceful co-existence between enemies provoke shared, felt or hidden anxiety, and therefore shared psychological obstacles against peaceful solutions because they threaten existing large-group identities, despite the fact that at times the population may appear to favour such changes. As a way of handling the opposing large groups' anxiety, the facilitating team pays attention to *two basic principles* that govern the interactions between enemies. These two principles are:

1. Two opposing large groups need to maintain their identities as distinct from each other (principle of non-sameness) and
2. Two opposing large groups need to maintain an unambiguous *psychological* border between them. If a political border exists between the enemies, it becomes highly psychological.

Both principles relate to the fact that people in one large group have a tendency to externalize, project, and displace certain unwanted elements onto the other. Imagine "mud" is thrown onto the "other's" huge tent's canvas, and it sometimes leaves a "stain". There is, however, also anxiety that the "mud" could be hurled right back at the sender. The two principles exist to prevent the "mud" from coming back, thus helping each side's identity remain cohesive. The act of paying attention to differences, including minor ones, between two large groups in conflict can be seen as a way of shoring up the psychological border between the two large groups' identities. This differentiation helps lessen each group's anxiety, since, with the border in place, a clear distinction between the two large groups is maintained, diminishing the anxiety that one large group's identity will become diluted or lost in the other's. This emphasis differentiates this facilitating team's strategy from many other peace-making

persons' or teams' insistence that in order to make peace the opposing groups are required to be friendly and that enemies need to
"love" each other in order to make peace.

When two opposing groups perceive threats against their large-
group identities, *minor differences* (Freud, 1917, 1921; Volkan, 1988,
1997, 2006) between them assume increasing psychological importance. Many symbols that mark large-group identities have been
involved in accentuating minor differences. For example, the inhab-
itants of Andhra Pradesh in India often wear scarves around their
necks, whereas members of the neighbouring group with whom
they sometimes fight, the Telanganas, do not. Between Croats and
Serbs, dialect differences—such as the Croat *mlijeko* (milk) vs. the
Serb *mleko*—carry a heavy political-cultural load. In times of stress
and violent outbreaks, identifying minor differences may have
deadly implications. Sinhalese mobs in the Sri Lankan riots of 1958,
for example, relied on a variety of subtle indicators—such as the
presence of earring holes in the ear or the manner in which a shirt
was worn—to identify their enemy Tamils, whom they then attacked
or killed (Horowitz, 1985).

During the application of the Tree Model the participants from
the opposing large groups may suddenly experience a rapproche-
ment. This closeness is then followed by a sudden withdrawal from
one another and then again by closeness—coming together and then
pulling apart like an accordion. Denying and accepting derivatives
of aggression within the participants towards the "enemy" large
group, even when they are hidden, and attempts to protect large-
group identities underlie this behaviour. Effective discussion of real-
world issues cannot take place unless one allows the "accordion
playing" to continue for a while so that the swing in sentiments can
be replaced by more secure feelings about participants' large-group
identities.

Clinical psychoanalysis provides us with models to apply towards
establishing a psychoanalytically informed methodology for finding peaceful solutions between enemies. Consider, for example, an
individual with a very traumatic childhood. He comes to analysis as
an adult with defences against shame and humiliation, murderous
rage, and a need to be understood and accepted as a human being
by fellow human beings. After a while this person, during his sessions, gives up his defences and adaptation to his internal conflicts.

The analyst becomes a transference figure and the patient experiences the analyst as some important figure from his childhood, such as a person on whom the patient depends and for whom he experiences rage. Such developments are part of analytic treatment, and for it to work properly, a "therapeutic space" has to be formed and maintained in the analyst's office.

Let us visualize such a space with an imagined effigy representing the analyst sitting in the middle of it. The patient sends verbal missiles to mutilate and kill the effigy and the analyst tolerates the attack. The next day, the analyst-effigy is placed in the therapeutic space again, showing the patient that his childhood rage did not commit a murder. A mental "game" is played in this space until the patient learns how to "kill" a symbol and not a real person, how to relinquish devastating guilt feelings, how to tame other intense emotions, and how to separate fantasy from reality. The patient also learns to establish a firm continuity of time, but with an ability to restore feelings, thinking, and perceptions to their proper places: the past, the present, or the future. In other words, the burdens of the past can be left behind, and a hope for a better future can be maintained. There should be no damaging intrusions into this space. For example, the patient does not really hit the analyst, but only his or her effigy, and the analyst does not have real sex with the patient who wishes to be loved, but only shows the patient that the latter is "loved" because the analyst has always protected the therapeutic space.

The Tree Model aims to create such a "therapeutic space" between warring enemy large groups where they can "play" a serious and deadly game while always killing the effigies rather than one another. This is of course very difficult and perhaps impossible to establish if enemy groups constantly invade this space with real bullets, missiles, torture, and live bombs—like suicide bombers. However, our experiences with this model have shown us that it works in situations when wars are over or when international conflict has become chronic. I also believe that some of the Tree Model principles, especially those connected with the large-group psychology pertaining to large-group identity, can be and sometimes should be considered even when the conflict is "hot" and deadly. I have reached the conclusion that as psychoanalysts, if we choose to be involved in fieldwork and collaborate with others from different disciplines, such as diplomats, our clinical knowledge can make us significant contributors to international relationships. During the meeting celebrating Freud's 150th birthday in Vienna that I mentioned at the beginning of this chapter, participants also shared this view.

References

Arlow, J. (1973). Motivations for peace. In: H.Z. Winnik, R. Moses & M. Ostow (Eds.), *Psychological Basis of War* (pp. 193–204). Jerusalem: Jerusalem Academic Press.

Blos, P. (1979). *The Adolescence Passage: Developmental Issues.* New York: International Universities Press.

Blum, H. (1985). Superego formation, adolescent transformation and the adult neurosis. *Journal of the American Psychoanalytical Association,* 4: 887–909.

Eckstaedt, A. (1989). *Nationalismus in der "zweiten Generation": Psychoanalyse von Hörigkeitsverhältnissen (National Socialism in the Second Generation: Psychoanalysis of Master-Slave Relationships).* Frankfurt: Suhrkamp Verlag.

Erikson, E.H. (1956). The problem of ego identification. *Journal of the American Psychoanalytical Association,* 4: 56–121.

Fornari, F. (1966). *The Psychoanalysis of War.* A. Pfeifer (Trans.). Bloomington, IN: Indiana University Press, 1975.

Freud, S. (1913). *Totem and Taboo. S.E., 13:* 1–165. London: Hogarth.

Freud, S. (1917). *Taboo of Virginity. S.E., 11:* 191–208. London: Hogarth.

Freud, S. (1921). *Group Psychology and the Analysis of the Ego. S.E., 18:* 65–143. London: Hogarth.

Freud, S. (1927). *The Future of an Illusion. S.E., 21:* 5–56. London: Hogarth.

Freud, S. (1930). *Civilization and its Discontents. S.E., 21:* 59–145. London: Hogarth.

Freud, S. (1932). *Why War? S.E., 22:* 197–215. London: Hogarth.

Glower, E. (1947). *War, Sadism, and Pacifism: Further Essays on Group Psychology and War.* London: Allen and Unwin.

Grubrich-Simitis, I. (1979). *Extremtraumatisierung als kumulatives Trauma: psychoanalytische Studien über seelische Nachwirkungen der Konzentrationslagerhaft bei Überlebenden und ihren Kindern* (Extreme traumatization as a cumulative trauma: psychoanalytic studies on the mental effects of imprisonment in concentration camps on survivors and their children). *Psyche, 33:* 991–1023.

Hendrick, I. (1958). *Facts and Theories of Psychoanalysis.* New York: Knopf.

Herzfeld, M. (1986). *Ours Once More: Folklore, Ideology and the Making of Modern Greece.* New York: Pella.

Horowitz, D.L. (1985). *Ethnic Groups in Conflict.* Berkeley: University of California Press.

Jokl, A.M. (1997). *Zwei Fällezum Thema "Bewältigung der Vergangenheit". (Two cases referring to the theme of "mastering the past".)* Frankfurt: Jüdischer Verlag.

Kakar, S. (1996). *The Colors of Violence: Cultural Identities, Religion and Conflict.* Chicago: University of Chicago Press.

Kernberg, O.F. (2003a). Sanctioned political violence: A psychoanalytic view—Part 1. *International Journal of Psychoanalysis, 84:* 683–698.

Kernberg, O.F. (2003b). Sanctioned political violence: A psychoanalytic view—Part 2. *International Journal of Psychoanalysis, 84:* 683–698.

Kestenberg, J. (1982). A psychological assessment based on analysis of a survivor's child. In: M.S. Bergman & M.E. Jucovy (Eds.), *Generations of the Holocaust* (pp. 158–177). New York: Columbia University Press.

Klein, M. (1946). Notes on some schizoid mechanisms. In: J. Riviere (Ed.), *Development of Psychoanalysis* (pp. 292–320). London: Hogarth.

Klein, M. (1961). *Narrative of a Child Analysis: The Conduct of the Psychoanalysis of Children as Seen in the Treatment of a Ten-Year-Old Boy.* London: Hogarth, 1975.

Koliopoulos, J.S. (1990). Brigandage and irredentism in nineteenth-century Greece. In: M. Blinkhorn & T. Veremis (Eds.), *Modern Greece: Nationalism and Nationality* (pp. 67–102). Athens: Sage-Eliamep.

Loewenberg, P. (1995). *Fantasy and Reality in History.* London: Oxford University Press.

Markides, K. (1977). *The Rise and Fall of the Cyprus Republic.* New Haven, CT: Yale University Press.

Mitscherlich, A. & Mitscherlich, M. (1975). *The Inability to Mourn: Principles of Collective Behavior.* New York: Grove Press.

Niederland, W.C. (1961). The problem of survivors. *Journal of Hillside Hospital, 10:* 233–247.

Niederland, W.C. (1968). Clinical observations on the "survivor syndrome." *International Journal of Psychoanalysis, 49:* 313–315.

Rice, A.K. (1965). *Learning for Leadership: Interpersonal and Intergroup Relations.* London: Tavistock, 1965.

Shapiro, E. & Carr, W. (2006). Those people were some kind of solution: Can society in any sense be understood? *Organizational & Social Dynamics, 6:* 241–257.

Streeck-Fischer, A. (1999). Naziskins in Germany: How traumatization deals with the past. *Mind and Human Interaction, 10:* 84–97.

Turquet, P. (1975). Threats to identity in the large group. In: L. Kreeger (Ed.), *The Large Group: Dynamics and Therapy* (pp. 87–144). London: Constable.

Volkan, V.D. (1979). *Cyprus—War and Adaptation.* Charlottesville, VA: University Press of Virginia.

Volkan, V.D. (1981). *Linking Objects and Linking Phenomena: A Study of the Forms, Symptoms, Metapsychology, and Therapy of Complicated Mourning.* New York: International Universities Press.

Volkan, V.D. (1987). *Six Steps in the Treatment of Borderline Personality Organization.* Northvale, NJ: Jason Aronson.

Volkan, V.D. (1988). *The Need to Have Enemies and Allies: From Clinical Practice to International Relationships.* Northvale, NJ: Jason Aronson.

Volkan, V.D. (1991). On chosen trauma. *Mind and Human Interaction,* 4: 3–19.

Volkan, V.D. (1997). *Bloodlines: From Ethnic Pride to Ethnic Terrorism.* New York: Farrar, Straus and Giroux, 1997.

Volkan, V.D. (1999). The tree model: A comprehensive psychopolitical approach to unofficial diplomacy and the reduction of ethnic tension. *Mind and Human Interaction,* 10: 141–210.

Volkan, V.D. (2004). *Blind Trust: Large Groups and Their Leaders in Times of Crisis and Terror.* Charlottesville, VA: Pitchstone Publishing.

Volkan, V.D. (2006). *Killing in the Name of Identity: A Study of Bloody Conflicts.* Charlottesville, VA: Pitchstone Publishing.

Volkan, V.D. (2009a). The next chapter: Consequences of societal trauma. In: P. Gobodo-Madikizela & C. van der Merve (Eds.), *Memory, Narrative and Forgiveness: Perspectives of the Unfinished Journeys of the Past* (pp. 1–26). Cambridge: Cambridge Scholars Publishing.

Volkan, V.D. (2009b). *Cyprus—War and Adaptation* (Revised Edition). Istanbul: OA Press.

Volkan, V.D., Ast, G. & Greer, W. (2001). *The Third Reich in the Unconscious: Transgenerational Transmission and its Consequences.* New York: Brunner-Routledge.

Volkan, V.D. & Fowler, C. (2009). *Searching for a Perfect Woman: The Story of a Complete Psychoanalysis.* New York: Jason Aronson.

Volkan, V.D. & Itzkowitz, N. (1994). *Turks and Greeks: Neighbours in Conflict.* Huntingdon, England: Eothen Press.

Volkan, V.D. & Zintl, E. (1993). *Life After Loss: The Lessons of Grief.* New York: Charles Scribner's Sons.

ACT II

THE FINANCIAL CRISIS
AND THE DISAPPEARING CONTAINERS

In Act II the safety provided by "containment" has been lost, swept away. Nothing can be relied upon in the same way as before. None of the systems, organizations, or the established financial institutions can now be trusted.

How and where can a sense of trust and security develop?

Oedipus Rex at Enron: Leadership, Oedipal struggles, and organizational collapse[1]

Mark Stein[2]

Abstract

This article is intended to contribute to our understanding of the December 2001 collapse of Enron. The existing literature on Enron's demise falls largely into two broad areas, involving either "micro" psychological explanations or "macro" accounts that emphasize the workplace and its environment; this paper is an exploratory study that focuses on a new interpretation which links the two areas more closely together. It is proposed that Enron's culture was influenced

[1] Paper revised June 25, 2007 for: *Human Relations*.
First published by Sage Publications in *Human Relations*, September 2007, author Mark Stein.
Paper reprinted in full by permission of Sage Publications.
[2] Acknowledgements: the author is grateful to the Advance Institute of Management and British Academy of Management for the co-sponsored research workshop in which he received much useful feedback on early ideas in his examination of the Enron case. He also wishes to thank Yiannis Gabriel, William Halton, and Antje Netzer-Stein as well as associate editor Barbara Townley for their comments and guidance on drafts of this paper. The Tavistock Institute of Medical Psychology provided a personal bursary that supported this research and for this he owes much gratitude. The responsibility for the views expressed in this paper is entirely the author's own.

by both "micro" and "macro" factors: an experience of unsuccessful paternal authority figures within the family history of Enron's leaders, coupled with an experience of problematic government and regulatory regimes associated with the gas industry. Drawing on concepts from psychoanalysis and its application to organizational dynamics, it is argued that these "micro" and "macro" factors helped to generate an Oedipal mindset in Enron's leaders according to which external authority was seen to be weak and not worthy of respect, and that this contributed to Enron's demise. Implications for theory are examined.

Introduction and outline

Six times *Fortune* magazine's "Innovative company of the year", Enron was consistently admired in Wall Street and applauded elsewhere. Its collapse in December 2001 surprised almost everyone, shocking the business, regulatory, and academic communities. While major corporate debacles such as those at Barings Bank, WorldCom, and Parmalat have preceded and followed the one at Enron, the nature and magnitude of Enron's demise—the biggest corporate failure at that point in history—may lead it to become "the most analyzed business case in the history of capitalism" (Boje et al., 2004, p. 751). Despite this interest, there is little consensus on how we should understand the Enron case. With the intention to bridge the different areas of explanation that are offered in this case, a new perspective based on the concept of the Oedipus complex is offered in this paper.

The sequence of the paper is as follows. Following this introduction, the methodology section outlines the sources of data used and the manner in which they were analysed. In specifying the methodology, a link with the burgeoning literature on text-based research is established. An examination of the existing literature follows, in which it is noted that existing explanations for Enron's collapse fall into two broad categories, "micro" and "macro". The rationale for this paper—involving a new explanation that makes a stronger link between the "micro" and "macro" aspects—is then outlined. Following this, a precis of the Enron case relates the background and key events leading up to the collapse of the company. The theoretical framework—drawing on the psychoanalytic concept of the Oedipus complex and its application to organizational dynamics—is then specified. Having outlined the theoretical framework, the analysis section involves the postulation and exploration of an interpretation that uses the above framework and is intended to contribute to our understanding of Enron's collapse. This interpretation begins with an exploration of the personal histories of the two key leaders at Enron and then goes on to examine the peculiar and highly problematic regulatory history of the gas industry. It is then argued that these two sets of factors coalesced to incline the leaders to undermine, thwart, and deride Enron's regulators in a way that ultimately contributed to the collapse of the company. In the discussion and conclusion, the theoretical implications of the Oedipus argument are examined.

Methodology

The analysis offered in this paper is inspired, at least in part, by the growing interest in text-based research in organization and management studies (Gephart, 1993; Brown, 2003, 2005; Brown & Jones, 2000; Weick, 1993). A wide range of textual sources were used to provide data for the case. First, books on the Enron debacle were examined: these include "insider" perspectives by Cruver (2002) and Swartz and Watkins (2003), as well as other accounts by Bryce (2002), Eichenwald (2005), Fox (2003), Fusaro and Miller (2002), Jenkins (2003), and McLean and Elkind (2003), which, collectively, draw on many hundreds of interviews with key players in and around Enron. Second, specialist books on Enron and its context were also read. These include Mehta's account of Enron's Dabhol project (1999); a book by Cannon (1993), a historian of the US gas industry; a book by MacAvoy (2000), an expert on the regulation of the gas industry; a volume on the oil industry, edited by Share (1996); and a volume by Partnoy (2003), a professor of law who testified to the US Senate's Enron hearings. Third, a variety of papers and academic journal articles focusing specifically on Enron's collapse were examined. Fourth, using keyword searches, the websites of a number of newspapers and periodicals were scrutinized. This yielded not only hundreds of newspaper articles on Enron's demise but also many pieces that appeared in the years prior to its downfall. Fifth, a variety of other relevant websites were examined.

Data from these sources were collected together in a thematically organized, typed document, with each entry being followed by a page reference to the original source (book, article etc.) from where it came. Following Burgess (1991), as well as substantive (observational) notes, methodological notes (concerning impressions) and analytic notes (concerning preliminary analysis) were taken. These themes were then subject to further examination by being linked together, discarded, modified, or further refined (Burgess, 1991; Creswell, 1994; Robson, 1993). References to the various texts were re-read and links were pursued so that the thematic document was modified and extended. By the time the last iteration of this process was undertaken a single-spaced typed document of 29 pages had been created. Consistent with Brown's textual method, a qualitative rather than quantitative analysis of these themes was undertaken because it allows for "the highlighting of nuances of meaning and sensitivity to language used" (Brown, 2003, p. 108); this is also consistent with the psychoanalytic approach mentioned below.

The theme titles used in the analysis included relatively straightforward topics such as "whistleblower" and "bribery"; the names of key actors (for example, "Lay" and "Skilling"); and more explanatory concepts such as "the shadow"; "the gang"; "narcissistic organization"; and "Oedipal phenomena". Such explanatory concepts bear some similarity to the "formal, analytic" themes described by Hammersley and Atkinson (1983, p. 226). Using these ideas, the themes referred to above were therefore used to construct plausible rival hypotheses (Yin, 1994) or interpretations that were juxtaposed with the ambition of developing alternative explanations. After several iterations, the Oedipal theme—which provides the opportunity for a closer linking of "micro" and "macro" aspects—was selected and refined into a provisional interpretation intended to contribute to an explanation of Enron's downfall.

While great care was taken in the writing of this paper, there is no suggestion that the account provided here offers the only plausible view of the Enron debacle. Following the work of authors such as Hammersley and Atkinson (1983) and Gill and Johnson (1991), this study is "reflexive" in the sense that it is conceived with the knowledge that the researcher is necessarily part of the social world explored here. Not only must this paper reflect the interests of the author, but it inevitably privileges some voices rather than others

(Pentland, 1999), and is "conceived and executed within a particular scholarly discourse" (Brown & Jones, 2000, p. 659).

Explanations from the literature

An examination of the existing literature shows that studies of Enron's demise may be grouped into two broad categories. On the one hand are "micro" psychological arguments that focus largely on personal characteristics within Enron's leadership. On the other hand are "macro" arguments that focus largely on issues connected with the workplace and its environment. Specific analyses within these broad categories of analysis, "micro" and "macro", are explored below.

One key "micro" theme is that of greed. The centrality of greed in the Enron literature is evidenced by the fact that the term finds a place in the title or subtitle of three of the books on the company's collapse (Bryce, 2002; Cruver, 2002; Partnoy, 2003). Further, Boje et al., depict "Enronization" as a "script of greed" (2004, p. 766) with Fox (2003) arguing that Enron is emblematic of modern, corporate greed. Cruver's account of the role of greed exemplifies this approach: he argues that greed fuelled those who "dreamed of colossal bonuses" and "millions in stock options" (Cruver, 2002, Introduction xv). Levine (2005) articulates some of the psychology of this by arguing that Enron's leaders experienced a "relentless greed" (2005, p. 728) that required them to be the recipients of an endless and uninterrupted flow of all those things that they valued. Cruver concludes that "greed ... pushed Enron to ignore the very same risk strategies that it was preaching to the world" and led it "to ignore—or even punish—the messengers of bad news" (2002, Introduction xv–xvi). According to this view, therefore, greed was a major factor in leading to Enron's collapse.

Articulated by Carr and Downs (2004, 2005), a second "micro" theme suggests that the activities of certain of Enron's leaders can be seen through the prism of psychoanalytic ideas of "transitional objects" (Winnicott, 1971) and "splitting" (Klein, 1980). In particular, some of Enron's financial structures known as Special Purpose Entities (SPEs) are understood to be akin to a child's playful "transitional objects" that represent a particularly schizoid or split view of the world. Thus, some SPEs were given "good" *Star Wars* names such as "Chewco" and "Jedi" while others were given "bad" names such as "Raptor" and "Condor" from the film *Jurassic Park* (Carr & Downs, 2005, p. 5). Carr and Downs suggest that these structures may have represented a timeless internal drama that had its origins in the history of leaders at Enron (2005, p. 3). It follows, therefore, that the creation and design of these structures pivoted on a distorted view of reality and that this thereby contributed to the demise of the company.

A third "micro" theme focuses on the issue of narcissism: this notion suggests that Enron's problems occurred as a result of highly inflated hubristic feelings among the leadership that convinced them that great success was guaranteed. Long, for example, argues that "narcissistic … grandiose *individual players*" at Enron created an organizational system that was "illusory, self-deceptive" and "in denial" (2002, p. 195—emphasis in original). Levine takes this further by arguing that Enron's leaders were motivated by the desire to "extract from others the admiration needed to protect a fragile sense of self" (2005, p. 729). He goes on to suggest that their desire for "ultimate narcissistic fulfillment" (2005, p. 728) was associated with a contemptuous view of others, a theme demonstrated in earlier studies of organizational narcissism (Stein, 2003). Narcissism within Enron's leadership is therefore seen as having played a major role in the company's collapse.

Turning to the "macro" themes, several authors—noting the debacles in companies such as Barings, WorldCom, and Parmalat—argue that Enron's demise can be explained by certain features of modern organizations and their relationships in the wider environment. Deakin and Konzelmann, for example, maintain that Enron's business model was focused on short-term profits and "exemplifies the pathology of the 'shareholder value' system" that has become "dominant in Britain and America in the 1980s and 1990s" (2003, p. 584). It is noteworthy that concern about the short-term focus of public, listed companies is particularly pronounced in relation to Enron's area of core competence, that of the oil and gas industries (Share, 1996, p. 405). In spite of the 2002 Sarbanes–Oxley Act (passed in the US in response to the Enron collapse), Deakin and Konzelmann conclude that the strong emphasis on short-term profits will lead to further scandals unless more substantial regulatory changes make this model unattractive.

Other "macro" writers focus on how, following the payment of financial contributions to political parties, governments and regulators have colluded with modern work organizations (Conrad, 2003); popularized by Ralph Nader, this view is consistent with a thread running through parts of the regulation literature according to which there is persistent evidence of the "capture" of regulatory agencies by business (see especially the volume by Baldwin et al., 1998). "Macro" views of the collusion of regulators and government are paralleled by similar views of the role of auditors. Specifically, some regard the highly questionable methods of Arthur Andersen (Enron's auditors) as the central source of the problem, arguing that this was part of a wider pattern which benefited other big audit firms (Grey, 2003; Eisenberg & Macey, 2004), with similar accounting violations having occurred in other high profile cases, including WorldCom (Tinker & Carter, 2003).

At an even broader level, however, certain "macro" authors believe that Enron is representative of a range of work organizations which are part of the wider "corporate meltdown" of modern capitalism. Enron, WorldCom, and Parmalat are not just "a few bad apples" (Conrad, 2003, p. 553), but rather instances of widespread, socially irresponsible "turbo-capitalism" (Grey, 2003, p. 573). Such "turbo-capitalism" is seen to be supported by business schools that promote the ambition for capital accumulation in the absence of any concern for the ethics used to achieve it, as well as a business press which has a similar disregard for moral issues when it evaluates and gives awards to those who have succeeded in this quest. The "macro" literature on the pathology of the "shareholder value" system; regulatory capture; questionable accounting methods; and "turbo-capitalism", are consistent with the view that Enron's collapse was an "accident waiting to happen"; to borrow Perrow's (1999) term, Enron's collapse could thus be seen as a "normal accident".

Rationale for this paper

The literature review thus provides a clear picture of two broad but distinctive ways of explaining the demise of Enron. First there are the "micro" arguments that focus on the personal, psychological characteristics of the company's leaders: these arguments suggest that characteristics such as greed, narcissism, or the use of primitive "splitting" and "transitional objects" swayed the leaders to behave in highly irrational ways that led to the company's downfall. Second, and by way of contrast, are the "macro" arguments that focus on the workplace and its environment; these concern, for example, the relationship between Enron and external agencies such as regulators as well as the shaping of this by the economic and social forces pervasive in late 20th century capitalism.

Having noted the two broad streams of literature on Enron, the problematic of this paper gradually emerged and was formulated around the following question: could a stronger argument be made if the two streams were to be brought closer together? In particular, "micro" issues concerning the psychology of Enron's leaders are more likely to have put the company at greater risk if they were paralleled by other, related "macro" pressures that influenced the organization in its environment. Conversely, while "macro" factors may have put many organizations at risk, they would have had a greater impact on companies which were made more vulnerable by related "micro" factors; after all, many large companies exist in similar environments to Enron, but only a small proportion have collapsed. The problematic of this paper thus eventually emerged as the quest for a closer link between the two streams in order to provide a more powerful argument.

With the ambition to bridge the gap between the "micro" and "macro", the more specific aim was thus to identify a "generating mechanism" (Pentland, 1999) or deep structure explanation that makes a strong connection between the two sets of factors. Such a generating mechanism was found in the concept of the Oedipus complex (Freud, 1933, 1915–17), one that occupies a place in the literature on psychoanalysis and its application to organizational dynamics (French & Vince, 1999; Gabriel, 1998; Hirschhorn, 1988, 1997; Kets de Vries & Miller, 1987, 1989; Obholzer & Roberts, 1994; Schwartz, 1990; Stein, 2000, 2003), also known as systems psychodynamics (Gould et al., 2001). While psychoanalytic views of transitional objects, splitting, and narcissism have already been mentioned, the idea of the Oedipus complex was selected as a theoretical base for this study because it contains the concept of a relation to authority figures and is therefore capable of linking "micro" individual and family dynamics with "macro" societal structures.

The Enron case

Both companies that merged in 1986 to create Enron—Houston Natural Gas (HNG) and InterNorth—had long and largely success-ful histories in utilities and in the gas industry in particular. HNG had contributed significantly to the wealth and development of its home town, Houston; by the early 1980s, it was one of the most profitable companies in the city (Bryce, 2002, p. 23). When it joined with the much larger, Omaha-based, InterNorth, the merged com-pany owned the largest gas distribution system in the US. While HNG and InterNorth had witnessed many profitable years in the gas business, incompetent government regulation during the 1970s and 1980s created difficulties for them and for the gas sector in general; it was only during the late 1980s/early 1990s, following the merger to form Enron, that the crisis abated (McLean & Elkind, 2003, p. 9).

From the outset, with Kenneth Lay as chairman and CEO, Enron showed signs that it had an inclination to condone illegal activity and ignore, undermine, or snub its regulators. For example, the company gave implicit, on-going support to Borget and Mastroeni, the Enron traders whose illegal actions in 1987 landed the company in $1.5 billion debt and almost bankrupted it. Then there were Lay's dealings with dubious individuals such as Michael Milken—the man "at the epicentre of Wall Street's crime wave in the 1980s" (Eich-enwald, 2005, p. 281)—whose illegal use of junk-bonds had led to a 10-year jail sentence. Milken's company Drexel Burnham Lambert underwrote Enron's debt at the time of the merger, and Lay contin-ued to have contact with him over many years.

Soon after Enron was created, the company diversified within the utility sector. Having held senior positions in companies such as Florida Gas and Transco, Lay himself had much experience in utilities. At Enron, Lay used this experience to initiate a number of large ventures in the electricity and water industries in particular. In due course, and under the leadership of Rebecca Mark, this would include the massive Dabhol India electricity project—a "sordid saga" (Mehta, 1999, p. 178)—that so outraged others that it involved 24 separate lawsuits and led to the victory of the Hindu nationalist coalition in Maharashtra state campaigning with the slogan that it wanted to "push Enron into the Arabian sea" (McLean & Elkind,

2003, p. 81). The biggest foreign investment in India's history, the project was a disaster both for Enron and India.

At the same time as this utility focus, Enron also diversified into the rather different areas of trading and finance; this move was directly influenced by Jeffrey Skilling, who had joined the company from McKinsey consulting. Beginning with Skilling's brainchild known as the "Gas Bank", Enron would in due course trade in weather derivatives, coal, pulp, paper, plastics, metals, and bandwidth capacity. Its massive Houston headquarters had vast trading floors where its culture was closer to Wall Street than to a traditional utility company. Skilling also embarked on an active campaign to thwart and undermine Enron's regulators. In 1991, for example, at Skilling's insistence, Enron introduced highly questionable mark-to-market accounting methods. In 1993, also under Skilling's influence, the company gained exemption from regulation by the Commodity Futures Trading Commission (CFTC). These changes, together with a variety of other practices, would later allow chief finance officer Andrew Fastow to create a variety of illegal and highly problematic financial structures called special purpose entities (SPEs).

Skilling championed the trading side of the business and did his best to diminish Enron's interests in utilities. His position was considerably strengthened in 1996 when he took over as chief operating officer from the relatively cautious Rich Kinder. At this point, Skilling vastly increased the trading business, and its recorded profits and revenues soared. In August 2000, Rebecca Mark, head of the utility side of the business, was forced to resign, enabling Skilling to further shut down Enron's interests in this area. At the time of Mark's resignation, Enron's recorded revenues reached a massive $100 billion (almost entirely based on its purported revenues in trading), making it the seventh largest company in the Fortune 500. However, this image disguised a chaotic reality characterized by an absence of regulation; the collusion of auditors Arthur Andersen; a range of illegal practices; intense internal rivalry; and highly dangerous risk taking.

During this time, a wide range of parties and stakeholders celebrated Enron as one of the most promising companies in the US, praising it as an organization with an exemplary "innovative" quality. Business academics such as Harvard's Gary Hamel, for example, wrote of Enron as having "the almost magical mix of entrepreneur-ship with the ability ... to get things done" (quoted in Beard, 2003). This adulation lasted almost until Enron's collapse, and it was only in the latter part of 2001 that suspicions about Enron's activities became widespread. In August 2001, negative publicity was generated fol-lowing an anonymous memo warning of an imminent accounting scandal, and in October 2001 the Securities and Exchange Commis-sion (SEC) began an investigation.

Finally, the "straw that broke the camel's back" (Jenkins, 2003, p. 7) was Enron's November 8 filing re-stating its financial state-ments showing massive reductions in reported earnings of 91% in 1997, 16% in 1998, 28% in 1999 and 13% in 2000 (Jenkins, 2003). Enron's stock price slumped dramatically, from nearly $80 at its peak to $11 at the end of October, and later to $1 at the end of November. By December 2001, Enron filed for bankruptcy, its stock worthless; at the time, this was the largest corporate bankruptcy in history. The consequences were widespread: thousands of Enron employees lost their jobs, their pensions ruined; Arthur Andersen (one of the "big five" accounting firms) laid off thousands of workers and finally col-lapsed; the US Justice Department started a criminal investigation; senior Enron executives were in substantial legal and personal trou-ble, with one committing suicide; and the US business community was rocked to the core.

Theoretical framework

As mentioned earlier, the thrust of this paper is to supplement exist-ing accounts by establishing an explanation that makes a stronger link between certain of the "micro" and "macro" dimensions that led to Enron's demise. Such an explanation was found in Freud's theory of the Oedipus complex (Freud, 1933, 1915–17). Sophocles' play *Oedipus Rex*, which inspired Freud's idea, involves a young man who murders his father and marries his mother. While Sophocles' work is full of the drama and tragedy of classic Greek mythology, its core idea was used by Freud (1933) to represent more ordinary rela-tionships between children and parents, as well as, via the "transfer-ence", relationships between adults and authority. There are several aspects to the psychoanalytic notion of the Oedipus complex that are relevant here.

First, Freud postulated that the growing child's development involves an intense struggle with the parent of the same gender and an unconscious desire to replace that parent. Central to Freud's notion is the idea that the child invariably experiences more ordinary feelings of competitiveness, hostility, and rivalry towards the same-sex parent. Although the "complete" Oedipus complex involves struggles with both parents (Laplanche & Pontalis, 1973, p. 283), the relationship with the parent of the same gender is especially at issue; in this paper, we focus particularly on the relationship between the son and the father.

Second, the successful resolution of such feelings within the son requires the father to be a strong, continuing presence who is able to provide for the well-being of the family and also withstand this rivalry. This is likely to include the father being able to provide in a number of different areas, such as emotional, developmental, and material aspects, in catering for the needs of the son. When the son feels safe enough to be able to compete against—and simultaneously, to identify with and feel love for—the father, the Oedipus complex could be said to have reached some resolution. The strong father figure enables the son to (a) identify with and aspire to be like him, and (b), to remain a son and accept the father's authority over him.

Third, problems are likely to occur when the father is unable to create a reasonably secure environment for the son. While some areas of failure may be compensated for by other areas of success, problems may occur if the father is unable to understand and address the son's emotional needs, cater adequately for his developmental needs, and provide materially for him. Such problems may lead to a strengthening of the boy's (conscious or unconscious) desire to replace the father rather than model himself on him. The son therefore develops a premature competence and—in the absence of the maturity to do so—"becomes" the father in the family, so that he is unable to accept the actual father's authority over him. In such circumstances the Oedipus complex is not adequately resolved. It should be noted that quite different problems (such as an excessively strict or tyrannical father) may also impede the resolution of the son's Oedipus complex, but this lies beyond the scope of the present paper.

Fourth, when premature competence occurs and the Oedipus complex remains unresolved, problems may also develop in later life. Via the transference, the relationship with a weak father figure is unconsciously transferred elsewhere, resulting in a repetition of the same pattern of relationship with a variety of authority figures. Attempts are therefore made by the son at thwarting, undermining and effectively "getting rid of" those who unconsciously represent the father's authority because they challenge the son's idea that he is the father himself. This transference can occur in relation to people or authorities who may outwardly appear quite different from the father, but who, by virtue of their authority positions, unconsciously represent him. In organizational settings, such transference may occur in relation to figures of authority within the organization or those outside it.

Fifth, the psychoanalyst Melanie Klein has added to these ideas by arguing that, through the transference, such fathers may evoke not only the desire to undermine later "parental authorities", but also feelings of contempt and the inclination to deride them (Klein, 1945). In essence, the desire to demean—and to show oneself to be superior to—these authorities are fuelled by an unconscious wish to do this to the father.

Sixth, the consequences may be very damaging. Individuals struggling with unresolved Oedipus complexes are likely to find it difficult to evaluate and differentiate between the helpful and unhelpful aspects that authority may provide, a lack which renders them vulnerable to danger. Their thwarting of authority thus involves an undermining of those who could provide the helpful restraints that protect them and prevent self-harm, as well as those who may in some other way support their well-being.

Analysis

Drawing on the above theoretical framework, my argument is that a culture in which external authority was seen to be weak and not worthy of respect emerged in Enron because it was unconsciously influenced by an experience of failed parental authority figures within Enron's leaders, coupled with failed government and regulatory regimes associated with the gas industry.

Leaders' personal backgrounds

One of the most striking aspects of the downfall of Enron concerns its relationship with its "parental" institutions: from its inception, the senior leaders of Enron mounted a vigorous and sustained attack on the authority of its regulators, leaving the company vulnerable to the dangers that these institutions were tasked with protecting it against. The interpretation offered in this paper proposes that there were two factors that account for why this happened. The first are "micro" psychological factors that concern Lay and Skilling, two highly influential leaders who had played a central role in shaping Enron's culture (Tourish & Vatcha, 2005): it is proposed here that, through the transference, their relationships with their fathers unconsciously influenced Enron's connections with its "parental" authorities in an especially problematic way.

Beginning with Lay, his father's main ambition in life was to become a Baptist preacher and, in the jobs he took in order to earn a living, he was singularly unsuccessful. The consequences for the family were considerable, with Lay's father spending some years selling stoves door-to-door and "bouncing his family around" from one place to another, "but never seeing enough success to make ends meet" (Eichenwald, 2005, p. 20). Lay's father seemed to be endlessly engaged in a search for a new job and a better life elsewhere, but, with each change, life for him and the family almost invariably got worse. As a result, Lay had no permanent home and he grew up "dirt poor" (McLean & Elkind, 2003, p. 4). During his first 11 years, for example, he never lived in a house with indoor plumbing (McLean & Elkind, 2003, p. 4); he had to start bringing in money from the age of nine by driving tractors and delivering newspapers (Fox, 2003, p. 7); at one point, when a deliveryman crashed a truck belonging to Lay's father, the resulting loss led to the bankruptcy of his business (Swartz & Watkins, 2003, p. 22).

Following the bankruptcy, Lay's father was forced to take to the road again as a travelling salesman, with the family moving from town to town; finally, they had no option but to move in with in-laws (McLean & Elkind, 2003, p. 4). Further, during one Christmas, they were so poor that they had to eat baloney sandwiches for their festive meal (Swartz & Watkins, 2003, p. 22). In the wake of his father's failure, as Swartz and Watkins argue, Lay became a "determined, almost frenetic worker" (2003, p. 22) and felt forced to take on major parental roles at an early age. The onset of Lay's early adult role was witnessed by his sister, who commented that "[i]t's hard for me not to think Ken was an adult when he was a child" (McLean & Elkind,

2003, p. 4). In sum, Lay's family depended on his help to earn income and provide support because his father had brought them close to financial ruin.

In the case of Skilling, although his father was trained as a mechanical engineer, he was in effect a salesman who sold valves to utilities and other industries. With a father who was very disappointed in his own career and who "wasn't around much" (Eichenwald, 2005, p. 26), Skilling grew up a "shy, awkward kid" (Eichenwald, 2005, p. 26), a "tortured soul" (McLean & Elkind, 2003, p. 29), as one friend described him. Skilling's mother clearly felt dissatisfied with her husband's career. She reported: "I've read where my husband was a high-falutin' executive. I don't want to say he was just a salesman, but he was a salesman. He traveled a lot. We had to be very frugal" (Bryce, 2002, p. 48).

Over the duration of his career Skilling's father waited for a promotion which never happened; his being overlooked was said to have had a "devastating" effect on the family, forcing them to move to Chicago (Swartz & Watkins, 2003, p. 41). The journey to Chicago was itself traumatic: Skilling's father was already there, so that his mother and four children had to pack up the contents of the house and travel by car across country. Young Skilling helped read the map and filled water bottles to stop the engine from over-heating (McLean & Elkind, 2003, p. 29). Skilling's mother "never quite recovered from the disappointment" of the move to Chicago, and it was the young Skilling who "held the family together" (Swartz & Watkins, 2003, p. 41), finding a job at the age of 14, and supporting the family through the trauma of their move. Further, throughout his years at high school, Skilling felt compelled to work "upward of 50 hours a week" (McLean & Elkind, 2003, p. 29), taking on jobs in which he was "in charge, dictating how the work should be accomplished" (Eichenwald, 2005, p. 27). Thus, as with the Lays, Skilling's father's lack of business success had led to the son taking on major, early responsibilities and providing support prematurely for the family.

It is interesting to note that Skilling's later considerations about his career also seem to have been influenced by a negative view of his engineering-trained father, as well as associated thoughts about failed heavy industry. Skilling's father suggested he consider engineering and he took him to see his alma mater, Lehigh University, set in the Pennsylvanian "Rust Belt". It was a recession year (1970), and, according to McLean and Elkind, the young Skilling had "an immediate visceral reaction" to the sight of "aging, decrepit steel mills" (2003, p. 29). As Swartz and Watkins put it, when he saw "the skeletons of abandoned steel mills ... [he] ... felt the promise of his life seeping away" (2003, pp. 41–42). He ultimately developed an enthusiasm for finance and studied it at Southern Methodist University in Dallas, one of the few thriving US cities at the time. He later went on to become a Harvard MBA Baker scholar, following which he joined McKinsey consulting and became its youngest ever partner.

It is thus argued here that Lay and Skilling both had unresolved Oedipus complexes and that this had an important impact on them. First, both grew up in families where there was a perception of a father who had fallen significantly short in his career and in his capacity to provide support for the family. In both cases, these problems involved the fathers making changes that led not to the abatement of the difficulties, but to the creation of new ones. In some cases, it also involved decisions to move the family in difficult circumstances, decisions which had problematic and unforeseen consequences for them. The young Lay and Skilling had therefore been forced to take on premature responsibility, making it difficult for them to identify with a good and capable paternal authority. Second, their perception of their fathers is likely to have made them ambivalent about those who take authority over them. It should be added that, while it is not argued that their fathers' shortcomings made this situation inevitable, it is suggested that it predisposed Lay and Skilling to this attitude.

Institutional background

The interpretation also suggests a second set of explanatory factors, proposing "macro" issues relating to the organization and its environment as a parallel to the family background. Thus, it is argued, the highly problematic role of the US government and its regulatory agencies strengthened Lay's and Skilling's negative predispositions towards authority. Specifically, government legislation and regulatory organizations caused havoc in the gas industry during the 1970s and '80s. This led to a performance in the gas industry that was poorer than any other regulated industry in the country for two decades (MacAvoy, 2000, Preface xiii), as well as to major adverse effects on customers. One of the difficulties was the creation of an extraordinarily complex price structure so that "it is unlikely that anyone … understood the rules at any given time" (Cannon, 1993, p. 283). Another problem was that—in attempting to secure the provision of gas at low, fixed prices over a substantial period of time—the regulators made gas production highly uneconomic. As a consequence, by the mid-1970s there were major shortages that exceeded all levels previously witnessed in energy markets, resulting in consumers incurring losses of $13 billion and producers losing in excess of $44 billion (MacAvoy, 2000, p. 74). These shortages led to schools and factories closing for weeks at a time in the East and Great Lakes states and were "politically intolerable" (Cannon, 1993, p. 291).

Then, in 1978, in a "desperate attempt" (Cannon, 1993, p. 291) to deal with the problem, the government shifted direction and passed a new law which simultaneously decreased and increased regulation in different parts of the industry. Once again, this only made matters worse. One result of the legislation was an even greater "tangled web of producer categories and differing prices for different gases" which led to "weird consequences" that "resulted in gas from different reservoirs in the same general area selling to the same buyer for prices ranging from 50 cents to $10 per thousand cubic feet" (Cannon, 1993, pp. 292–293). Another difficulty was that, while the new law led to a substantial increase in gas production, problems were simply transferred to the pipeline companies who were forced to enter into "take-or-pay" deals which guaranteed that they would purchase gas at a fixed price from the producers. The difficulty was that, for a variety of reasons, demand for gas fell, with the consequence that companies such as Transco (which Lay had joined in 1981) were saddled with large quantities of gas that they had purchased but could not sell. As Fox argues, "[i]f Ken Lay the economist has wanted an illustration of how badly the government could screw up a market, he picked the right time to join Transco" (2003, p. 11).

In 1985, shortly after Lay moved to Houston Natural Gas (HNG), the US government changed direction again by introducing further legislation encouraging pipeline companies to make their lines available to all gas utilities, but they did not allow the pipeline companies to unburden themselves from their take-or-pay contracts. This "made a bad situation even worse" by placing the pipeline companies "in an impossible position … between a rock and a hard place" (McLean & Elkind, 2003, p. 9): over the course of the next few years, many pipeline companies got into difficulty, became insolvent, or went bankrupt. By 1985, when, with Lay as chairman and CEO, HNG and InterNorth merged, it reported losses of $14 million (Fox, 2003, p. 14). To add to the humiliation, when in April 1986 the merged company adopted the name "Enron", Lay was forced to announce that the company would lose 1500 jobs and would need to save $70 million a year (Fox, 2003, p. 15), a substantial sum at the time. "Lay's new business" as McLean and Elkind put it, "had more than $1 billion in take-or-pay liabilities" (2003, p. 13). In something of an understatement, Lay later summed up the situation by saying that "[t]hroughout the '70s and part of the '80s, Congress kept chipping away at the [energy] industry" (Lay, 1996, p. 360). Unsurprisingly, by January 1987, Enron's credit rating was downgraded to junk status, and it was only in the late 1980s and early 1990s that the situation for it, and the gas industry in general, stabilized.

It is important to note that, although not directly employed by Enron until 1990, Skilling was centrally involved in the gas industry and with Enron from the outset. Working for McKinsey, Skilling had played a major role in advising Lay and others on the 1985 HNG/ InterNorth merger. By the late 1980s, he was spending about half his time on Enron work (McLean & Elkind, 2003, p. 33). Skilling's comments give voice to his view of the gas industry and its relation to government and regulators at the time. He said: "It was the screwiest business I'd ever seen in my life. All the rules were written in Washington. It was like *Alice in Wonderland*" (McLean & Elkind; 2003, p. 33). This is consistent with the view of Cannon, a gas industry historian, who argues that "[i]t is difficult … to document a more confused and economically destructive regulatory history than that of natural gas regulation" (1993, p. 289).

Thus, the interpretation of this paper proposes that the two leaders' personal histories in relation to their fathers' incompetence intersected with—and were reinforced by—the institutional history of Enron in its environment, where governmental and regulatory authorities caused havoc over a substantial period of time. These two factors therefore coalesced in Lay and Skilling to promote a frame of mind in which they would see such authorities as so incapable that they would be more likely to cause the collapse of the pipeline companies than to support them. It is argued here that this frame of mind in Lay and Skilling influenced Enron's culture, where, as argued below, the two held considerable sway over how things were done.

Consequences for Enron

We move now to explore the consequences of this. It is suggested here that these "micro" and "macro" factors coalesced and influenced Lay and Skilling's treatment of the authorities above them. As Lay was at the apex and Skilling very senior in Enron, the transference occurred principally in relation to external rather than internal authorities: they thus behaved as if external authorities were a threat to survival and would ruin their chances of success. The target of this undermining, government and their regulators, was always reasonably clear: as Lay wrote, "governments should stay out of the energy business" (Lay, 1996, p. 360). However, the explicit and official theme of Lay's writing and speeches—"rule breakers get to the future first" (Swartz & Watkins, 2003, p. 118)—only hinted at the depths to which he would go in legitimizing the undermining and ignoring of rules. This is evident, for example, in his treatment of two rule breakers (traders Borget and Mastroeni) who landed Enron in $1.5 billion debt and almost bankrupted it in 1987, early on in the company's history. Despite prison sentences for Borget and Mastroeni as well as clear advice for Lay that he should terminate their contracts, he kept them on the payroll because, according to Bryce, "he need[ed] their earnings" (2002, p. 39). A telex to the two was also sent by Enron's Mick Seidl, a close friend and colleague of Lay's (as well as his former number two), in which he thanked Borget and Mastroeni for their perseverance, adding "[p]lease keep making us millions" (McLean & Elkind, 2003, p. 20).

Lay's contempt for the law and for his regulators is also evident from his long-standing working relationship with Michael Milken. Milken, who was described by Lay as "innovative" (Cruver, 2003, p. 235), ran Drexel Burnham Lambert, the company that had underwritten over half a billion dollars of debt when Enron was formed in 1987 (Cruver, 2003, p. 17). Despite Milken being sentenced to 10 years in jail 1990 for his firm's illegal deals, Lay kept in contact with him years after his release, viewing him as "a kind of role model"

(Fusaro & Miller, 2002, p. 8), and inviting him to a private meeting in May 2001 to drum up support for Enron's unsavoury and illegal tactics in the California energy crisis.

Milken aside, the broader picture of the Californian energy crisis reveals further the degree to which Enron would undermine its regulators. It is now well established that Enron utilized deceptive and fraudulent strategies in order to create chaos in the Californian energy markets during the heat wave of the summer of 2000. Enron booked massive profits on the back of this crisis, while the people of California were forced to endure spiralling prices as well as rolling blackouts, the first such since the Second WorldWar. In the absence of any guilt, concern, or sense of responsibility for their role in the affair, Enron executives and traders lambasted the state and its regulators: they described California's regulatory policies as a "freak hybrid" (Eichenwald, 2005, p. 115) and a "disaster" (Eichenwald, 2005, p. 116), with Skilling comparing the system to that of the Soviet Union and Lay speaking of it being "doomed to failure" (McLean & Elkind, 2003, p. 281). Skilling rubbed salt into the wound during a conference speech by joking that the difference between California and the *Titanic* was that "[a]t least the lights were on when the *Titanic* went down" (Eichenwald, 2005, p. 281).

Returning to the early days of Enron, Skilling also played a dominant role in steering the company along a path which involved persuading, cajoling, evading, or corrupting its regulatory authorities. This began with Enron's attempts to gain permission to use highly questionable mark-to-market accounting practices; this was "a lay-my-body-across-the-tracks issue" (McLean & Elkind; 2003, p. 39), as Skilling called it, so fundamental that using this method was a condition of his joining the company. Following intensive lobbying, the Securities and Exchange Commission (SEC) sent a letter granting permission for the method to be used from 1992 in Enron's natural gas business; Enron was the first non-financial company to be given this approval. In principle, this method of accounting is open to abuse: as Swartz and Watkins argue, mark-to-market accounting enabled Enron to have the freedom to ensure that "mathematical formulas could be adjusted to come up with virtually *any* desired calculation" (Swartz & Watkins, 2003, p. 94—emphasis in original), thereby undermining the Commission's capacity to control its activities. However, Enron took this abuse further, by replying to the SEC's letter that it was going to ignore the approval date and begin using mark-to-market accounting from the start of 1991 (a full year earlier), stating that this change was "not material" (Bryce, 2002, p. 67); and, further, in explicit contradiction to the permission granted, it used the method in all its businesses and not just in natural gas.

Soon after this, guided by Skilling and with Lay's explicit support, Enron set to work to attempt to gain an exemption from regulation by the Commodity Futures Trading Commission (CFTC), another of its regulators. It succeeded in January 1993 when—five weeks before the end of her tenure as chairman of the CFTC—Wendy Lee Gramm granted a full exemption. A short while later, Gramm joined Enron's board, providing her with a substantial annual salary that rose to $119,292 by 2001. The exemption put Enron in a unique position: not being a bank, it did not answer to the Federal Reserve; however, on account of the Gramm exemption, neither did it answer to the CFTC. Representative Glen English, chairman of the House agricultural committee, which had jurisdiction over the CFTC, said that in his "18 years in Congress [the Gramm exemption] is the most irresponsible decision I have come across" (Bryce, 2002, p. 84). By undermining its regulators, as well as treating accounting rules with contempt (Levine, 2005, p. 727), Enron opened up the possibility of excessive and highly dangerous risk-taking, ultimately leading to derivatives liabilities of over $18.7 billion.

In sum, it is argued here that the experience of failed father figures, reinforced by the incompetence of its "parental" regulatory authorities, led Lay and Skilling to steer Enron towards a relationship in which its regulators were undermined and treated with contempt. While Lay and Skilling may have understandably been concerned about problems in the gas industry's regulation during the 1970s and 1980s, their actions—treating the regulators of all industries with great disdain—reveal a response that takes this much further. Lay's inclination to actively condone and support those engaged in illegal activity both within and outside Enron is one indication of this. In the case of Skilling, not only does his insistence on mark-to-market accounting suggest a determination to use methods which would render regulatory scrutiny almost useless, but Enron's ignoring of the approval date and its application in areas it was not authorized for implies a treatment of the SEC characterized by contempt. Further, suggestions of the bribery of CFTC officials imply a taking over and thwarting of its regulatory apparatus. From a theoretical point of view, therefore, it is proposed here that personal histories that were influenced by unresolved unconscious Oedipal struggles were reinforced by a damaging experience of the regulatory regimes, leading to a culture in which "parental" institutions were seen to be highly problematic and contemptible failures, deserving to be taken over, thwarted, and undermined. Ultimately, the lack of regulation in both its utilities and financial services divisions gave Enron the freedom to adopt unsound business practices that finally led to bankruptcy and collapse.

Discussion and conclusion

We now turn to examine the implications of an explanation based on the Oedipus complex in more detail. In arguing that the similarity between the "micro" issues (concerning the psychology of the leaders) and the "macro" issues (concerning the workplace and its environment) was underpinned by Oedipal factors, the central argument of this paper thus provisionally suggests a new "generating mechanism" (Pentland, 1999) as an explanation for Enron's collapse. Thus, while similar to the "theoretical memoranda" (Brown, 2003, p. 108) used elsewhere in the literature on text and discourse, this paper also adds the further dimension of a deep structure interpretation that draws inspiration from a particular theoretical perspective. In particular, the undermining of regulators and the consequent exposing of the company to major risk is linked with Lay and Skilling's unresolved Oedipus complexes. These unresolved Oedipus complexes—in which the central problem is one not just of relationships (Sapochnik, 2003, p. 182) but specifically relationships to authority—concern the manner in which such relationships influenced the direction and functioning of the company, and are thus suggested as "motors" that contributed to Enron's downfall.

The argument of this paper has implications for various perspectives emerging from a range of sources. One such source is the contemporary debate on risk, a diverse set of focusesi—the "risk archipelago" (Hood et al., 1992)—that examine risk, defined broadly as the likelihood of the occurrence of adverse events. Turner and Pidgeon (Turner, 1976; Turner & Pidgeon, 1997), who made a key contribution to the risk debate, found that disasters rarely emerge *ex nihilo*; instead, they argue, disasters are invariably preceded by an "incubation period" during which warning signs are known about but not adequately heeded. The Enron case lends support to this notion. That certain of the warning signs were in the public domain—a sure sign of an incubation period—is indicated, for example, by Partnoy's observation that "[w]hen I testified before the US Senate, the things they found most outrageous were things I had got out of reading Enron's annual report" (Partnoy, quoted in Gold, 2003). However, the connections made in this paper extend the incubation period argument and take it in a new direction because they suggest that difficulties originating many years earlier in leaders' personal histories may influence the outcome of the firm they joined. If this is the case, it could be suggested that aspects of the incubation preceded the formation of the company.

The ideas developed in this paper also have implications for the debate between, on the one hand, the "conflict" or "pluralist" frame of reference (Fox, 1973), and, on the other, the "consensual" or "mutuality of interest" frame of reference, especially as it concerns the issues of regulation (Hutter, 1997; Baldwin et al., 1998). Focusing on power relations and the differences of interests in and between organizations, the "conflict" frame views organizations as populated by a variety of groups that have legitimately different interests and compete against each other—as well as external groups—for domination. Following this line of thinking, Enron's leaders may be seen to have acted in their own interests in trying to thwart and disencumber the company from its regulators. In response, it needs to be acknowledged that Enron's leaders did indeed flex their power over the regulators in a struggle for power and domination, and that they succeeded in severely diminishing their influence.

However, while the "conflict" frame and the view offered in this paper are by no means mutually exclusive, one of the key contributions of this paper lies in its assertion that, valuable though a "conflict of interest" type of explanation may be, it should be tempered by an understanding of the "mutuality of interest" that also pertains in the Enron case. The "mutuality of interest" frame is particularly appropriate here: it highlights the importance of regulatory authorities not only as powerful forces that control the regulated company, but also as institutions that protect it and others against its own excesses. Viewed in this light, not only was the leaders' extreme thwarting of the regulators contrary to the company's own interests, but it was central to its downfall. It is thus much to be regretted that the "mutuality of interest" frame is "[o]ften decried as old fashioned" (Baldwin et al., 1998, p. 10), as its relevance in the Enron case is especially poignant.

The Enron case is also of significance because it draws our attention to a particular issue within the "mutuality of interest" perspective. It is noteworthy that traditional justifications for regulation—the control of monopoly power and excess profits, compensation for spillovers, inadequate information, and excessive competition (Breyer, 1998)—are focused largely on the need to protect parties "external" to the enterprise such as consumers, rival companies, and the wider public. While these justifications are clearly important, they concentrate rather less on the need to protect the "internal" parties that were so severely damaged in the Enron saga. These "internal" parties include thousands of workers who lost their jobs, many current and former employees who found their pensions reduced to nothing, and the unwitting shareholders (the owners of the company) who witnessed Enron equity become worthless overnight.

Finally, the Enron case suggests that leaders delude themselves when they are of the opinion that being largely unregulated represents a kind of freedom that would allow the unfettered growth of a business. On the contrary, the Enron story reminds us that the substantial subversion of regulatory regimes destroys important safeguards and is thus simultaneously a subversion of the organization itself, diminishing its capacity to survive. Enron needed its external regulators and, having rid itself of them, catastrophe ensued. In the wake of this, it is incumbent upon us to attempt to learn from this case so that the likelihood of its repetition is diminished. It is hoped that this paper takes us some way in this direction.

References

Baldwin, R., Scott, C. & Hood, C. (Eds.) (1998). *A reader on regulation.* Oxford: Oxford University Press.

Beard, M. (2003). Bosses gather for audience with Enron admirer. *The Independent*, March 29.

Boje, D.M., Rosile, G.A., Durant, R.A. & Luhman, J.T. (2004). Enron spectacles: A critical dramaturgical analysis. *Organization Studies*, 25(5): 751–774.

Breyer, S. (1998). Typical justifications for regulation. In: R. Baldwin, C. Scott & C. Hood (Eds.), *A reader on regulation* (pp. 59–92). Oxford: Oxford University Press.

Brown, A.D. (2003). Authoritative sensemaking in a public inquiry report. *Organization Studies, 25*(1): 105–122.

Brown, A.D. (2005). Making sense of the collapse of Barings bank. *Human Relations, 58*(12): 1579–1604.

Brown, A.D. & Jones, M. (2000). Honourable members and dishonourable deeds: Sensemaking, impression management and legitimation in the "Arms to Iraq affair". *Human Relations, 53*(5): 655–689.

Bryce, R. (2002). *Pipe Dreams: Greed, Ego and the Death of Enron.* Oxford: PublicAffairs.

Burgess, R.C. (1991). Keeping field notes. In: R.G. Burgess (Ed.), *Field Research: A Sourcebook and Field Manual* (pp. 191–194). London: Routledge.

Cannon, R.E. (1993). *The Gas Processing Industry: Origins and Evolution.* Tulsa, OK: Gas Processors Association.

Carr, A. & Downs, A. (2004). Transitional and quasi-objects in organization studies: Viewing Enron from the object relations world of Winnicott and Serres. *Journal of Organizational Change Management, 17*(4): 352–364.

Carr, A. & Downs, A. (2005). ENRON: Taking our cue from the world of object relations. *Tamara Journal of Critical Postmodern Organization Science, 3*(2): 1–15.

Conrad, C. (2003). Stemming the tide: Corporate discourse and agenda denial in the 2002 "corporate meltdown". *Organization, 10*(3): 549–560.

Cresswell, J.W. (1994). *Research design: Qualitative and quantitative approaches.* Thousand Oaks, CA: Sage.

Cruver, B. (2002). *Anatomy of greed: The unshredded truth from an Enron insider.* London: Hutchinson.

Deakin, S. & Konzelmann, S.J. (2003). After Enron: An age of enlightenment? *Organization, 10*(3): 583–587.

Eichenwald, K. (2005). *Conspiracy of Fools: A True Story.* New York: Broadway.

Eisenberg, T. & Macey, J.R. (2004). Was Arthur Andersen different? An empirical examination of major accounting firm audits of large clients. *Journal of Empirical Legal Studies, 1*(2): 263–300.

Fox, A. (1973). Industrial relations: A social critique of pluralist ideology. In: J. Child (Ed.), *Man and Organization* (pp. 185–233). London: Allen and Unwin.

Fox, L. (2003). *Enron: The rise and fall.* Hoboken, NJ: John Wiley and Sons.

French, R. & Vince, R. (Eds.) (1999). *Group relations, management and organization*. Oxford: Oxford University Press.

Freud, S. (1915–17). *Volume 1. Introductory Lectures on Psychoanalysis*. London: Penguin, 1973.

Freud, S. (1933). *Volume 2. New Introductory Lectures on Psychoanalysis*. London: Penguin, 1973.

Fusaro, P.C. & Miller, R.M. (2002). *What went wrong at Enron*. Hoboken, NJ: John Wiley and Sons.

Gabriel, Y. (1998). The hubris of management. *Administrative Theory and Praxis*, 20(3): 257–273.

Gephart, R.P. (1993). The textual approach: Risk and blame in disaster sensemaking. *Academy of Management Journal*, 36(6): 1465–1514.

Gill, J. & Johnson, P. (1991). *Research methods for managers*. London: Paul Chapman.

Gold, K. (2003). Bulls and blaspheming beasts. *The Times Higher Education Supplement*, May 16.

Gould, L.J., Stapley, L.F. & Stein, M. (Eds.) (2001). *The Systems Psychodynamics of Organizations: Integrating the Group Relations Approach, Psychoanalytic and Open Systems Perspectives*. London: Karnac.

Grey, C. (2003). The real world of Enron's auditors. *Organization*, 10(3): 572–576.

Hammersley, M. & Atkinson, P. (1983). *Ethnography: Principles in Practice*. London: Routledge.

Hirschhorn, L. (1988). *The workplace Within: Psychodynamics of Organizational Life*. Cambridge, MA: The MIT Press.

Hirschhorn, L. (1997). *Reworking Authority: Leading and Following in the Post-modern Organization*. Cambridge, MA: The MIT Press.

Hood, C.C. et al. (1992). Risk management. In: *Risk: Analysis, Perception and Management* (pp. 135–192). London: The Royal Society.

Hutter, B.M. (1997). *Compliance: Regulation and Environment*. Oxford: Clarendon.

Jenkins, G.J. (2003). *The Enron collapse*. Upper Saddle River, NJ: Pearson Education.

Kets de Vries, M.F.R. & Miller, D. (1987). *The Neurotic Organization: Diagnosing and Changing Counterproductive Styles of Management*. San Francisco: Jossey-Bass.

Kets de Vries, M.F.R. & Miller, D. (1989). *Unstable at the Top: Inside the Troubled Organization*. New York: Mentor.

Klein, M. (1945). The Oedipus complex in the light of early anxieties. In: M. Klein, *Love, Guilt and Reparation and Other Works, 1921–1945* (pp. 370–419). London: Hogarth, 1981.

Klein, M. (1946). Notes on some schizoid mechanisms. In: M. Klein, *Envy and Gratitude and Other Works 1946–1963* (pp. 1–24). London: Hogarth, 1980.

Laplanche, J. & Pontalis, J.-B. (1973).*The language of Psychoanalysis.* London: Hogarth.

Lay, K.L. (1996). A new vision. In: J. Share (Ed.), *The Oil Makers: Insiders Look at the Petroleum Industry* (pp. 351–365). College Station, TX: Texas A&M University Press.

Levine, D.P. (2005). The corrupt organization. *Human Relations, 58*(6): 723–740.

Long, S. (2002). Organisational destructivity and the perverse state of mind. *Organisational and Social Dynamics, 2*(2): 179–207.

MacAvoy, P.W. (2000). *The Natural Gas Market: Sixty Years of Regulation and Deregulation.* New Haven, CT: Yale University Press.

McLean, B. & Elkind, P. (2003). *The Smartest Guys in the Room: The Amazing Rise and Scandalous Fall of Enron.* London: Viking.

Mehta, A. (1999). *Power Play: A Study of the Enron Project.* Hyderabad, India: Orient Longman.

Obholzer, A. & Roberts, V.Z. (Eds.) (1994). *The Unconscious at Work: Individual and Organizational Stress in the Human Services.* London: Routledge.

Partnoy, F. (2003). *Infectious Greed: How Deceit and Risk Corrupted the Financial Markets.* London: Profile.

Pentland, B.T. (1999). Building process theory with narrative: From description to explanation. *Academy of Management Review, 24*(4): 711–724.

Perrow, C. (1999). *Normal Accidents: Living with High-risk Technologies* (2nd edition.) Princeton, NJ: Princeton University Press.

Robson, C. (1993). *Real World Research: A Resource for Social Scientists and Practitioner-researchers.* Oxford: Blackwell.

Sapochnik, C. (2003). Corruption: Oedipal configurations as a social mechanism. *Organizational and Social Dynamics, 3*(2): 177–190.

Schwartz, H.S. (1990). *Narcissistic Process and Corporate Decay: The Theory of the Organizational Ideal.* New York: New York University Press.

Share, J. (Ed.) (1996). *The Oil Makers: Insiders Look at the Petroleum Industry.* College Station, TX: Texas A&M University Press.

Stein, M. (2000). The risk-taker as shadow: A psychoanalytic view of the collapse of Baring Bank. *Journal of Management Studies, 37*(8): 1215–1229.

Stein, M. (2003). Unbounded irrationality: Risk and organizational narcissism at Long Term Capital Management. *Human Relations, 56*(5): 523–540.

Swartz, M. & Watkins, S. (2003). *Power failure: The rise and fall of Enron.* London: Aurum.

Tinker, T. & Carter, C. (2003). Spectres of accounting: Contradictions or conflicts of interest. *Organization, 10*(3): 577–582.

Tourish, D. & Vatcha, N. (2005). Charismatic leadership and corporate cultism at Enron: The elimination of dissent, the promotion of conformity and organizational collapse. *Leadership, 1*(4): 455–480.

Turner, B.A. (1976). The organizational and interorganizational development of disasters. *Administrative Science Quarterly, 21*: 378–397.

Turner, B.A. & Pidgeon, N.F. (1997). *Man-made Disasters* (2nd edition). Oxford: Butterworth-Heinemann.

Weick, K.E. (1993). The collapse of sensemaking in organizations: The Mann Gulch disaster. *Administrative Science Quarterly, 38*: 628–652.

Winnicott, D.W. (1971). *Playing and Reality.* London: Tavistock.

Yin, R.K. (1994). *Case Study Research: Design and Methods.* Thousand Oaks, CA: Sage.

Narcissism project and corporate decay: The case of General Motors

Howard S. Schwartz

Note: This paper was first published in 1990, as part of my book *Narcissistic Process and Corporate Decay: The Theory of the Organization Ideal* (New York University Press). It is reprinted herewith with explicit permission of NYUP.

Given the present condition of General Motors, it seems opportune to republish it now. The paper has been condensed for reasons of space and I have changed a few terms for theoretical clarity. It is written so that the citations of my own work refer to the original published sources, rather than to other chapters of the book, but otherwise I have left it basically as it was. One addition to the text is in order. I report below that, at the original time of writing, GM's share of the US market was 35%. Following that, except for a brief period after the 2001 attacks on the US World Trade Center, GM's US market share declined monotonically, averaging almost 7% per year. It has not been profitable since 2004 and in 2008 lost 30.9 billion dollars. On June 1, 2009, General Motors filed for bankruptcy. On June 10, it was bought by a new entity that is owned primarily by the United States government.

Introduction

When I left graduate school and began teaching organizational behaviour courses, I was struck by the irrelevance of what I had learned to the actual organizational experience of my students. My students experienced and understood organizational life as a kind of "vanity fair", in which individuals who were interested in "getting ahead" could do so by playing to the vanity of their superiors. One needed to do this in two respects. One needed to flatter the superior as an individual and as an occupant of the superior role. This latter process tended to trail off into an adulation of the organization in general. Work either fitted into this process of adulation, in which case it made sense; or it did not, in which case it did not make sense. Work which did not make sense in this way, my students felt, was best left to the suckers who had not figured out yet how to get ahead and who deserved whatever torment this system led them to inherit. If, through this process, important, valid information was lost to the system by being withheld or simply unappreciated, that was not their concern. Through luck or guile, the consequences would, or could be made to, occur on somebody else's watch.

At first glance, my students' attitude looked to me like cynicism. But closer analysis suggested that, although they had a great deal of cynicism in them, they were not simply being cynical, for they believed in the righteousness of what they were doing.

For them, getting ahead was a moral imperative, which justified any means necessary for its accomplishment. But more than this, the system itself which called upon subordinates to idealize it was held to be morally sacrosanct. A person who refused to go along with the system was seen as not only stupid and naive, but as morally inferior. And this was so even if the individual in question was offering a point of view that was essential for the organization to do its work effectively and efficiently.

It thus seemed to me that, for my students, the organization's processes were held to define moral value. As defined by its processes, the organization seemed to exist in a moral world of its own, which served to justify anything done on its behalf, and which did not require justification on any grounds outside itself. This view was inconsistent with a view of the organization as an instrument to do work. For my students, the organization did not exist in order to do work; it did work in order to exist.

Yet even while holding this point of view, many of my students did not appear to have a deep loyalty to the organizations which they so supported. On the contrary, for the most part they were willing to change organizations with no regrets or guilt. Their loyalty, if that is what it was, seemed to be to an abstract idea of organization, an idea of the organization as a vehicle for the revelation of their own grandiosity. Ultimately, therefore, their loyalty appeared to be directed at themselves.

Over time, trying to be a good empiricist, I came to take their stories about organizational life increasingly seriously. I made the assumption that organizational life was just what my students, whom I came to consider my research subjects, and sometimes informants, appeared to be living. Relegating what I had learned in graduate school to the status of a fantasy, I tried to fashion a theoretical conception that would explain this organizational reality. Following Shorris (1981), I called the syndrome "organizational totalitarianism" (Schwartz, 1987a).

I first understood organizational totalitarianism in moral terms, in terms of the psychological damage done to the individuals involved (Schwartz, 1987a). But as time went by it became more and more clear to me that the processes I was coming to understand must have practical consequences as well—consequences for the effective functioning, the efficiency, the profitability, the competitiveness of organizations. In a word, it did not seem to me that organizations as I understood them could possibly be successful even in terms of the narrowest economic criteria, without regard to the moral costs involved. So, when American industry seemed to be incapable of competing with foreign enterprises, I did not find myself at all surprised.

Getting beyond my students' accounts to gain evidence of the systemic effects of the process, however, proved to be a problem. There is a kind of "uncertainty principle" that applies here. Organizational participants who are in a position to be able to describe these systemic effects have given up the moral autonomy that would have enabled them to perceive them. Participants who insist on retaining their moral autonomy are typically excluded from important positions in the system precisely because of that insistence. Thus, the closer one is to the data, the less likely one is to be able to see it.

Accordingly, in the present paper I have relied heavily on one of the very few accounts that I know of by a highly positioned insider who became alienated from the system and reported on its processes to the outside. This is a book by John Z. De Lorean, co-written by J. Patrick Wright and published by the latter under his own name, called *On A Clear Day You Can See General Motors* (1979). (Passages from the book are reproduced with the explicit permission of J. Patrick Wright.) There is also a more recent account of GM by Maryann Keller (1989). I will be using her work to lend secondary support to my case.

Organizational totalitarianism and the theory of the organization ideal

The theory I shall use to discuss organizational totalitarianism begins with the premise that, for people like my students, the idea of the organization represents an ego ideal—a symbol of the person one ought to become such that, if one were to become that person, one would again be the centre of a loving world as one experienced one-self as a child, in the condition that Freud called "primary narcis-sism" (Freud, 1955, 1957; Chasseguet-Smirgel, 1985). It represents an end to the anxiety that entered our lives when we experienced ourselves as separate from our apparently all-powerful mothers; it is a phantasy of a return to fusion with her.

With regard to organizations, this means that individuals rede-fine themselves as part of an organization, conceived of as perfect. Thus, the image of such an organization is one in which members are perfectly integrated into a collectivity which is perfectly adapted to its environment. An image of an organization serving as an ego ideal may be called an "organization ideal" (Schwartz, 1987a, b, c). The organization ideal thus represents a project for the return to maternal fusion and primary narcissism.

The problem with the organization ideal, like any ego ideal, is that it can never be attained. It represents a denial of our separation, finitude, vulnerability, and mortality; but these remain with us by virtue of our existence as concrete individual human beings (Becker, 1973; Chasseguet-Smirgel, 1985; Schwartz, 1987b).

Given the importance of maintaining belief in the possibility of attaining the ego ideal, organizations often attempt to generate a way of preserving the illusion of the organization ideal in the face of the failure of the organization to exemplify it. The attempt to manage an organization by imposing this illusion is what I call "organizational totalitarianism".

Organizations attempt this imposition in a number of ways. As Klein and Ritti (1984) observe, they give and withhold information to create a myth of the organization as more effective than it really is. They impose patterns of speech and behaviour on participants that make them seem more integrated than they really are. They promote the attribution that their problems are due to forces which do not belong in the world, which is to say to "bad" forces. And they generate an image of a gradient of Being, an "ontological differentiation", in the organization (Schwartz, 1987a, b, c; also see Sievers, 1987, and Schwartz, 1987d) which idealizes the higher figures in the organization (Klein & Ritti, 1984, pp. 170–172) as individuals who have fulfilled the project of the return to narcissism and become centres of a loving world. This provides the drive to climb the hierarchy that my students experience as the central spirit in their moral world (Schwartz, 1987a). Moreover it delegitimates those who are farther down (Sennett & Cobb, 1973). This makes it possible for organizations to maintain the idea of the perfection of the organization's core and blame its imperfections on peripheral elements.

Organizational decay

The problem is that such symbolic manipulation places falsehood right at the core of organizational functioning and therefore cannot help but lead to a loss of rationality. For the attainment of the ego ideal is impossible, short of psychosis (Chasseguet-Smirgel, 1985), and therefore organizational totalitarianism means the superimposition of a psychosis upon organizational functioning. Ultimately, whatever the gains in motivation, such a loss of rationality leads to generalized and systemic organizational ineffectiveness.

Moreover, I suggest that this condition of generalized and systemic ineffectiveness has a unity to it, and therefore represents something like an organizational disease. I would like to give it the name "organizational decay", with the intention being to convey the impression of an internal process of rot, not occasioned by outside forces; and with the intention as well to give the impression of a holistic process, not taking place in isolated parts of the organization but typically and increasingly sapping the vitality of the organization as a whole. This decay eventually may manifest itself in any of a number of ways. I shall discuss a few of them, relying on De Lorean's and Keller's books about General Motors to provide illustrations.

Some causes of decay

Commitment to bad decisions

Perhaps the most obvious symptom of organizational decay is the commitment to bad decisions. Staw (1980) has noted that the tendency to justify past actions can be a powerful motivation behind organizational behaviour and can often run counter to rationality. As he notes, the justification process leads to escalating commitment. When mistaken actions cannot be seen as mistaken actions, the principle on which they are based is not seen as being mistaken. Worse still, our feeling that it is a valid principle becomes enhanced through our need to defend our decision and subsequent decisions made on the basis of it.

This process must be especially lethal in the case of the totalitarian organization, where the idea of the perfection of the organization provides the organization's very motivational base. Here, the assumption of the identity of the individual decision maker and his or her organizational role turns the tendency to justify past actions from a defensive tendency on the part of individuals to a core organizational process—a central element of the organization's culture.

The case of the Corvair illustrates the process of commitment to bad decisions. Modelled after the Porsche, the Corvair was powered by a rear engine and had an independent, swing-axle suspension system. According to De Lorean, any car so powered and so suspended is going to have serious problems—problems which were "well documented inside GM's engineering staff long before the Corvair ever was offered for sale." (p. 65). The questionable safety of the car caused a massive internal fight among GM's engineers... . On one side of the argument was Chevrolet's then general manager, Ed Cole... . On the other side was a wide assortment of top-flight engineers.... . One top corporate engineer told me that he showed his test results to Cole but by then, he said, "Cole's mind was made up." Management not only went along with Cole, it also told dissenters in effect to "Stop these objections. Get on the team, or you can find someplace else to work." The ill-fated Corvair was launched in the fall of 1959. The results were disastrous (p. 66).

The Corvair demonstrated itself to be unsafe almost immediately. However, despite the fact that a stabilizer bar costing only $15 a car would have provided a solution, GM did not correct the problem until the release of the 1964 models. By that time numerous lives had been lost and millions had been spent in legal expenses. Even so, "The corporation steadfastly defends the car's safety, despite the internal engineering records which indicated it was not safe, and the ghastly toll in deaths and injury it recorded" (p. 67).

*Advancement of participants who detach themselves
from reality and discouragement of reality-oriented
participants who are committed to their work*

When core organizational process becomes the dramatization of the organization and its high officials as ideal, the evaluation of individuals for promotion and even for continued inclusion comes to be made on the basis of how much they contribute to this dramatization. This means that, increasingly, promotion criteria shift from achievement and competence to ideology and politics.

Thus, De Lorean says that whether or not someone was promoted often depended on something other than competence:

> That something different was a very subjective criterion which encompassed style, appearance, personality and, most importantly, personal loyalty to the man (or men) who was the promoter, and to the system which brought this all about. There were rules of this fraternity of management at GM. Those pledges willing to obey the rules were promoted. In the vernacular, they were the company's "team players." Those who didn't fit into the mold of a manager, who didn't adhere to the rules because they thought they were silly, generally weren't promoted. "He's not a team player," was the frequent, and many times only, objection to an executive in line for promotion.

It didn't mean he was doing a poor job. It meant he didn't fit neatly into a stereotype of style, appearance and manner. He didn't display blind loyalty to the system of management, to the man or men doing the promoting. He rocked the boat. He took unpopular stands on products or policy which contradicted the prevailing attitude of top management. (p. 40)

Keller (1989) adumbrates this point in a number of places, for example this about recently retired chairman Roger Smith:

> For 31 years, Smith moved up through the ranks of GM as the consummate corporate player—the GM culture coursed in his veins. Admiration for and loyalty to the organization was at the core of his being. He was one of a new breed of corporate politicians whose success depended on their ease in wearing the corporate mantle. Translated, that meant, "Above all, be loyal to your superior's agenda". (p. 66)

One result of this will be that those individuals who are retained and promoted will be those who will know very well how things are supposed to look, according to the viewpoint of the dominant coalition, but who will know less and less about reality insofar as it conflicts with, or simply is independent of, this viewpoint. The problem is, of course, that since no organization is, or can be, the organization ideal, this means that those individuals who are retained and promoted will be those who can cut themselves loose from discrepant reality.

Another result of this sort of selection must be that realistic and concerned persons must lose the belief that the organization's real purpose is productive work and come to the conclusion that its real purpose is self-promotion. They then are likely to see their work as being alien to the purposes of the organization and must find doing good work increasingly depressing and pointless.

> In any system where inexperience and even incompetence exists in the upper reaches of management, lower-echelon executives become demoralized and dissatisfied. They see a system which impedes rather than enhances decision making. Their own jobs become frustrating. Divisional managers reporting to a group executive who is uneducated in their businesses must literally

try to teach the business to him before getting decisions from
him on their proposals. We often waltzed our bosses on the
14th floor through a step-by-step explanation of each program
proposal—what it meant, how it related to the rest of the business and what it would do for the company. Even after this,
their judgment most often was based on what GM had done
before. (p. 255)

And he gives this example of the clash between the incompetent
who have been promoted and their competent but discouraged
subordinates:

Increasingly, group and upper managers seemed to look upon
their jobs in such narrow terms that it was impossible to com-
petently direct broad corporate policy. Often misplaced, unpre-
pared or simply undertalented, these executives filled their
days and our committee meetings with minutiae. After one
particularly frustrating meeting of the Administrative Committee, John Beltz and I were picking up our notes when he looked
down at the far end of the conference table at the corporate
management and said to me, "I wouldn't let one of those guys
run a gas station for me." It was a bitter and sad indictment
of our top management by one of the then young, truly bright
lights of General Motors management. (p. 256)

A third effect, made obvious by this point, is that higher management is effectively isolated from criticism, or even serious discussion, of its thought and actions. De Lorean gives this account:

This system quickly shut top management off from the real
world because it surrounded itself in many cases with "yes
men". There soon became no real vehicle for adequate outside
input. Lower executives, eager to please the boss and rise up the
corporate ladder, worked hard to learn what he wanted or how
he thought on a particular subject. They then either fed the boss
exactly what he wanted to know, or they modified their own
proposals to suit his preferences.

Original ideas were often sacrificed in deference to what the
boss wanted. Committee meetings no longer were forums for

open discourse, but rather either soliloquies by the top man, or conversations between a few top men with the rest of the meeting looking on. ...The rest of the team would remain silent, speaking only when spoken to. When they did offer a comment, in many cases it was just to paraphrase what had already been said by one of the top guys. (p. 47)

Indeed, as organizational promotion and retention criteria shift towards the dramatization of the perfection of the organization, this shapes the very job of the subordinate into what Janis (1972) calls "mindguarding"—the suppression of criticism.

Keller (1989) also comments on the conflict between what one needs to do to get promoted and the quality of one's work:

One retired executive rails against a system that creates vertical thinkers and cautious leaders. "The whole system stinks once you're in it. You continue to want to make vertical decisions: 'What is it that I should decide that will be good for me. Never make a horizontal decision based on what is good for the company. I want to get promoted.'"

"So you get promoted because you're sponsored by someone; you get promoted before they catch up with you. I can go through a litany of those clowns. They go from this plant to that complex and then, all of a sudden, they've got plaques all over the walls that say how great they've done—but the plant's falling apart and the division's falling apart". (p. 34)

The creation of the organizational jungle

The more successful the organization is at projecting the image of itself as the organization ideal, the more deeply must committed participants experience anxiety. For the image projected, the image of the individual as perfectly a part of the perfect organization, is only an image; and the more perfect it is, the more acute the discrepancy between the role and the role player. Given the importance of the organization ideal in the individual's self-concept, some way must be found in which the individual can reconcile the discrepancy between the centrality in a loving world he or she is supposed to be experiencing and the wretchedness he or she in fact feels. As we have seen above, the typical way is to attempt to deepen the identity of self and organization by rising in the organization's hierarchy and by fighting off what are perceived as threats to the organizational identity one has attained—perceived threats which are often projections of one's own self-doubts.

The result of this is that individuals become obsessed with organizational rank. They become compelled to beat down anyone who threatens or competes with them in their pursuit of higher rank or who is perceived as threatening the rank they have already acquired. Thus, ironically, behind the display of the organization ideal, of everyone working together to realize shared values, the real motivational process becomes a Hobbesian battle of narcissism project against narcissism project. The consequences of this for coordination, co-operation, and motivation are clear enough.

De Lorean says:

> Once in a position of power, a manager who was promoted by the system is insecure because, consciously or not, he knows that it was something other than his ability to manage and his knowledge of the business that put him in his position... . He thus looks for methods and defense mechanisms to ward off threats to his power. (p. 49)

Isolation of management and rupture of communications

A related problem is that the greater the success of the totalitarian manager, the more the manager is isolated from his or her subordinates. The world that the subordinates live in is the world of the organization ideal as created by the totalitarian manager. The world that the totalitarian manager lives in is the world of the construction of the image of the organization ideal. These two worlds are incommensurable and it cannot help but happen that communication and trust must break down between them. For communication and trust mean two different things to these groups. Indeed, for totalitarian management, communication to subordinates is not communication at all—it is deception.

In this fashion, the organization comes to be stratified in an insider/outsider dimension that has been likened to the structure of an onion (Shorris, 1981; Arendt, 1966) and which serves the same function as party membership in the totalitarian state.

Development of hostile orientation towards the environment

If the totalitarian manager is successful, as we have seen, organiza-tional participants take the organization as an organization ideal. It must follow, in their thinking, that such an organization will be successful in its dealings with the world. This poses a difficulty of interpretation for the necessarily problematic relationships between the organization and its environment.

Thus, in the nature of things (Katz & Kahn, 1966) the environment places constant demands on the organization. Failure to meet them will result in the organization's death. But from the standpoint of the totalitarian manager committed to portraying the organization as the organization ideal, this sort of reasoning cannot be acknowl-edged. From this point of view it is the organization that is the cri-terion of worth. The environment is not conceived of as existing as an independent environment at all; it exists only in order to support the organization. From this standpoint the demands of the environ-ment must be presented as hostile actions on the part of bad exter-nal forces—hostile actions to which a legitimate response is equally hostile action.

The General Motors Corporation, in response to Ralph Nader's (1965) book about the Corvair, *Unsafe At Any Speed*, hired private detectives to find ways to discredit him. Sending private detectives to find out the dirty details of his private life suggests something about their attitude towards him. It suggests that they expected to find something to show that he was a bad person. He had to be a bad person: he had attacked GM, hadn't he?

Again:

> Criticism from the outside is generally viewed as ill-informed. General Motors management thinks what it is doing is right, because it is GM that is doing it and the outside world is wrong. It is always "they" versus "us". (p. 257)

And when Peter Drucker wrote *The Concept of a Corporation* (1946), a work which was generally regarded as decidedly pro-business and pro-GM, "he was resoundingly criticized within the com-pany for daring to criticize the organization of the corporation" (p. 258).

Thus, the picture of the organization as organization ideal leads to an orientation towards the world that can best be described as paranoid. It is clear enough that such a conception must degrade the relationships with the environment that ultimately the organization requires for its survival.

The transposition of work and ritual

When work, the productive process, becomes display, its meaning becomes lost. Its performance as part of the organizational drama becomes the only meaning that it has. Accordingly, the parts it plays in the organization's transactions with the world become irrelevant. When this happens, it loses its adaptive function and becomes mere ritual.

At the same time, those rituals which serve to express the individual's identification with the organization ideal, especially those connected with rank, come to be infused with significance for the individual. They become sacred. Thus, reality and appearance, signified and signifier, trade places. The energy that once went into the production of goods and services of value to others is channelled into the dramatization of a narcissistic fantasy in which the organization's environment is merely a stage setting.

Consider how this shows up in the matter of dress. One can easily make a case that patterns of dress among organizational participants often have some functionality. But when the issue comes to be invested with great meaning, one must suspect that ritual has supplanted function. Thus, De Lorean describes how half of his first meeting as a GM employee was taken up in a discussion of how a vice-president had been sent home for wearing a brown suit (p. 40).

The dynamics of the ways in which ritual comes to assume the importance work should help to explain the dynamics of the ritualization of work. For the willingness to allow one's behaviour to be determined by meaningless rituals comes to be justified by an idealization of the organization that elevates its customs above, and discredits, one's values—one's sense of what is important. This willingness to subordinate and delegitimate, in a word to repress, one's own sense of what is important, even about matters that should be within the competence of anyone's judgment, must have its consequences magnified when the matters in question become more abstruse and difficult to make judgments about, as is the case with real executive work. Then the repression of one's values deprives one of any basis for making such judgments, and leads naturally to a superimposition of the rituals with which one is familiar, even where, patently, they do not belong.

Thus, De Lorean recalls that when he was elevated to the 14th floor, GM's executive suite, as group executive in charge of the domestic Car and Truck Group:

> ...I saw that the job ... often consisted only of ... little, stupid, make-work kinds of assignments, things which I thought should have been decided further down the line.
>
> Some of these things, which had little or no impact on the business, were an insult to a person's intelligence... . As I recall, [for example, my boss] asked me to catalogue service parts numbers and to prepare reports on the size of parts inventories. (pp. 26–27)

De Lorean, feeling that a person at his high level should be involved in planning, rather than in trivia, set up a meeting with vice-chairman Thomas Murphy to straighten out his job assignment. But Murphy found nothing peculiar, and:

> I suddenly realized that what I felt was a weakness of life on the 14th floor, he and others thought was "business as usual." They were quite happy to let their jobs drag them from one place to the next, trying to solve problems as they came up, but not getting into the kind of long-range planning that 14th floor executives were supposed to be doing. (p. 33)

Loss of creativity

The delegitimation of one's sense of what is important gives rise to a special case of the ritualization of work—the loss of creativity. Thus, Schein (1983) describes the condition of "conformity" which follows from an insistence by the organization that all of its norms be accepted as being equally important. Under that condition, the individual "can tune in so completely on what he sees to be the way others are handling themselves that he becomes a carbon-copy and sometimes a caricature of them".

And he notes: "The conforming individual curbs his creativity and thereby moves the organization toward a sterile form of bureaucracy" (p. 197).

Maslow (1970) gives us insight into the psychodynamics of this when he observes that creativity is characteristic of both ends of the continuum of personality development, but not of the stages in the middle (pp. 170–171). Creativity, this suggests, is a function of spontaneity, a function of taking seriously our actual affects and interacting in the world in consideration of our spontaneous feelings. But as the self comes to be dominated by a concern for how things appear to others, which is characteristic of the middle stages of personality development (Schwartz, 1983), creativity disappears as a mode of interacting with the world. As the organization requires that the individual subordinate his or her spontaneous perception to an uncritical acceptance of the ideal character of the organization, it thus determines that the affective basis of creativity will be repressed.

The lack of creativity, since it is a lack of something, cannot be positively demonstrated. As an experience, it makes itself known as a feeling of missing something different that has not occurred, even though one does not know what the different element would have been. Thus, De Lorean found himself introducing a "new" crop of Chevrolets that were not really new at all:

> This whole show is nothing but a replay of last year's show, and the year before that and the year before that. The speech I just gave was the same speech I gave last year, written by the same guy in public relations about the same superficial product improvements as previous years.... Almost nothing has changed ... there was nothing new and revolutionary in car development and there hadn't been for years. (pp. 60–61)

In benign times, one may experience boredom: the consciousness of a sameness, a lack of originality. When circumstances are harsh, partly as a result of the lack of creativity that the organization needed if it was to have adapted, one may simply experience the intractability of the situation. Adding up the figures in the usual way simply shows one, again and again, how hopeless the situation is. One may then experience the loss of creativity as a wish for a saviour who will make the organization's problems disappear.

In the hard times, I suspect, one rarely comes to recognize that the ideas that the organization needed in order to have avoided its present hopeless state may have been upon the scene a long time ago. But the individuals who had them might have been passed over for promotion because they were not "team players", or perhaps they were made to feel uncomfortable because they did not fit it in, or maybe they were scapegoated whenever the organization needed a victim. Indeed, ironically, the very ideas that were needed might have been laughed at or ignored because they were not "the way we do things around here".

Dominance of the financial staff

Another hypothesis may be used to account for the emergent dominance of the financial function of the corporation that De Lorean finds in General Motors and that others, for example Halberstam (1986) have partly blamed for the decline of American industry.

As envisaged by Alfred P. Sloan, the financial function and the operations side of the corporation were both supposed to be represented strongly at the top level of the corporation. But, as De Lorean notes, over time, and specifically through the rise of Frederick Donner, the financial side came to dominate the corporation. Why?

I propose that finance, rather than operations, offers the greater narcissistic possibilities. As Nader and Taylor (1986) note, operations, the productive process, tends to temper grandiosity. The recalcitrance of matter, so to speak, exerts a humbling influence. Not so with finance. I suggest that the financial world-view can be understood as a kind of latter-day Pythagoreanism in which the world is seen as mere instantiation of number, and as imposing no bounds on the imagination's flights. Everything seems possible as long as the numbers can be made to work, and the one who can make them work can take this as a sign of omnipotence. When the matter comes to competitive elevation of the organization ideal, who can do it better, who can represent it better, than the officer whose bonds to earthly substance are the lightest. Who better than the specialist in finance? Keller's analysis is similar:

> The tyranny of the number crunchers has evolved, to a great extent, from GM's reluctance to hear bad news about itself.

If the finance guys can present the right numbers, everyone breathes a sigh of relief, and the finance people look like heroes. There's no incentive for executives in finance positions to give bad news; the more facile they can be with numbers, the higher their fortunes rise. (pp. 27–28)

Cynicism and corruption or self-deception and the narcissistic loss of reality

Referring to the ways people are related to their own presentations, Goffman (1959, p. 17–18) notes that one can either be taken in by one's own performance or not taken in by it, using it only "to guide the conviction of his audience ... as a means to other ends". In the latter case we refer to the individual as a cynic. Such persons disassociate themselves from discrepant information consciously and through deception. In the former case, the individual "comes to be performer and observer of the same show". Goffman adds:

It will have been necessary for the individual in his performing capacity to conceal from himself in his audience capacity the discreditable facts that he has had to learn about the perform-ance; in everyday terms, there will be things he knows, or has known, that he will not be able to tell himself. (p. 81)

Goffman notes that these persons cut themselves loose from discrepant information through repression and disassociation, a point which corresponds perfectly with psychoanalytic theory concerning the maintenance of the ego ideal.

We may refer to such individuals as self-deceptive. Thus, in the totalitarian organization, no matter what its espoused values, promotion and even continued inclusion will tend to go to deceptive cynics whose moral involvement in their organizational activity is attenuated, or to self-deceptive persons whose involvement in reality is attenuated.

Of the two, it is difficult to say which is to be preferred. Cynics at least know what is going on around them; and if their moral involvement in their organizational role is attenuated, that does not seem inappropriate in an organization as deceptive as one which is managed by totalitarian means. Indeed, in organizations which have seriously degenerated as a result of these processes, it is often only the cynics who can get anything done at all.

Nonetheless, there is no doubt that cynicism tends toward corruption. Corruption does not play a major role in De Lorean's picture of General Motors, but he does note its presence (p. 83).

For the present analysis, I think the more serious problem comes in with those who deceive themselves and distance themselves from reality. For as the processes I have described operate, and as the organization degenerates accordingly, it becomes increasingly difficult to see it as the ideal, and individuals who are able to do so must become increasingly self-deceptive. A point must come when such individuals may be said not to be psychologically living in the same world as the real organization. What makes this even worse is that, since this capacity for self-deception is an important advantage in the race for promotion, the total dissociation of the individual from organizational reality is likely to be correlated with the individual's position in the hierarchy. Then the most important processes within the organization come to be under the authority of people who are not operating in the real world as far as the organization's requirements are concerned.

Keller hints at this:

> During the 1970s, a writer for *Fortune* magazine set out on a quest for dissenting views at General Motors, and found it hard "to find a top executive at GM who does not evidence enthusiasm for what he or the company is doing." One view might hold that GM had achieved a state of management consensus that would be the envy of any company. But more likely, the lack of dissension was motivated by self-interest. It was managerial suicide to be the person who got labeled a naysayer. There was also an element of denial; in the same way that children of alcoholics often refuse to accept their parents' addiction, GM employees refused to admit the truth about their corporate parent. They didn't want to believe. (pp. 65–66)

Overcentralization

The narcissistic loss of reality among those at the top of the corporation may be a major cause of overcentralization of operational decision making. De Lorean found this overcentralization to characterize General Motors, and with it the tendency to provide simplistic answers to complex questions. The idea that, having risen to the top of the corporation, individuals would hold themselves as bearing all of its knowledge and virtues follows immediately from what we have been saying.

From this would follow the tendency of top management to believe themselves more capable than anyone else of providing answers to any questions that arise. Having no command of specific details beyond those in their imaginations, the answers which they give, and which would come to bind the rest of the corporation, would necessarily be simplistic and inappropriate. Moreover, as the decay process continues, and as the competence of top management declines accordingly, both their tendency to impose simple answers to complex problems, and the specific inadequacy even of the simplistic answers they propose, would tend to increase. Moreover, the capacity of the system to correct itself would tend to decrease, since the increasing power of the higher echelons of the corporation, and their increasing narcissism, would tend towards an attribution of blame to the lower levels of the organization. This would delegitimize those whose judgment would be necessary to reverse the decay process.

De Lorean and Keller provide a number of examples of this. This one, from De Lorean, will serve our purpose:

> ...the corporate program for maximum standardization of parts across product lines was a knee-jerk cost-cutting reaction to the incredible proliferation of models, engines and parts which took place in the uncontrolled and unplanned boom of the 1960s. However, the program was not intelligently thought out. It was not thoroughly analyzed for its actual effect on the company. On paper the concept looked good and seemed like a sure way to save money. In reality it wasted money. The car divisions rebelled at various stages of the standardization program. Their cries were unanswered. When Chevrolet rebelled against using the new corporate U-joint ... Keyes told me, "Use the corporate one or I'll get someone in Chevy who will".
>
> We used it, at an investment of about $16 million in tooling, and our costs rose $1.40 per car. In addition, the corporate

design failed in use and Chevy paid out about $5 million extra in warranty claims.

Instead of saving money, the standardization program at GM wound up costing the corporation about $300 million extra per year... .

The last straw came in 1972, however, when management asked us: "Why is the cost of building a Chevrolet $70 closer to Oldsmobile today than it was in 1964?" The question from the top was offered in the usual "You aren't doing your job" manner. The irony was incredible. (252–253)

An overview

Before concluding this discussion of the practical consequences of totalitarian management, it is worthwhile to note a characteristic that the consequences mentioned have in common: they are all cumulative and interactive with each other. They all tend to build within the system and, interacting with each other, take over the system bit by bit. This is the way in which the ineffectiveness characteristic of the decadent organization becomes systemic and generalized. Thus, for example, the accumulation of bad decisions taken within the system suggests that those who manifest belief in it as an organization ideal must increasingly be self-deceptive or cynical, which in turn decreases the retention of realism and concern for work, leading to a further increase in bad decisions, further degradation of the relationship with the environment, and so on.

The result of this is that the rate of decay will tend to accelerate. On the basis of this the fact that GM's market share took six years to decline from 46% to 41%, but only three more years to go to 35% (Ingrassia & White, 1989), comes to make a certain chilling sense.

Conclusion: On averting organizational decay

There is no doubt that fantasy plays an important part in our mental lives. To say this one does not need either to approve of fantasy or to regret its inroads into the psyche. Fantasy simply is. So it is with the ego ideal, which is a particularly central fantasy in our lives.

But the same cannot be said for organizational totalitarianism and organizational decay. These are not either necessary or inevitable features of organizational life. They become features of organizational life when the desire to be the centre of a loving world becomes a demand and when the power is available to turn this demand into a programme of action.

What this suggests is that (1) organizational totalitarianism and organizational decay, which first appeared to us as systemic problems that concern the organization, are at their root existential, moral, even spiritual problems which concern the individual; and (2) these problems at the individual level become systemic problems for the organization when organizational power is used to effect this transformation.

Putting the matter this way enables us to perceive a continuity between our analysis of organizational decay, on one hand, and the Greek conception of tragedy, on the other. What we see in both cases is the horror that comes from the claims of powerful mortals to be more than mortal. The Greeks called this hubris and they knew that the gods, whom we might refer to as reality, do not stand for it. They demand humility.

References

Arendt, H. (1966). *The Origins of Totalitarianism*. New York: Harcourt, Brace and World.

Argyris, C. & Schon, D.A. (1974). *Theory in Practice*. San Francisco: Jossey-Bass.

Becker, E. (1973). *The Denial of Death*. New York: Free Press.

Burns, J.M. (1978). *Leadership*. New York: Harper and Row.

Chasseguet-Smirgel, J. (1985). *The Ego Ideal: A Psychoanalytic Essay on the Malady of the Ideal* (1st US edition), P. Barrows (Trans.). New York: Norton.

Chasseguet-Smirgel, J. (1986). *Sexuality and Mind: The Role of the Father and the Mother in the Psyche*. New York: New York University Press.

Freud, S. (1914). *On Narcissism: An Introduction*. S.E., 14. London: Hogarth.

Freud, S. (1921). *Group Psychology and the Analysis of the Ego. S.E., 18*. London: Hogarth.

Goffman, E. (1959). *The Presentation of Self in Everyday Life*. New York: Doubleday Anchor.

Halberstam, D. (1986). *The Reckoning*. New York: William Morrow.

Hummel, R.P. (1987). *The Bureaucratic Experience* (3rd edition). New York: St. Martin's.

Ingrassia, P. & White, J.B. (1989). "Losing the Race: With Its Market Share Sliding, GM Scrambles to Avoid a Calamity," *Wall Street Journal*, December 14.

Janis, I. (1972). *Victims of Groupthink: A Psychological Study of Foreign-Policy Decisions and Fiascoes*. New York: Houghton-Mifflin.

Katz, D. & Kahn, R.L. (1966). *The Social Psychology of Organizations*. New York: Wiley.

Keller, M. (1989). *Rude Awakening: The Rise, Fall, and Struggle for Recovery of General Motors*. New York: William Morrow.

Klein, S.M. & Ritti, R.R. (1984). *Understanding Organizational Behavior* (2nd edition). Boston: Kent.

Luthans, E., Hodgetts, R.M. & Rosenkrantz, S.A. (1988). *Real Managers*. Cambridge, MA: Ballinger.

Maslow, A.H. (1970). *Motivation and Personality* (2nd edition). New York: Harper and Row.

Nader, R. (1965). *Unsafe At Any Speed*. New York: Grossman.

Nader, R. & Taylor, W. (1986). *The Big Boys: Power and Position in American Business*. New York: Pantheon.

Schein, E.H. (1983). Organizational socialization and the profession of management. In: B.M. Staw (Ed.), *Psychological Foundations of Organizational Behavior* (2nd edition). Glenview, IL: Scott, Foresman.

Schwartz, H.S. (1983). Maslow and the hierarchical enactment of organizational reality. *Human Relations*, 36(10): 933–956.

Schwartz, H.S. (1987a). On the psychodynamics of organizational totalitarianism. *Journal of Management*, 13(1): 38–51.

Schwartz, H.S. (1987b). Antisocial actions of committed organizational participants: An existential psychoanalytic perspective. *Organization Studies*, 8(4): 327–340.

Schwartz, H.S. (1987c). On the psychodynamics of organizational disaster: The case of the Space Shuttle *Challenger*. *The Columbia Journal of World Business*, XXII(1): 59–67.

Schwartz, H.S. (1987d). Rousseau's Discourse on Inequality Revisited: Psychology of work at the public esteem stage of Maslow's Hierarchy. *International Journal of Management*, 4(2): 180–193.

Schwartz, H.S. (1988). The symbol of the Space Shuttle and the degeneration of the American Dream. *Journal of Organizational Change Management*, 1(2): 5–20.

Searle, J.P. (1969). *Speech Acts: An Essay in the Philosophy of Language*. London: Cambridge University Press.

Sennett, R. & Cobb, J. (1973). *The Hidden Injuries of Class*. New York: Vintage.

Shorris, E. (1981). *The Oppressed Middle: Politics of Middle Management/Scenes from Corporate Life*. Garden City, NY: Anchor Press/Doubleday.

Sievers, B. (1986). Beyond the surrogate of motivation. *Organization Studies*, 7(4): 335–351.

Staw, B.M. (1980). Rationality and justification in organization life. In: B.M. Staw & L.L. Cummings (Eds.), *Research in Organizational Behavior* (Vol. 2) (pp. 45–80). Greenwich, CT: JAI Press.

Wright, J.P. (1979). *On a Clear Day You Can See General Motors: John Z. De Lorean's Look Inside the Automotive Giant*. New York: Avon.

SCENE SIX

Beneath the financial crisis[1]

Burkard Sievers[2]

> This thing we're in doesn't yet have a name. It is variously
> called, in placeholder shorthand, the global financial meltdown,
> the financial crisis, the credit crisis, the recession, the great
> recession, the disaster, the panic, or the bust.

> —Paumgarten (2009, p. 42)

What first appeared as a financial crisis limited to US banks soon
spread and began to threaten national economies around the world.
The collapse of banks, the dramatic increase in unemployment rates,
the critical state of the entire automobile industry, the decrease in
national GNPs (gross national product) for this and next year, and
other factors have forced us to face a world that is no longer what
it used to be—or at least the one we experienced during our life-

[1] This paper was first presented at the 26th ISPSO (International Society for the Psychoanalytic Study of Organizations) annual meeting, June 22–28, 2009, in Toledo,
Spain: "Differences at Work: Towards Integration and Containment".
[2] I am very grateful to Rose Mersky for her help in editing this paper.

117

time. And nobody is able to predict with any certainty how long the economic crisis will last.

The predominant public discourse on the financial crisis and its aftermath appears to be broadly limited to a political and economic one. It thus is focused on finding the appropriate choice of financial and economic means to diffuse the actual and potential damage and thus to encourage banks to offer credit both between themselves and to their customers, to boost production and consumption, and to bail out financial and economic enterprises which threaten to collapse without huge government support.

Although there is broad consensus that the financial industry needs stricter international regulations in order to reduce or prevent future global disasters, we are permanently made to believe that the present capitalist system based on free markets must and will survive. Any serious concern that capitalism, as such, may ultimately lead to the death of freedom and what we regard as democracy and humanity is either broadly ignored or derogated as a pipe-dream (or a nightmare) of those people who never get it right. Thus there is quite some reason to be afraid "that the predominant narrative of the financial crisis will not help us wake up from a dream but will enable us to continue dreaming" (Žižek, 2008, p. 10).

In the media, the discourse regarding the crisis and its outcome has been broadly restricted to financial and economic facts and explanations, the apportioning of blame on apparently responsible parties, and the analysis of appropriate measures to prevent the very worst. The insight, however, that the financial crisis—like all bubbles and busts of financial markets—"was essentially psychological in origin" (Shiller, 2008, p. 24) is not broadly shared—neither in the media nor in most of the literature—although it is gaining traction. In our attempt at a deeper understanding of the subprime crisis from a socio-analytic perspective, we thus are in a sense, broadly "handicapped...by economists' understanding of human beings" (Bain, 2009, p. 1). Even Alan Greenspan, former Federal Reserve chairman was supposed to say: "Unless somebody can find a way to change human nature, we will have more crises" (*Time* magazine, September 21, 2009).

From a psychoanalytic perspective, "there is a crisis ... when speech, discourse, the words, the figures, the rites, the routine, all the symbolic apparatus, prove suddenly impotent to moderate a real which makes as it pleases. A crisis, it is the real unchained, impossible to control" (Miller, 2008). Even though a crisis on the societal level often appears comparable to hurricanes, tsunamis or earthquakes in so far as it "periodically recalls mankind of its precariousness, of its land frailty" (ibid.), the present financial crisis—like countless others before it (e.g., Ferguson, 2008)—differs significantly because it was a disaster caused by man, not nature.

Robert Shiller, professor of economics at Yale University (2008, pp. 43f., 55, 57, 62), explains the extent to which the crisis originated from contagious collective thinking that is similar to an epidemic. This collective thinking was coined by a whole range of unalterable assumptions—quite similar to those that Bion (1959) describes as "basic assumptions": the exorbitant increase in house prices and the real estate boom would never end; the financial market was based on economic rationality; one could rely on financial experts as well as rating agencies (Shiller, 2008, p. 69). Only when the bubble of speculation began to burst in 2007 did it become obvious to what an extent this collective thinking was based on unchecked assumptions and was, to a high degree irrational. One is reminded of Bion's (1959, p. 189) view of basic assumptions as having "the characteristics of defensive reactions to psychotic anxiety".

While bankers on occasion contemptuously refer to financial instruments as being quite simple and easy for anyone to understand, the financial system appears from the outside as magical financial engineering. And, as a matter of fact, the financial industry as a whole seems to a large extent based on magic thinking and manic defences. This magic thinking and manic defences can also be detected in the state's response to the current crisis, as in the UK the use of "quantitative easing" as a magical way to overcome the crisis.

As Winnicott (1935, p. 132, quoted in Kirsner, 1990, p. 42) states, the manic defence embodies "omnipotent manipulation or control and contemptuous devaluation". Among other things, the manic defence is characterized by "denial of inner reality, a flight to external reality from inner reality, holding the people of the inner reality in 'suspended animation', denial of the sensation of depression … by specifically opposite sensations" (Winnicott, ibid.). Rycroft (1972, p. 86) adds the tendency towards "identification with objects from whom a sense of power can be borrowed".

Towards a socio-analysis of the present financial crisis

Though it would be quite fascinating to look at the historical, economic, and political background and development of the present financial crisis in more detail (cf. e.g., Shiller, 2008; Sievers, 2009; Soros, 2008), I have to restrain myself on this occasion from such a venture. I will refer instead to some of the phenomena, to various dynamics, and to critical episodes of the crisis in this attempt to contribute possible answers to the question of how the crisis can be perceived and understood from a socio-analytic perspective.

I am working with the double assumption that any attempt at understanding the crisis from a socio-analytic perspective should go beyond the obvious "facts and figures" to the development of hypotheses about the various unconscious dynamics that contributed to the present escalation, and that any adequate socio-analytic attempt at understanding this crisis and its underlying unconscious dynamics would be more than one socio-analytic scholar could cope with.

My main intent is thus not to suggest a comprehensive socio-analysis of the crisis. Instead I will examine some existing socio-analytic approaches and theories and attempt to articulate how they may contribute towards an understanding of global finances and the present crisis in particular. Thus the previous work of scholars may offer possible directions for thinking about what so far broadly appears to be unthinkable and unknown.

Based on the assumption that both the socio-analysis of the financial industry and its markets and that of the present crisis in particular are yet to be written, my idea for this paper is to attempt a kind of preface for a venture at understanding.

The following selection of psychoanalytic and socio-analytic approaches and theories is, however, a subjective one; it does not claim to be complete. I will stay faithful to a large extent to the original voices of the authors to whom I refer. Though this may not be the "royal road" in academic writing, it represents the writers as they represent themselves.

Manic-depressive—illusion/disillusion

Psychoanalytic attempts at understanding a financial and economic crisis, its reactions, and effects appear to be practically non-existent until the 1990s. The only source I have found is an article by W. Béran Wolfe (1932) on the Great Depression. Wolfe was an American psychoanalyst of Austrian origin. Making the questionable assumption that "nations react to calamity exactly as individuals" (ibid., p. 209), Wolfe offers the thesis that "any national disaster is likely to produce national reactions comparable to those generated by the breakdown of a romantic life-formula in an adolescent confronted with his first frustration by reality" (ibid.). Although Wolfe's limited perspective refers to a nation as a collective of individuals, most of the neurotic reactions towards the crisis that he describes—e.g., perceiving the depression as "normal", denial of hopelessness, "frantic search for new magical formulas" (ibid., p. 211), "cult of devil-chasing and scapegoat-baiting" (ibid.), and suicide—broadly mirror contemporary reactions to the present financial and economic crisis.

Douglas Kirsner (1990)—through whom I became aware of Wolfe's article—appears to be the first contemporary scholar who explicitly elaborates some of the psychoanalytic aspects of a recent financial crisis, i.e., the stock market crash of 1987. While the financial world before the crash (in the USA in particular) was based on the illusion of unlimited growth of the share market on the side of "bankers, brokers and freelance financial geniuses" (Galbraith, 1987, p. 65), Kirsner takes the view that "the crash of 1987 was viewed by many as a pestilence visited upon us from outside the system... . This was achieved through an inappropriate conviction that the economic system was intrinsically sound, through a defensive disavowal of economic reality and a splitting of the economic system into good and evil, where the evil was seen as coming from outside while the good was viewed as intrinsic. ... In fact the potential for the crash was often denied and fear of a crash was regarded as irrational" (Kirsner, 1990, p. 34f). Even when the crash came, it was initially denied and the technocratic myth was confirmed by many "that everything could be manipulated and controlled by the right interventions" (ibid., p. 41). And as it continued, "many people were involved with a manic denial of reality in which they refused to accept that there were some fundamental transformations in the market, with enormous consequences for the world economy. ... The *Zeitgeist* of the market had been that of disavowal" (ibid., p. 43).

"The common zeitgeist drives", as Shiller (2008, p. 43) states, "common opinion among the members of society at any point in

time and place, and this zeitgeist changes as new ideas gain promi-
nence and recede in importance within the collective thinking. Spec-
ulative markets are merely exceptionally good places in which to
observe the ebb and flow of the zeitgeist."

"The stock market crash inflicted a large narcissistic blow to delusions of omnipotence, together with an attendant refusal to face the
unnamed terrors on unknown situations. The reaction of many is not
a depressive anxiety which can experience impotence and ignorance
and thereby possibly repair any emotional damage. There is, rather,
a denial of the external reality of loss, powerlessness and uncertainty,
and a replacement with an even more omniscient and omnipotent
phantasy that yes, we can foretell the future in general and control it" (Kirsner, 1990, p. 48). Referring to Freud's notion (1927a) of
"fetishism", Kirsner (1990, p. 51) states that "disavowal can be the first
stage of perversion in adults—the neurotic represses the demands of
the id, whereas the psychotic begins by disavowing reality". A predominant reaction to the crash was "manic defence" in the sense that
"omnipotent manipulation was used as a substitute for reality, which
was denied and replaced with wishful thinking" (ibid., p. 52).

Narcissistic processes and corporate decay

Howard Schwartz (1990a/b) offers the concept of corporate decay
using the theory of the organizational ideal (see Scene 5 in this volume). Corporate decay is related to, if not an outcome of, narcissistic processes on the side of organizational role holders. His chosen
organization for analysis—General Motors—is of particular relevance, as it filed for Chapter 11 bankruptcy protection on June 1,
2009.

Schwartz's central thesis is that organizational role holders tend
to buy into a dramatized "fantasy about the organization's perfection" (Schwartz, 1990a, p. 1) which is "the return to narcissism, in
which the organization and its highest participants are seen as the
center of a loving world. Since the return to narcissism is impossible, orienting the organization to the dramatization of this fantasy
means that the organization loses touch with reality. The result is
organizational decay—a condition of systemic ineffectiveness. ...
Organizational decay may be compared with the consequences of
hubris" (ibid.).

The notion and theory of the ego-ideal, which Schwartz applied to organizations, could also increase our understanding of the function of money—both in general and in the present context. This is illustrated by Wolfenstein. He states: "Money is the measure of the man. This implies that psychical values are akin to commodities. This commoditization of the inner world extends to the ego itself. Money, that is to say, takes up residence in the super-ego or ego-ideal. The super-ego is monetized. The ego, which is judged by and measures itself against the super-ego, is thus commoditized. Dimensions of selfhood that are not commoditized—that can not be measured by money—are alienated and devalued" (Wolfenstein, 1993, p. 302). Money appears to have taken up residence in the ego-ideal of the financial market.

Toxicity, miasma and the inconsolable organization

In several of his writings, Mark Stein (e.g., 2000, 2003, 2004, 2007) (see Scene 4 in this volume), has focused on the (mis)use of money and capital in corporations and capital management. Though these articles certainly are important sources for a socio-analysis of finances and financial disasters, I would like, in the present context of the global financial crisis, to pay special attention to his more recent paper on "Toxicity" (Stein, 2008).

Even though Stein does not explicitly refer to money or finances in this paper, it is the notion of toxicity itself that offers a direct link to the financial crisis and its aftermath, in so far as it may contribute to a better conceptualization and understanding of what has broadly become known as "toxic assets".

There is quite some reason to assume that the toxicity ascribed in a metaphorical sense to assets in the aftermath of the bank crisis is not limited to these assets themselves but refers to financial institutions—(investment) banks, hedge funds, private equity firms etc.—and the financial market at large; it may even have tainted wide areas of the economy. The fear of contagion has led to an enormous loss of trust and thus caused enormous regression in both financial and economic activities.

Yiannis Gabriel's (2008a/b) concept of "organizational miasma" provides a further leading perspective on toxicity in systemic contexts.

[Gabriel] analyses some of the inevitable burdens that organizations place on their members but also some of the surplus privations and sufferings that many of them inflict. ... [He] develops a theory of organizational miasma, a concept that describes a contagious state of pollution, material, psychological and spiritual, that affects all who work in particular organizations. [Gabriel]... delineates the fundamentals of organizational miasma, as a theoretical concept describing and explaining numerous processes of certain organizations. These include a paralysis of resistance, an experience of pollution and uncleanliness, and feelings of worthlessness and corruption. (2008a, p. 52)

Howard Stein's (2007) notion of the "inconsolable organization"—like his writings on organizational downsizing (e.g., 1999, 2001; Allcorn et al., 1996)—throw further light on some of the unconscious dynamics of the financial crisis and its impact on many organizations in its aftermath. Drawing on Gabriel's work on miasma, mentioned above, Stein (2008, p. 91) proposes "the new metaphor and concept of an 'inconsolable organization'" that refers to "a state of affect paralysis in the face of massive, often sustained, loss that cannot be mourned" (ibid.). He elaborates the thesis that "when organizational loss is not acknowledged, and mourning is proscribed, inconsolable grief and miasma follow. The various forms of 'managed social change' create these in their long wake" (ibid.).

Corruption and perversion

Corruption seems to be an increasingly hot topic both in organizational practice and the discourse of organization theory. Corporations like Enron, Adelphia, WorldCom, Siemens, MAN and many others have been striking examples in the recent past (e.g., Chapman, 2003; Eisold, 2004; Lawrence, 2009, pp. 11f.; Levine, 2005; Long, 2008a, pp. 36ff., 2008b; M. Stein, 2007). Though it seems at first sight that the phenomenon of organizational corruption might have only a minor impact on the financial crisis and its aftermath, some of the socio-analytic literature on corruption may be relevant for understanding the unconscious dynamics in the present context.

Jane Chapman (2003) explores the relatedness of task hatred and task corruption in organizations. Task hatred may emerge from avoidance of the organization's primary task. Task corruption happens if "the change in the nature of the task ... [is] destructively motivated, whether at the conscious or the unconscious level" (ibid., p. 46).

What Chapman describes as "task corruption by simulation" appears to me most relevant in the present context. Task simulation:

> is where the system or individual adopts the appearance of task engagement precisely in order to avoid task engagement. ... The corruption derives from the destructive intent: not only is real task killed off and system energies devoted to the appearance of the tasks being done, but task values are subverted and task power becomes abusive. Simulating organisations, i.e., those which behave as if they are a system engaged in a real task in order to avoid becoming a system engaged in a real task, are characterised by poor morale, low system energy, high levels of politicking, questionable ethics, and high levels of conflict" (ibid., pp. 46f.).

What Chapman describes as "task corruption by simulation" is of special relevance to the major changes banks have gone through during the recent financial boom. Traditionally, commercial banks were committed to the role of "monetary" intermediates to their customers by helping them make deposits and take loans to pursue their personal interests as either consumers or producers, while modestly profiting themselves. Meanwhile, however, many banks gave only the appearance of undertaking their original task. In a sense the aim has become the primary task, i.e., to make as much money as possible and to "own" it for the sake of megalomaniac prestige and power as a financial institution on the world market. To the extent that banks began gambling in the international casino of finance, they betrayed not only most of their customers but also their original primary task and thus were in danger of becoming corrupt organizations.

David Levine (2005, p. 729) states, "the essence of the corrupt organization is ... [the] failure to separate organization from self, a failure driven by the domination in the personality of the hope for the ultimate fulfilment and the treatment of the organization as nothing more than a vehicle for realizing that hope". It seems that the organizational culture of many financial institutions/organizations during the boom has been tainted—if not dominated—by corruption, in that the bonuses of individual role holders served as vehicles to fulfil their hopes of becoming rich (cf. Eisold, 2004, 2008).

Susan Long (2008a), in her recent book on the "perverse organization", illustrates how corruption may often be a bedfellow of perversion: "Perverse dynamics eventually lead to corrupt behaviours within the system" (ibid., p. 2). "Organised corporate corruption is a conscious manifestation, the iceberg tip of an unconscious perverse societal structure and dynamic. Corruption builds on an underlying social fabric of perversity" (ibid., p. 3).

Though this concept was developed before the financial crisis reached its crescendo with the September 2008 collapse of Lehman Brothers, the perverse organization makes an important contribution to the understanding of the blindness about organizational risk grounded "in the collective emotional life of people in organisations" (Long, 2008b). Long's emphasis:

> is on perversity displayed by the organisation as such, rather than simply by its leaders, or other members, even though they may embody and manifest perverse primary symptoms to the extent that they at times engage in corrupt or criminal behaviours. What is explored is a group and organisation dynamic, more deeply embedded than conscious corruption. Within the perverse structure some roles become required to take up corrupt positions. They become part and parcel of the way things work. The *person* may condemn certain practices, but *the role* requires them. Tensions between person and role may mean that the person *in* role acts as they would not while in other roles. Such tensions may lead to the dynamics of perversity. (Long, 2008a, book jacket)

Although Susan Long focuses on the "narrow" frame of organizations and corporations in particular, one may extend beyond this frame by exploring the extent to which perversion is ingrained in the financial world—and thus in the capitalist system at large—and how this global perversion can be perceived and understood in order to extend the range of our thinking as well as our concern and responsibility. Needless to say, this will make us more aware of the helplessness, powerlessness, and despair to which this exploration may inevitably lead.

Unconscious phantasy relationships, states of mind, and unconscious group functioning

Not least due to the fact that *behavioural economics* is broadly restricted to theoretical and rational explanations of *behaviour* in situations of decision-making, uncertainty, and time pressure, Richard Taffler and David Tuckett propose "an interdisciplinary set of theories presently labelled *emotional finance*" (Tavistock Policy Seminars, 2008). With this new paradigm, the authors emphasize "the key role of the emotions as drivers of investors['] behaviour. … It aims to provide an understanding of financial market behaviour and investment processes by formally recognising the role unconscious needs and fears play in all investment activity. … One core insight is that thoughts create feelings, and that feelings create thoughts" (Taffler & Tuckett, 2007, p. 18).

In their article "Phantastic objects and the financial market's sense of reality" Tuckett and Taffler (2008) focus primarily on the internet bubble between 1995 and 2000. Whereas internet stocks had at first been phantastic objects, they later became reviled, "stigmatized and felt to be a massive liability" (ibid., p. 403) once the stock market dramatically crashed in April 2000.

> In the crash, investors suffer the return of the repressed. Knowledge that their investments were based on very risky assumptions had always been there; but such doubts were unconscious while an idealized love affair was in progress. Investors became conscious of the knowledge and feelings hitherto split off, including perhaps the anxiety stirred by their previous activities. They are now forced to own the experience of risk and to notice facts that had always been there. … The phantastic object was now an unconscious persecutory object (ibid., pp. 403f.).

"The study questions a fundamental assumption of mainstream economic models—that investment decisions are rationally motivated by competing, self-interested individuals. These models fall down, argue the authors, in uncertain dynamic conditions such as those

created by the rise of new technology, when emotion and unconscious impulses drive decision-making as much as any dry reading
of growth forecasts. In bubble situations, banks and financial institutions should be as wary of 'emotional inflation' as they are of fiscal
inflation" (The Hero, n. d. (a website, which meanwhile has been
closed)).

Psychosis unlimited

On a previous occasion, in my paper "Your money or your life?
Psychotic implications of the pension fund system: Towards a socio-
analysis of the financial services revolution" (Sievers, 2003), I focused
on the psychotic thinking and dynamic underlying pension funds
systems and shareholder value optimization. My conceptualization of psychosis comes from Lawrence (2000, pp. 4f.), who regards
psychosis in general as "the process whereby humans defend themselves from understanding the meaning and significance of reality,
because they regard such knowing as painful. To do this, they use
aspects of their mental functioning to destroy, in various degrees,
the very process of thinking that would put them in touch with reality" (cf. Sievers, 1999, 2006, 2008).

Though Welch, former CEO of General Electric and once one
of the biggest promoters—if not "the father"—of the "shareholder
value" movement, has now renounced it and declared it as a
"dump idea" (Guerrera, 2009), pension funds are still playing a significant role in the financial market. They have—both as actors and
as "victims" or "casualties"—been heavily involved in the present
crisis and its aftermath, not least with the result that millions of
people are made to fear for their pensions, and consequently for
their future.

The working hypothesis of this paper was that:

> [T]he pension fund system, because of its inherent defenses
> against persecutory and depressive anxieties, is based on psy-
> chotic dynamics. Participation in the pension fund system
> encourages a psychotic dynamic; the expected pension after
> retirement is seen to protect one from a "miserable" way of life,
> from deprivation, from annihilation and feelings of dependency,
> gratitude, love, and guilt. As people increasingly strive for an

affluent retirement, commoditized money nurtures the illusion that the more money one accumulates the more certain death will be kept away. It further [is] ... argued that the psychotic dynamic inherent in the pension funds system is not limited to those who invest in the funds, but further finds an expression or "resonance" in the organizations that manage the funds and their respective role holders. Money paid into a pension scheme serves—in addition to its "pecuniary" function—as a "conductor" of psychotic anxieties. As a consequence, pension funds have become the main players in a kind of global marshalling yard where underlying anxieties are transferred and shifted in various ways. Loaded with their customers' expectations and anxieties about adequate pensions after retirement, pension fund organizations tend to maintain and spread a globalized collusion of psychotic thinking. (Sievers, 2003, p. 187)

On this occasion, I can only briefly sketch some socio-analytic aspects of the financial crises, which I have previously developed more fully (Sievers, 2009). My current thoughts are based on the *working hypothesis* that the thinking of various actors in the real estate and financial markets has been, to a high degree, psychotic—and to some extent still is. This hypothesis comes from the assumption that it is not so much individual persons or their actions through which the "reality" of organizations and markets is coined, but instead through the thinking of role holders in their respective contexts and organizations, e.g., house buyers, employees of banks, insurance companies, private equity firms, hedge and pension funds, economists, and politicians.

The decisions of home buyers, investment and commercial banks, real estate agencies, hedge funds etc. during the real estate market boom were based on the unshakable assumption that this boom—in comparison to all previous ones, e.g., the 1987 stock market crash and the "dotcom" boom and bust of 1995–2000—was the very first in the history of mankind that would last indefinitely. The unshakable belief that real estate prices would, with almost certainty, rise permanently was based, in part, on the limited available land for development and the expected increase in population and economic development in the US (Shiller, 2008, p. 69). This has proven to be a myth. The belief that it would go on infinitely is, however, typical for almost every boom—as long as it continues. This belief is based on an illusion, which, as Freud (1927b, p. 31, quoted in Kirsner, 1990, p. 31) indicates, exists "when a wish-fulfilment is a prominent factor in its motivation, and in doing so we disregard its relations to reality, just as the illusion itself sets no store by verification".

The thinking in the financial world was not least coined by a collectively shared manic defence, a psychotic process by which countless role holders unconsciously felt impelled to mobilize their personal manic parts to a much higher degree than they would do in other role and systemic contexts. On this occasion I must confine myself to a few examples:

- Many governments—first and foremost the Bush one in the US—emphasized vehemently at the beginning of the financial crisis that this crisis would not lead to catastrophic consequences. The fact that the public was again and again reassured that a disaster like the Great Depression of 1929 would not recur may have had a calming effect on some people but, at the same time, made the high level of anxiety and apprehension more obvious. And many banks reacted in a similar way long before they ultimately became aware of what they actually had on their books.
- The frantic pace by which some national governments reacted to the burst of the financial bubble appears to be more an expression of manic defence against immense helplessness and anxiety than of thinking and reflection.
- The nationalization of banks and their takeover by their states can be understood more as a manic defence than as an alleged strategy to "conquer" (and better run) them.
- The astronomic cost of credit securities and buyouts as well as economic stimulus programmes supplied by some states—without any estimate of the middle and long term consequences for national budgets and future generations, not to mention the question of how these national deficits could ever be reduced—is further evidence for my assumption.
- The fact that some banks were bailed out and thus rescued by their states mirrors a degree of state intervention unknown in the capitalist world at least since World War II. It "implies something about the fact that we might have imperceptibly and globally entered into a new and unchartered phase of capitalism when the

prevailing economic system has in effect become a 'State-Assisted Capitalism'" (Brunning, 2009). It thus seems as if the state suddenly becomes the only reliable container not only for the free floating toxic debenture bonds but also for the anxiety and the despair concomitant with them. At present, it is unknown what these temporary solutions will stimulate in us as citizens and in the world globally (ibid.)—and, I would add, for our perception of the future of democracy.

- The unswerving conviction that the present financial crisis was caused by disturbances within the system and does not take into account the possibility of a systemic crisis of capitalism itself (Wade, 2008, p. 39; Žižek, 2008, p. 10) seems to indicate a denial of reality.

- Last but not least, the media and the literature on the financial crisis seem to neglect the fact that "a house of one's own" or "one's home" is just not a commodity, but, foremost, a "phantastic object" (Tuckett & Taffler, 2008), a "symbol for life and death, freedom and dependency" (Hirsch, 2006; cf. Bourdieu, 2005). This neglect is surprising, since the Bush government, especially since 9/11, intensively propagated national programmes to encourage people—minorities in particular—to purchase their own homes. When the bust hit, hundreds of thousands of American home buyers realized they could not repay their subprime mortgages and that they would probably be evicted from their homes. Thus a long cherished (and propagated) dream became a nightmare, and countless people became despairingly aware that what they were seduced to take on as reality was actually an illusion. The endless despair and the traumata of countless home buyers—not to mention the growing number of unemployed people—are not acknowledged anywhere in the financial discourse; their fate, if it is considered at all, is most likely seen as "collateral damage" which, for example, was also the term used for those innocents killed in the Iraq War.

Looking at the thinking regarding the financial crisis and its aftermath from the perspective chosen here, there is ample evidence to suggest that vast parts of the world and its economy are in a globalized collusion of psychotic thinking and thus in a state of "psychosis unlimited".

A brief synopsis—and some concluding considerations

Even though my choice of the six approaches sketched above is limited (and selective), it becomes obvious that there is already quite a body of psychodynamic/socio-analytic theory that may be of further help in developing an understanding of some of the unconscious dynamics of the financial world and the present financial crisis in particular.

In retrospect, it appears to me that the map drawn here leaves many open questions that have not yet been raised and which, from my point of view, are still in search of thinkers and require further thinking. These open questions concern—above all—a deeper socio-analysis of the contemporary predominance of the financial world both in the economy at large and in our lives, our "images of man" and our world views.

It seems that socio-analytic contributions explicitly dealing with the unconscious dynamics of capitalism are scarce, if not non-existent, in the field of psychoanalytic study of organizations. Despite the discontents we may have with capitalism it appears that we have made peace with it. Even the hardened ex-communist powers like Russia and China are busily building capitalist systems of their own. We all profit and suffer without making a deeper attempt to illuminate the implications of our discontents. Like "the main stream of the psychoanalytic movement", we broadly appear "to accept capitalist society, equating it with civilization itself" as Hansen (1956) once stated, drawing on Marcuse's (1955) *Eros and Civilization*.

Not only were many—if not most—role holders in the financial industry unable to calculate the risk of their transactions, much less to understand the instruments and products they were dealing with, even the majority of economists, academics, and politicians, seem—according, for example, to Heinsohn (2009)—to have ignored their own not-knowing regarding the foundations of economic theory, i.e., how the market actually works and how it is constituted: "The politics of economics in the crisis resemble emergency surgery without any knowledge of anatomy. We still deceive ourselves about the basics of interest, money and market" (Heinsohn, 2009).

Apparently there still seems much to be done in order to better understand the world in "the time of financial crisis". In doing so, a capacity for not-understanding may be a virtue rather than an indication of incompetence. As Gotthold Ephraim Lessing (1772), the German poet at the time of the Enlightenment, states in his "bourgeois tragedy" *Emilia Galotti*: "He who does not loose his mind about certain things, does not have a mind to loose."

In concluding, I want to sketch at least two of the many open questions to be further elaborated in the present context: risk management and the function of the financial industry in contemporary societies and the world.

It appears that, despite the fact that risk is of manifold relevance to the financial crisis, we broadly seem to have left the notion of risk and risk management to the experts (and supposed acrobats) in the global financial world. Instead of conceptualizing and further elaborating "risk in depth and at large", we tend to extrapolate and project it into the future, the outer world and the financial one in particular (cf. e.g., Hirschhorn, 1999; Pelzer, 2009; Pelzer & Case, 2007; M. Stein, 2003).

Another question worth exploring is whether and, if so, to what extent, the financial system as a societal or global sub-system is at present serving as a kind of container (and a "scapegoat" or cover story) for various other virulent issues and broadly neglected problems, both on the level of societies and the world at large: e.g., fundamentalism and the "war on terror", the increasing scarcity of natural resources, the north-south divide, widespread famine, and our increasing inability to understand the world in which we live—to mention just a few. The financial world seems at present to be the most obvious domain in which psychotic thinking as an expression of the "normality of madness" can most easily be hidden behind the "rationality" of the market. Shafer (2001) adds a further hypothesis to this thought: "The institutionalised power of money is currently a defence against rapidly increasing powerlessness and diminished faith in personal and institutional authoritative leadership."

To the extent that we and the world at large seem broadly unconcerned with such not-knowing and lack a willingness to understand, the financial crisis and the world of finance in general thus may serve as a container for the toxicity in the world at large—and one might assume—in ourselves, which we, for understandable reasons, do not want to face.

References

Allcorn, S., Baum, H.S., Diamond, M. & Stein, H. (1996). *The Human Costs of a Management Failure: Organizational Downsizing at General Hospital*. Westport, CT: Quorum.

Bain, A. (2009). *The Economic Crisis as Manic Depression. A few thoughts*. http://www.acsa.net.au/articles/The%20Economic%20Crisis%20as%20Manic%20Depression.pdf. (May 9, 2009).

Bion, W.R. (1959). *Experiences in Groups*. New York: Basic Books.

Bourdieu, P. (2005). *The social structures of the economy*. Cambridge: Polity Press.

Brunning, H. (2009). Private e-mail communication, May 14, 2009.

Chapman, J. (2003). Hatred and the corruption of task. *Organisational and Social Dynamics*, 3(1): 40–60; first published 1999 in *Socio-Analysis*, 1(2): 127–150.

Eisold, K. (2004). Corrupt Groups in Contemporary Corporations: Outside Boards and Inside Traders. *Journal of Psycho-Social Studies*, 3(1): 4. http://www.martinzager.com/eisold/wp-content/uploads/2009/01/corrupt.pdf (November 29, 2009).

Eisold, K. (2008). What makes traders trade?—and how it is changing in the digital age [paper presented at the 2008 ISPSO Symposium, Philadelphia].

Elias, N. (1985). *The loneliness of the dying*. Oxford: Basil Blackwell.

Freud, S. (1927a). Fetishism. *S.E., 11* (pp. 152–157). London: Hogarth.

Freud, S. (1927b). The future of an illusion. *S.E., 11* (pp. 5–56). London: Hogarth.

Gabriel, Y. (2008a). Organizational miasma, purification and cleansing. In: A. Ahlers-Niemann, U. Beumer, R. Redding Mersky & B. Sievers (Eds.), *Organisationslandschaften. Sozioanalytische Gedanken und Interventionen zur normalen Verrücktheit in Organisationen* (The normal madness in organizations: Socio-analytic thoughts and interventions) (pp. 52–73). Bergisch-Gladbach, Germany: Verlag Andreas Kohlhage.

Gabriel, Y. (2008b). Oedipus in the land of organizational darkness: preliminary considerations on organizational miasma. In: M. Kostera (Ed.), *Organizational Epics and Sagas: Tales of Organizations* (pp. 51–65). Basingstoke, England: Palgrave.

Galbraith, J.K. (1987). The 1929 parallel. *Atlantic Monthly*, January: 62–66.

Guerrera, F. (2009). Welch rues short-term "obsession". *Financial Times*, May 12. http://us.ft.com/ftgateway/superpage.ft?news_id=fto031220091430053057 (May 11, 2009).

Hansen, J. (1956). A psychoanalyst looks for a sane society. *Fourth International*, 17(2), Spring: 65–69. http://www.marxists.org/archive/hansen/1956/xx/psych.htm (May 18, 2009).

Heinsohn, G. (2009). *Die nächste Blase schwillt schon an. Frankfurter Allgemeine Zeitung*, May 20, No. 116, p. 31.

Hirsch, M. (2006). Das Haus. *Symbol für Leben und Tod, Freiheit und Abhängigkeit*. Giessen, Germany: Psychosozial-Verlag.

Hirschhorn, L. (1999). The primary risk. *Human Relations, 52*(1): 5–23; again in: B. Sievers (Ed.), *Psychoanalytic Studies of Organizations: contributions from the International Society for the Psychoanalytic Study of Organizations (ISPSO) 1983–2008* (pp. 153 174). London: Karnac, 2009.

Kirsner, D. (1990). Illusion and the stock market crash. Some psychoanalytic aspects. *Free Associations, 19*: 31–58.

Lawrence, W.G. (2000). Thinking refracted. In: W.G. Lawrence: *Tongued with fire. Groups in experience* (pp. 1–30). London: Karnac.

Lawrence W.G. (2009). Authority examined in contemporary times [unpublished manuscript].

Lessing, G.E. (1772). Lessings Emilia Galotti. Charleston, SC: BiblioLife, 2008.

Levine, D.P. (2005). The corrupt organization. *Human Relations, 58*(6): 723–740.

Long, S. (2008a). *The perverse organisation and its deadly sins*. London: Karnac.

Long, S. (2008b). The perverse organisation and its deadly sins. http://www.karnacbooks.com/AuthorBlog.asp?BID=69 (May 14, 2009).

Marcuse, H. (1955). *Eros and Civilization. A Philosophical Inquiry into Freud*. Boston: The Bacon Press.

Miller, J.-A. (2008). The Financial Crisis. http://www.lacan.com/symptom/?page_id=299 (November 30, 2008).

Paumgarten, N. (2009). The death of kings. Notes from a meltdown. *The New Yorker*, May 18: 40–57.

Pelzer, P. (2009). The displaced world of risk: Risk management as alienated risk (perception?). *Society and Business Review, 4*(1): 26–36.

Pelzer, P. & Case, P. (2007). The displaced world of risk management: covert enchantment in a calculative world. In: M. Kostera (Ed.), *Mythical Inspirations and Storytelling for Organizational Realities* (pp. 121–135). Basingstoke, England: Palgrave.

Rycroft, C. (1972). *A Critical Dictionary of Psychoanalysis*. Harmondsworth: Penguin.

Schwartz, H.S. (1990a). Narcissism project and corporate decay: the case of General Motors. http://www.sba.oakland.edu/faculty/schwartz/GMDecay.htm (December 17, 2008).

Schwartz, H.S. (1990b). *Narcissistic Process and Corporate Decay: The Theory of the Organization Ideal*. New York: New York University Press.

Shafer, A. (2001). What is the value of money? [Seminar for the Australian Institute of Socio-Analysis series: "Money Talks!", November 30.] http://www.allanshafer.com/docs/What%20is%20 the%20Value%20of%20Money.doc (May 18, 2009).

Shiller, R.S. (2008). *The Subprime Solution: How Today's Global Financial Crisis Happened, and What to Do About it*. Princeton, NJ: Princeton University Press.

Sievers, B. (1999). Psychotic organization as a metaphoric frame for the socio-analysis of organizational and interorganizational dynamics. *Administration & Society, 31*(5), November: 588–615.

Sievers, B. (2003). Your money or your life? Psychotic implications of the pension fund system: Towards a socio-analysis of the financial services revolution. *Human Relations, 56*(2): 187–210.

Sievers, B. (2006). Psychotic organization—a socio-analytic perspective. *Ephemera, 6*(2): 104–120. http://www.ephemeraweb.org/journal/ 6–2/6–2 sievers.pdf (May 14, 2009).

Sievers, B. (2009). *Der "ganz normale" Wahnsinn. Zu einer Sozioanalyse der gegenwärtigen Finanzkrise. texte* 29(1): 81–106.

Soros, G. (2008). *The New Paradigm for Financial Markets. The Credit Crisis and What it Means*. London: PublicAffairs.

Stein, H.F. (1999). Downsizing, managed care, and the potlatching of America: A study in cultural brutality and its mystification. *Journal for the Psychoanalysis of Culture and Society, 4*(2), Fall: 209–227.

Stein, H.F. (2001). *Nothing Personal, Just Business: A Guided Journey into Organizational Darkness*. Westport, CT: Quorum.

Stein, H.F. (2007). The inconsolable organization: toward a theory of organizational and cultural change. *Psychoanalysis, Culture & Society, 12* : 349–368.

Stein, H.F. (2008). Traumatic change and the inconsolable organization. In: A. Ahlers-Niemann, U. Beumer, R. Redding Mersky & B. Sievers (Eds.), *Organisationslandschaften. Sozioanalytische Gedanken und Interventionen zur normalen Verrücktheit in Organisationen* (The normal madness in organizations: socio-analytic thoughts and interventions) (pp. 74–95). Bergisch-Gladbach, Germany: Verlag Andreas Kohlhage.

Stein, M. (2000). The risk taker as shadow: a psychoanalytic view of the collapse of Barings Bank. *Journal of Management Studies, 37*(8): 1215–1229.

Stein, M. (2003). Unbounded irrationality: risk and organizational narcissism at long term capital management. *Human Relations, 56*(5): 523–540.

Stein, M. (2004). The critical period of disasters: insights from sensemaking and psychoanalytic theory. *Human Relations, 57*(10): 1243–1261.

Stein, M. (2007). Oedipus Rex at Enron: Leadership, Oedipal struggles, and organizational collapse. *Human Relations*, 60(9): 1387–1410.

Stein, M. (2008). Toxicity and the unconscious experience of the body at the employee-customer interface. *Organization Studies, 28*: 1223–1241.

Taffler, R. & Tuckett, D. (2007). Emotional finance: understanding what drives investors. *Professional Investor*, Autumn: 18–20.

Tavistock Policy Seminars (2008). Markets, Meaning and Madness. November 20. London: The Tavistock and Portman NHS Foundation Trust. The Hero (n. d.): http://www.hero.ac.uk/uk/business/archives/2008/when_markets_go_mad_Jun.cfm (May 11, 2009—the site is now closed)

Tuckett, D. & Taffler, R. (2008). Phantastic objects and the financial market's sense of reality: a psychoanalytic contribution to the understanding of stock market instability. *International Journal of Psychoanalysis, 89*: 389–412.

Wade, R. (2008). *Systembeben. Neue Steuerungsinstrumente für die Weltwirtschat sind erforderlich. Lettre International, 83*, Winter: 35–40.

Winnicott, D.W. (1935). The manic defence. In: D.W. Winnicott, *Through Paediatrics to Psychoanalysis* (pp. 129–144). London: Hogarth, 1975.

Wolfe, W.B. (1932). Psycho-analyzing the depression. *The Forum and Century, 87*(4): 209–214.

Wolfenstein, E.V. (1993). *Psychoanalytic-Marxism. Groundwork.* London: Free Association, and New York: The Guilford Press.

Žižek, S. (2008). *Hoffnungszeichen. Doch die eigentliche Auseinandersetzung beginnt nach dem Sieg Obamas. Lettre International, 83*, Winter: 7–10.

ACT III

ON LEADERSHIP AND THE ILLUSION
OF CONTAINMENT

In Act III the search for containments continues. Hopes are raised and dashed. The yearning for salvation is vested in celebrated figures as well as modern and established institutions.

Can they offer any solution, or are they too just another illusive symbol of a failed leadership leading to failed dependency?

A dynamic reading of
The funeral of Diana,
Princess of Wales[1]

Wesley Carr

iana, Princess of Wales died in a motor accident in France in
1997. The news came out during the night. At about 6.20 a.m.
on a Sunday morning the phone rang in the Deanery at
Westminster, my home as Dean of Westminster. That world is one
with which few are familiar, so a little background information is
provided.

Westminster Abbey, one of the world's great religious buildings is
England's royal church and a national shrine. Monarchs are crowned
there; members of the royal family frequently attend services; thousands are memorialized and a million visit each year. The dean is
responsible for its work and is accountable to the monarch alone.

I had been appointed Dean of Westminster in February 1997 and
as such would be responsible for the order of service as well as being

---

[1] Parts of this chapter were explored in the Eric Miller Memorial Lecture 2009, now
published in the *Journal of Organisational and Social Dynamics, 9*: 2 (November 2009).
This essay was written against the background of the study of group relations in the
Tavistock tradition, where the psychoanalytical method is derived from and through
the study of group processes.

the minister who presided over the funeral of Diana, Princess of Wales.

It is difficult at this distance in time to recall the intensity of feeling that Diana's death aroused throughout the country and in large parts of the world. Yet although there were only five days to complete the funeral service, people were remarkably calm and seemed to be living with a subdued intensity. After the service, I went outside the abbey to talk to the people. They were milling around and not leaving. I had thought to open the abbey for a one way stream of visitors who could see the spot where the coffin had stood. It would not have been a problem to do. The crowd could not have looked less belligerent, but the police in charge ruled against me: the officers thought that they would not be able to control the riot that would probably ensue when I would eventually have to close the doors and not everyone had been through.

I spoke to a man who told me his story. He was single, middle-aged and an admirer of Diana. He had sat down in front of the television to watch the service when a strong feeling overwhelmed him that it was wrong and that he should be in London where the real funeral was. He lived in Stockport just outside Manchester and somehow had got himself to London. He knew he would miss the service, but was quite sure that the price was worth paying for being in London on such an historic day. This as we shall see is characteristic of dependence.

The opportunity to observe some of the underlying factors that go into the making of an institution and the growth of a society comes very rarely. This is the story of an international event that is unlikely to be repeated. It is an exploration of some of the current dynamics within British society, and in particular the roles of the monarchy. The episode also demonstrated the way that an institution may function on behalf of the society of which it is part. It involves death and bereavement and how these are socially managed. There is nothing more personal and individual than death; yet paradoxically no death could be more public and institutional than that of a prominent member of the family of the symbolic head of the nation and the mother of a presumed future king. This was Diana, Princess of Wales.

When people recall Diana, they tend to do so in personal terms— her beauty and style, her interest in others, and her skill of putting others at ease. But in fact much of her popular appeal seems to have been at least in part due to the way she handled complicated and competing roles, especially those which were suddenly thrust upon her. That exposed her to public examination. However wise or not, this functioned to bring her nearer ordinary people than, for example, some other members of the royal family. People seemed to feel an instinctive intimacy with her and, as an aspect of that, were prepared to ignore her weaknesses.

It was sometimes claimed that Diana had no one in the royal family with similar interests, but there were similarities between the princess and the queen mother—both were single, had many friends, had favourite servants, enjoyed light music, and undertook charitable work. ("Queen mother" is the title of the sovereign's mother should she be left a widow.)

People (and this included the media) were less forgiving of the behaviour of others involved in this story. We shall see something of this process later, but a small piece of evidence occurred from the start of the funeral week. Talking with people as they camped around the abbey precincts, I noted their surprise that the service was to be taken by someone who had never met her in real life. They openly wondered how I could do her justice and it did not occur to them that it is possible to work *in role*.

An interpretative stance

In dealing with human relations we need to adopt a stance by which we seek to interpret what is being said and done—an interpretative stance (Shapiro & Carr, 1978). For most everyday purposes, that kind of engagement will occur within a pair (myself and one other), a very small group (such as a family), or a small group gathered for some purpose, such as work or sport. But with that we seem to meet the limits of what is possible and such a stance might seem less applicable to an operation on the scale of this funeral. Millions around the world and more millions in Great Britain were involved. Who, then, could be said was consulting to whom and what interpretation with what outcome was possible? The answer lies in the areas of symbolism and liturgy.

Liturgy, the ordered form of music and word, is an interpretative medium. Its steady order and obvious structure provide a framework by which powerful feelings are not removed but are given a fresh context. In this instance the underlying order was that of the Church of England's Prayer Book. Ordered worship, even if only by offering a structure, can usually help people in disarray to address privately their disturbed self, but also as members of communities in a society. The steady security and relentless structure of a liturgy can reassure people, thus freeing them from anxiety to discover a new, more amenable life-style and often renewal. Music almost always plays a part in such transitional moments: it creates space for reflection without the oppression of silence.

At the time of writing (July 2009) the British Army was suffering heavy casualties in Afghanistan. One mother, whose son had been killed, movingly spoke of how hitherto she had always mocked the national Remembrance Service from the Royal Albert Hall with its parades and poppies as being "over the top". Today she can scarcely bear to watch it, she is so moved. This is obviously an intensely personal matter, but it is also an example of the shift in role from "mother" to "bereaved mother". This role change has exposed her to a new perspective on life and opened a new connection to the wider community. To this she gave service; from it she received recognition.

Diana herself presented a rich agglomeration of roles. In her brief public life she made friends among the "celebs"—singers, performers, actors, fashion designers, and dressmakers. She also acquired a reputation for charitable work, such as her campaign against land mines and her association with Mother Teresa of Calcutta. The princess's many roles were in fact the key to her funeral.

The hymns were taken from the four nations of the United Kingdom, thus emphasizing her royal role as a princess. The excerpt from Verdi's *Requiem* and Elton John's *Candle in the Wind* picked up the range of people whom she influenced and who influenced her. By their contrasting style they reminded the congregation of what she had achieved and her age. The traditional funeral sentences which were sung as the coffin was carried into the abbey established the first boundary to be negotiated, namely that between events to date and the specific activity of the funeral. John Taverner's haunting *Alleluias*, sung as the coffin left the abbey, brought the congregation back to Diana, the young woman, expressing final thanksgiving and hope. Thus in terms of process, the deceased was brought to the abbey;

through the liturgical structure of the service the congregation was presented with her various roles and their effect on the world; and the whole concluded with a reaffirmation of Diana the person. Even after her death her influence seemed to persist, at least for a while, although she no longer had the authority she had enjoyed.

A word that is widely used today, not least with reference to Diana, is *icon*. This describes pictures, old and new—whether early Christian paintings venerated in Orthodox churches or the images defining computer keys. But of a person it refers to their use by others to represent or hold some facet of life and in a sense sanctify it, i.e. have it recognized but not flaunted. How much of that definition is accurate about Diana? At this stage it is too early to tell.

The writing frenzy

With Diana's death the world appeared to go into shock. One way by which people seemed to manage this was through writing. Books of condolence were available at Buckingham and St James's Palaces and across the United Kingdom. (These two palaces are the main royal residences in London, the homes respectively of the queen and currently the Prince of Wales (although, at that time, the queen mother.)) The public called for such books and they wrote. Though their content remains private it was reported that many of the condolences were lengthy essays. People wrote of their experiences, usually of loss.

Letters also came to me at the abbey. They usually began with thanks for the service or, more frequently, a particular part of it, and then told a story (often of death or funerals) which had festered unspoken sometimes for 20 or 30 years. Why this writing should connect with Diana was not immediately clear. But it was apparent that unresolved grief required some attention and found it in the structure created for this funeral. Once again we may note the way in which authority functioned. Authority is always negotiated. In this case it had to be negotiated between Diana and the crowd. For reasons, some given above, that authority was implicit and she was the figure who gave permission to ordinary people to be normal—in this case to mourn. This was one outcome of the extraordinary number of symbolic roles that she was assigned. And the process seemed self-regenerating: the more charities she took on, the more charitable organizations approached her. The impact was world-wide. She was, for whatever reasons, a genuinely international icon.

It is a well attested observation that when people come to tend the grave of an ancestor they will sometimes sit by the headstone and hold a conversation with the deceased. Elsewhere such behaviours might be considered odd, even deviant, but tears are sanctioned by place. It may be that the writing at the time of Diana's death was a similar form of communication—public and private at the same time and legitimated by the place and the unique occasion. Continuing links are affirmed between the departed and the living and are actively explored as past behaviour is alluded to in personal conversation (Francis, Kellaher & Neophutou, 2005).

One poignant bit of writing deserves mention, for it sums up much about the funeral and about the princess. On the coffin, amid the flowers and royal regalia, there was a small card which simply read "MUMMY" that Prince Harry had put there. It was a reminder to all that while Diana the princess might have had multiple roles in society and was an iconic figure to the world, her primary role was that of mother and her children were not going to allow the world to forget it. I have not seen this point made elsewhere, but it has interesting resonances with part of Earl Spencer's address later in the service when he contrasted the huge demands that will fall on the princes with their need also for sustaining "ordinary" relationships.

Private and institutional bereavement

A distinction between private and institutional bereavement is necessary here. The death of a beloved person evokes conscious memories and stirs up unconscious feelings. Personal loss is also felt within the family group and in those who have close connections with it. The mourners gradually begin to recognize how the deceased represented dimensions of themselves. Others may seem to take the deceased's place; but he or she is at the moment irreplaceable. At this early stage of bereavement there is greater emphasis on the person than on roles. By contrast, in institutions there is naturally also grieving for the deceased, but quickly, indeed immediately, this goes beyond the personal into *the person in role*. The grieving is then, as it were, stored until needed, when it will be mobilized for work.

For instance, for reasons both of symbolism and political realism the USA cannot exist without a president. Thus, if the president dies or resigns the successor is sworn in immediately on behalf of the nation to ensure its continuance. Only after this essential step has been taken can friends and family turn to grieving for the person. This process was shown around the world at the death of President Kennedy through a notable photograph. It showed people gathered round the justice as he administers the oath to the new president, while off to the right stands Jackie Kennedy alone, gazing into the middle distance neither in nor out. The time for mourning had not yet arrived. The same is true of the British monarchy: the proclamation of the succession is "The king is dead; long live the king."

Institutions in the mind

Anyone who works in an institution or who is—through citizenship—related to society's institutions, has a picture of "the institution in the mind". This image is not consciously negotiated with others but is the unconscious product of many minds. It is, therefore, no surprise that when the basic grieving is over and mourning begins, fragments of residual or incomplete institutional loss remain for a while.

The week of Diana's funeral began with an unusually clear outline of what had to be addressed. Each person (including me) involved in any aspect of the organization of the event began with a blank sheet. At the point when the fact of Diana's death increasingly dawned, people turned to their public institutions, for leadership and containment. The Church was in demand in Westminster for a form of service that would allow many to mourn, most of whom had an idealized notion of the princess. The populist prime minister had already pre-empted the crowds' feelings by naming Diana "The People's Princess", a curious mix of regal and casual address. As I recall it was not a phrase widely used other than in the media. The prime minister also asked to read the scripture in the service and did so in an idiosyncratic fashion as if he were appointing himself the representative of the people. The military came into its own in managing the movements outside the abbey and the pall-bearing. This aspect was even changed up to the last minute. On the morning of the funeral the parade was extended by another mile and a half so that more of the crowds would see the funeral procession pass. The institutional church was the abbey.

Bion's theory modified

Those familiar with Bion's theory of groups and their relations may also be aware of a possible further hypothesis in which he relates the dynamics of groups to facets of society (1961). The group has an internal life with its unconscious dynamics; Bion invokes three—dependence (reliance on an individual), pairing (reliance on two people to produce the solution), and fight/flight. He speculates that these three dynamics are then taken up into society, where they are embodied in church and monarchy (dependence), pairing (aristocracy), and the armed forces (fight/flight). Thus, for example, during a war as much fight/flight as is possible is needed for the fighting and the soldiers should be able to leave the other dynamics for others to hold on their behalf. Consequently the dependent dynamic holds their dependency, so that, freed from those concerns, the military can concentrate on the task in hand. Usually in wartime clergy and doctors are the key focal points for dependence, since they may be believed to guard matters of love, life, and death.

Other basic assumptions have been proposed, although only one has stood up to examination: Turquet's perception of oneness—a group locks itself into an undifferentiated blob, with no prospect of examination. This is an even deeper level of unconscious inactivity. The group is being invited deliberately to become self-consciously dependent as a step towards facing necessary dependence (Carr, 2009). Even though Bion's speculation is obviously dated and calls for revision, the principle seems right. There are now numerous case studies to illustrate it. At the time of Diana's funeral the prevailing dynamic was profoundly dependent, focusing that dependence in the royal family (particularly the monarch) who were "absent" on location in Scotland.

Natural and intense dependency

In the face of our post-modern affirmations of individuality, autonomy, and independence, there still seem to be moments when the assumptions break down and we feel the need for something more solid upon which to rely. But this reliance inevitably involves dependence (Carr, 2001). Sometimes it seems that when a greater anxiety is generated we are invoking not one but two dependencies or two levels of dependency. This is not a state into and out of which we may or may not move. It is a permanent condition in which we live—we are always in this dependent state and the key to living with it is to be aware of it. Dependence is also qualitatively different from Bion's other two basic assumptions (fight/flight and pairing). It is as if the dependent mode operates in, or oscillates between, two levels in the unconscious mind itself. Much of the time it is just "there" and remains uninvoked; at other times it seems to peak to a powerful experience of explicit dependency. Group consultants, for example, can quickly detect dependence present in a group. They may use stratagems to encourage the group out of this dependent mode to return to managing the actual work. To do this they have to take into account both the natural dependence and its more intense form.

Bion's understanding of basic assumptions was not about alternative approaches to changing something. He was a psychoanalyst and knew about tasks and unconscious behaviour. But he saw that if left unaddressed, these unconscious dynamics could prevent work being done on the task. The same was true in the community in which he lived: the aim was to link the prevailing unconscious dynamic to the task in hand. This insight could also change perspectives, thus making effective work possible. The mode, however, from which there is no escape into work is the underlying dependence. And there is little point in drawing attention to this as it merely describes the *status quo*. But what if there were institutions that were specifically designed to focus this complicated dependence and in so doing to foster it? Reed's work on dependence, religion, and oscillation theory suggests that in the church and in the monarchy we have two such examples (Reed, 1978).

Regression

When an individual or group acknowledges their dependency, they do so in regression. Regression to what? Words such as "secular" and "materialistic" take much of their meaning from their context and a shift into overt dependence is only to another level or form of dependence. Yet the occasion of Diana's funeral seemed different. The emotional reactions, signs of genuine grief and the use of religious buildings and clergy and ministers by millions of people who "knew" the Princess only through the media were far greater than expected. Living did not come to a halt; but individual members of the public and various large organizations in the commercial and political worlds were required to manage themselves so as to allow time and space for mourning Diana and her public roles. In retrospect it is clear that something unique was happening. Her powerful presence, even in death, was such that it affected everything. Diana, never more potent than in her death, may even have been used to offer some shape to a society which knew itself to be broken but needed an example of such magnitude to become fully aware of it. Because of her significance in the nation Diana was used as a container of the stress that arises from living with multiple roles. Once again, although the issue looks different when viewed from a new vantage point, we have to examine Diana in her many roles rather than first as a person. There seems no doubt however, that the sense of loss was also to do with her as a person.

All of this occurred in a complicated interaction between what was personal and what was public. As we have seen, people used her public role as a focal point for their own mourning for family, friends and others. Millions used her public roles, with all their irrationality and impulsiveness, to represent aspects of their own lives in ways that surprised even them. The current trend in northern European societies seems to be towards minimizing ritual and emphasizing individuals and their own lives (Berger et al., 2009). Even death's power to disturb is often denied, that is, of course, until the persons concerned are themselves bereaved.

Societal dependency

The princess's death also illuminates aspects of societal dependency. The task was clear—to hold a state funeral for the princess. Of those directly involved, the queen and her family were at Balmoral Castle in Scotland on their annual summer holiday; the staff of the royal office was mostly at Buckingham Palace; Diana's family gathered at their home in Northamptonshire; the dean was at the abbey.

Although the royal family, including most importantly Diana's two sons, was in Scotland, it was not long before murmuring began: the nation "needed the queen" in the capital, London. The expression of primitive dependency became considerable: in childlike need bereaved people wanted "their queen" and the reassurance that they felt only she could provide. Leadership here meant testing pressure at the boundary between monarch and nation. The queen might reasonably have returned to London in response to the sense that her people needed her. And who would have gainsaid that? But weighing up the demands her decision appears to have been that she would ride out the waves of immature dependence and for the time being remain in Scotland. The choice was between her specific role as grandmother and a more general role as monarch.

For a few days people genuinely seemed to have a problem about the queen's role and that of the whole royal family. The role of monarch relates directly to the task of leading the nation. But in the days immediately following Diana's death the prevailing and powerful dependency required that someone was needed to give national permission for public grieving. People could not take their own authority to mourn because they could scarcely believe what had happened and the emotional turmoil that it stirred up in themselves. So they cast around dependently for a leader with sufficient authority. Because of the overwhelmingly powerful presence of Diana, it was difficult for such authority to be exposed. For a short while the people's claim on Diana was varied: "The People's Princess" (the phrase was Tony Blair's, the prime minister representing a democratic claim); "The Queen of Hearts" (a popular description endorsed by Diana herself); no longer "Her Royal Highness", yet given a state funeral (a claim perhaps fully to recognize the legitimacy of the succession in the light of her marital disarray). These taken together might have momentarily deprived even the monarch of her own authority to give that permission.

This was a protest against the monarchy, not of revolutionary intensity but sufficiently unfamiliar to feel uncomfortable. A further instance was the sense of protest. Dependency is all-pervading and when it is affronted the group surrenders any effort to work and turns in on itself with introverted anger which constitutes apathy. There was anger at Diana's death but it was not specifically located.

As a result it found its most formal expression in an unexpected happening.

The Earl Spencer, Diana's brother, gave the address, the content of which he had successfully kept secret. One passage was widely regarded, among a number of things, as an attack on the monarchy, specifically the queen. It was followed by applause beginning outside and then rolling up the nave to fill the abbey. Earlier, as I was entering the abbey to receive the coffin at the great doors, a marshal asked me whether I wanted them open or shut during the service. I said to keep them open "so that people outside might know that something live is happening in here". The reverse happened: the millions outside the abbey made their presence felt around and inside the building in which the queen and the whole royal family were worshipping. The incident was not easily dismissed and it became the point at which a number of boundaries coincided—outside/inside, angry/at peace, Spencer family/royal family, private grief/public grief, and so on. The comparatively minor decision on whether or not to leave doors open became a major issue because it represented a key part of any funeral: crossing from this world to the next—the ultimate boundary to transcend, death itself.

The queen had decreed that it would be a royal funeral. Thus she acknowledged Diana as mother of a future king, a role unique to her and indisputable. She further ordered it to be held in Westminster Abbey, the coronation church.

All these decisions met the dependent need of the people that she should do the "right" thing by Diana in her death. But as typical of people in a dependent mode, they wanted more—they wanted the sovereign herself. In these circumstances it would have been easy to discount such dependency. After so many centuries, ample material has been assembled in protocol documents to say what should or should not happen. But these are about precedent and take no account of any emerging or current wishes of the people.

In the week of the funeral there were many calls on the protocol departments and two very small adjustments were made. Each of itself might be considered (rightly in the eyes of many) trivial. But in a prevailingly complex setting such as this death and funeral they carry some significance: one is to do with flags, those banners that disclose identity, whether of an individual or a nation or some sub-sets of it; the other takes us back into the relationship that exists between the people and their sovereign and the relatedness between a citizen and the queen. It concerns the way she addressed the nation.

The flag

It had long been a tradition that only the royal standard was flown over Buckingham Palace and that only when the monarch was in residence. But it could never fly at half mast since, as we have seen, there is no moment when there is no monarch. The crowds, perhaps not aware of this and perhaps encouraged by the media, began to express discontent. London was overwhelmed by flags, as was much of the rest of the nation. The crowds therefore saw flags at half-mast everywhere, except at the palace, the queen's home. The royal household swiftly responded and the Union flag was flown at half-mast. This small but symbolic act signified royal acceptance of a role in the context of national dependence. It was not a major issue, but the speed of decision-making spoke of a body that could grasp the nature of dependence and respond accordingly. As a result, there is now a precedent and the Union flag flies at Buckingham Palace; the articulated voice of the people was heard and responded to at a time of great pressure on all concerned; and thirdly it demonstrates another small indicator of the dependency that the monarch has to absorb.

The queen's address

Before the funeral the queen addressed the nation. The setting of royal broadcasts (which are not frequent) usually shows the queen's desk and the picture is taken from the window looking in. This time, however, she stood with her back to the window and spoke against a live backdrop signifying that life goes on. By invoking the role of grandmother alongside that of queen in her opening, she addressed the complications at a stroke. For undoubtedly the public sympathy was above all with Prince William and Prince Harry. "As a mother" would have sufficed, but "grandmother" gave notice that this was a different sort of address. The symbolism of the pictures coupled with the sense of role in the word "grandmother" constituted a body of interpretative material for those who were considering the forthcoming funeral. Interestingly, there is an unresolved dispute about who proposed this phrase. But there is no doubt that the queen spoke it.

The subsequent funeral by its liturgical form allowed all concerned to examine their own dependence and so moving it from immature to mature dependence. The funeral was designed to create the conditions for people to make this move through an institution (the church), one function of which is to legitimize, even to encourage, the expression of dependence. To facilitate regression to dependence is a major function of religion. It takes us to that deeper level of unconscious activity where we feel existence, well-being and wholeness (Turquet, 1975). We have identified three aspects to this dependency—the "normal" everyday dependency; then basic assumption dependency which is identifiable and interpretable; and thirdly the deep dependency of "oneness", the comfortable, but not common, dependency that calls for interpretation, too. But the interpretation itself in the context of society has to be congruent with that context. It is no use offering individually focused consultation when the experience being used is not addressed to the individual.

The mourning was an international phenomenon, representing dependency on a large scale. It seems likely that without recognition of this the lives of many have remained in some sort of disarray.

The intensity of grief during the days leading up to the funeral was palpable. While I was writing this the death of Michael Jackson, the entertainer, was announced. It drew a world-wide response and the memorial service was held. But there was no obvious structure to it and it will be interesting to see what effect it has on the millions who feel bereaved. For ritual, as we have noted, is both a container and a form of non-verbal interpretation. It functions to facilitate a healing regression to dependence and a return to "normal" everyday life. There is little data on this.

One year on

As the anniversary of Diana's death approached we were uncertain about what, if anything, we needed to be prepared for at the abbey. We thought maybe people would want to visit the church where the funeral had been held. So we trained our staff, opened an area for flowers, set aside a place for quiet, and warned the duty chaplain to be ready to offer counsel. In the event, there was one bunch of flowers and fewer visitors than usual. There may be several explanations, but taking a psychodynamic perspective I find it difficult to find other than that the working at dependency through the funeral had enabled people to move to a more mature state, not forgetting the deceased but not needing to ritualize again.

After ten years the two sons arranged an anniversary event. Success and failure are not categories to be used in relation to that event; we can only say that it may have helped the princes, both of whom by then were far from the two young grandchildren with whom the queen had stayed in Scotland ten years previously. And so not just the remarks of the Bishop of London but also the whole event were about closure: "Let her rest in peace."

Ending

We are today in a no-man's land with regard to Diana, Princess of Wales. I was sitting with a group of young nurses and I asked them what Diana meant to them. They all had to think and the answers related only to some aspect of her life—first, that she died in a motor accident and second, that she had beautiful clothes. Otherwise they could say little about her. Yet at the time of the funeral, apart from the uncertainty surrounding her relationship with Mr Dodi Al-Fayed, she was undoubtedly an iconic figure. She was very much a woman of her time and with an unremarkable range of interests. But she, whether instinctively or not, made connections in a society where connecting becomes seemingly harder by the day. For example, she touched those afflicted with AIDS at a time when this condition was believed to be transmitted by touch and its virulence led to a swift and painful death. Her vulnerability is sometimes commented upon, but I wonder to what extent that is a projective interpretation. Similarly, at the time of her death she was being regarded by some as transcending this world and much of the post-death talk was heavy with religious overtones. At the same time, her youth contrasted with the age range of the royal family. It is difficult at this distance to think why Diana was so important in people's lives, but there is no alternative icon that has taken her place. One hypothesis might therefore be that she found herself made into an example of the sort of person that the crowd hoped would become the norm—she was educated sufficiently, she was attractive, she had an easy manner with people, she was the mother of two boys, one of whom already has his destiny fixed, and she was given to charitable works. She was obviously also able to enjoy life. Any mother might hope for as much for her children. The difference is that Diana was inserted into the royal family, thus putting these attributes at the heart of the symbolic governors of the country. It may be, therefore, that the unconscious behaviour of the crowd was ambiguous: on the one hand they recognized that she was in every sense unique and therefore offered nothing to which to aspire—you could only watch. On the other hand by locating her at the heart of the nation people were offering and being offered an ideal life which the politicians could promise but never deliver. In that sense we may say that she was used unconsciously to express the wishes of the people but not to carry hope. This would to some extent explain why, following the funeral, her influence now seems minimal and she has returned to obscurity. This role has proved unique: there can be no more Dianas. That was grasped by the crowd at the first anniversary of her death when they did nothing and left her in peace.

The "Diana phenomenon" then was exactly that—a phenomenon. Her personal relationships were complicated; and her roles varied. Because of her royal connections she was given a unique voice to articulate what it transpired many felt. She was not confined to any particular topics and she roamed freely through contemporary society—its fashions, styles, politics and its charitable beneficence. Two words that have been widely used of her are "vulnerability" and "transcendent". The former has been for all to see. The latter, however, is more difficult. Maybe it refers to her being used by the people to represent a wish for a society which is secular but not anti-religious, modern but not discarding the past, affirming the individual but not at the expense of the group—and vice versa.

At the wedding of Diana and Prince Charles the Archbishop of Canterbury talked about a fairy tale marriage. The phrase returned to haunt all involved in her death and funeral. "Once upon a time …" was not appropriate in the circumstances. That time now feels very long ago and Diana's influence has waned—except in one respect. The one role that without hesitation we can say was genuinely unique was that of mother of the future king. Barring a cataclysmic change in the governance of the United Kingdom, it seems probable that her voice may not be quite silenced yet.

References

Berger, P., Davie, G. & Fokkas, E. (2008). *Religious America? Secular Europe? A Theme and Variations*. Farnham, England: Ashgate.

Bion, W.R. (1961). *Experiences in Groups and Other Papers*. London: Tavistock.

Carr, A.W. (2001). The exercise of authority in a dependent context. In: L.J. Gould, L.F. Stapley & M. Stein(Eds.), The Systems Dynamics of Organisations (pp. 46–66). New York: Karnak.

Francis, D., Kelleher, L. & Neophutou, G. (2005). *The Secret Cemetery*. London: Berg.

Miller, E.J. & Rice, A.K. (1967). *Systems of Organisation*. London: Tavistock.

Reed, B.D. (1978). *The Dynamics of Religion*. London: DLT.

Shapiro, E.R. & Carr, A.W. (1987). *Lost in Familiar Places*. New Haven, CT: Yale University Press.

Turquet, P.M. (1975). Threats to identity in the large group. In: L. Kreeger (Ed.) (1975). *The Large Group: Dynamics and Therapy* (pp. 349–372). London: Constable.

Barack Obama's postpartisan dream: Leadership and the limits of the depressive position

Laurence J. Gould

> As soon as I started covering Barack Obama,
> I knew he was going to be in Trouble. …
> He was going to be the kind of guy who whipped you up and then,
> when you were all excited left you flat, and then, when you were
> deflated
> and exasperated and time was running out, ensorcelled you again
> with some sparkly fairy dust.
>
> (Maureen Dowd, "Less Spocky, More Rocky",
> *The New York Times*, September 9, 2009)

Introduction

As a sceptical supporter of Barack Obama suggests above, she and many others are troubled by what they increasingly regard as a potentially serious limitation—namely, raising impossible expectations that he either cannot or will not meet. Variations on this sentiment could, by now, be multiplied a thousand fold, and taken together form the core of what has become a consistent popular narrative about Obama's leadership. It is the purpose of this paper to recast this narrative in psychoanalytic terms. In this sense my aim is to contribute to the development of a general, psychoanalytically-informed theory of leadership capacities and personal requisites. As such, it is not about Obama's leadership *per se*, as it is an exemplification, writ large, of the issues I wish to address, refracted through the prism of his struggles. Specifically, I attempt to articulate a conception of how he takes up the role of the presidency internally (*the-role-in-the-mind*), on both the conscious and unconscious level, how it is enacted, and how one may understand this, with particular reference to M. Klein's theory (e.g., 1935, 1940, 1946) of *developmental positions*.

Before proceeding, however, a few caveats are in order. I will then turn to filling out the popular narrative of Obama's leadership, suggested by the opening quote. I will follow by providing a psychoanalytic transliteration, that explores the states of mind that I hypothesize animate this formulation, and conclude with some general considerations about leadership that can be extrapolated from it.

Caveats

- Given the above, what I say should not in any manner be construed as psycho-biographical in the traditional sense. I will have nothing to say regarding a genetic understanding of Obama's character. Rather, the psychoanalytic formulation I put forth is based exclusively on an appraisal of how he has exercised his leadership.

- For expository purposes, the emphasis will be on the problematic, both with regard to the popular narrative, and my psychoanalytic transliteration. I take as a given his extraordinary personal and political gifts.

- When writing about a public figure, judgments inevitably will infuse the discourse. I will try of course to keep these at a minimum, and either make them obvious, or expressly reference them, so that the reader may judge what I have to say. I emphasize this point especially in the context of some inevitable comparisons of Obama's leadership—both direct and implied—with that of his predecessor, George W. Bush. Disclosure: I was and continue to be an ardent admirer of Obama's, notwithstanding some serious disappointments and anxieties about his leadership, thus far.

Obama's leadership: the popular narrative
Synthesizing some of the main narrative lines, the picture that emerges can be organized around a number of interrelated themes. However, for the purposes of this paper, I will only focus on two, which I believe are the major orienting nodes of the narrative compass I elaborate below. I will take each in turn, and supply some relevant sources and commentary. Please note that I am articulating a synthesis of the dominant, left of centre, liberal narrative—the conservative narrative is another story altogether and not, except by implication, within the purview of this paper.

• Rationality and disappointment

This narrative theme is best captured in Dowd's (2009) op-ed piece, referred to above, titled "More Rocky, Less Spocky". The Rocky reference is to the tough, pugnacious, aggressive, single-minded boxer in his quest for the championship, lionized in the series of Rocky films. The Spock reference is to the hyper-rational, unflappable Vulcan first officer (or early on, commanding officer), Mr Spock of the Starship Enterprise, which is the central setting of the Star Trek series in its many television and film incarnations. In fact, after the release of the 2009 Star Trek film, Obama was often and quite directly compared with Spock in the media—examples are plentiful: *"Mr Obama has a bit of Mr Spock in him (and not just the funny ears); he has a Vulcan-like logic and detachment (note here, the now common "no drama Obama" characterization of his leadership style); and that Spock's cool, analytical nature feels more topical than ever now that we've put a sort of Vulcan in the White House"* (see Wikipedia—http://en.wikipedia.org/wiki/Spock).

The opposition of these two popular cultural icons is played out in the unfolding Obama leadership narrative. Initially the more Spocky-like representations dominated the public imagination, likely enhanced even further by comparison with Bush's image as "a shoot from the hip cowboy"; and, the "no drama Obama" reference could easily be extended, not only as a more thoughtful, rational, and measured alternative to Bush, but specifically as an opposition altogether to the previous administration's "dramatic initiatives". Such opposition would, simplistically to be sure, take the form of sound bites such as: no more wars; no more grand American exceptionalism and paeans to freedom, driving nation-building and regime change in the Middle East or the Third World; and, no more inflated rhetoric and belligerent stances against real and exaggerated enemies. However, within a fairly short time, following the election, as Obama began to confront tough political realities, the behaviour of the beloved Spocky Obama starts to raise concerns. Hence, the anxious lament of Dowd's title, reprised in her *crie de couer*: "Sometimes, when you've got the mojo, you have to keep your foot on your opposition's neck. When you're trying to get your Sisyphean agenda passed, it's good if people in the way—including rebellious elements in your own party—fear you." Spock would be befuddled by this suggestion, but Rocky would approve without hesitation!

- Obama's postpartisan dream and the rough edge of politics

Coupled with the above, and making its appearance quite early in the campaign, Obama clearly begins to articulate his postpartisan sensibility. Its major feature can be viewed as a dream in the aspirational sense. As such, it is a dream very much like the transformational creations of King Arthur's Camelot, and Cromwell's Parliament. In its most idealized form—Arthur's Round Table ("equals at a table")—it quite obviously symbolizes the wished for harmony of a world denuded of destructive conflict (Gould, 1999). Once again, it is likely that this wish was even further enhanced—for both Obama himself, the public at large, and the world—by comparison with the previous administration, noted for its extreme partisanship. In this context it is not difficult to understand and sympathize with Obama's postpartisan dream—a Camelot in modern dress—expressed variously, but perhaps in its most succinct form by one of his signature campaign slogans: "There are no red states or blue states—just the United States!" But quite quickly, his vow to bring the opposition along with him, oft repeated during the campaign, began to frustrate his supporters, who increasingly believe that what they perceive as an overzealous commitment to a postpartisan stance impedes the realization of any progressive transformational initiatives. Hence, a liberal editorialist (anonymous, 2009), pithily notes: "We believe that Mr Obama has been far too passive for the sake of unrequited bipartisanship..." and one prominent political wag says simply: "Obama needs to be more Bush!" (John Stewart, *The Daily Show*,

2009). Another telling and contentious example is Obama's insistence that his administration would look to the future and not the past, particularly in relation to holding the previous administration accountable for many putative crimes committed in the name of national security. As Bromwich (ibid.) points out: "The value of conciliation outweighed the imperative of truth. He stood for 'things that unite not divide us'. An unpleasant righting of wrongs could be portrayed as retribution, and Obama would not allow such a misunderstanding to get in the way of his ecumenical goals."

Much like the short tragic lives of Camelot and Parliament—Camelot ending, once and for all, in a bloody battle on Salisbury Plain, and Parliament being disbanded within three years, England eventually returning to a monarchy—sadly and ironically, within ten months of taking office, Obama's postpartisan dream is on the brink of shambles. Partisan politics, both within Obama's own party and between the parties, once again rule the land, perhaps even more so than previously, with the opposition party virtually voting as a block against every major initiative he launches (most notably an economic stimulus package, and a healthcare reform bill). But perhaps even more to the point, especially with regard to the healthcare bill, Obama seemed willing to accept, at least to many of his own party, excessive compromises in order to obtain the veneer of bipartisan support, even if this meant getting only a single supporting vote by a member of the opposition party! Twice Obama went to the bipartisan well, and twice he returned with half a bucket of water, plus at most, an additional drop or two. As Bromwich (ibid.) notes in this connection: "...the conceit of accommodating one's enemies inch by inch to attain bipartisan consensus seems with Obama almost a delusion in the literal sense: a fixed, false belief."

President Obama: The-role-in-the-mind

Taken together, the strands of the popular narrative suggest, either directly or implicitly, the major outlines of Obama's role conception as president—what I referred to as *the-role-in-the-mind*. I suggest that the first and foremost element in this conception is his fundamental relatedness to the *other*. If there were a formal term for this, it would likely be some variant of "counter-paranoid". There are seemingly no enemies in Obama's world, any evidence adduced to the contrary. It is as if he believes that all differences can be negotiated to the satisfaction of everyone concerned, and any doubts overcome by reason, conciliation, and good will. This is *Enlightenment Man in extremis*. As such, he acts on and proceeds in the political arena as if he is convinced, at bottom, that there are no political parties, nor differences within parties which need be taken into account. For Obama, political affiliations, in fact almost all affiliations of any sort, are epiphenomenal—incidental artifacts easily overcome by rational discourse. In his world, then, there are no boundaries that cannot be transcended. This attitude is highlighted by what may seem, at times, to be his grand vision of leadership: not only of a truly bipartisan domestic body politic, but of a postpartisan world—much more like the secretary-general of the United Nations, or more fancifully, the intergalactic head of an enlightened multiverse—than a grounded, practical, and partisan politician, struggling to lead party and country. I believe it fair to say that there is no political precedent for Obama's leadership vision. While, as a matter of course, virtually all US presidents and world leaders of liberal democracies have articulated similar views, none I think believed them in a way that at times makes Obama seem by comparison to minimize a fundamental dedication to country first. I do not mean this concretely, but rather as an unintended consequence of his underlying universalist sensibility, constrained only by the existential realities of time, place, culture, and history.

In light of the above, we can see quite clearly how Obama's postpartisan mind-set is manifested in his role enactments, as well as how problematic and confused this role definition has become. It goes without saying that this articulation of his role is certainly not the whole story, but in the context of what I have simply called the *rough edge of politics*, I suggest it has become increasingly dysfunctional. In Bromwich's (ibid.) elegant phrasing: "...his pattern has been the grand exordium delivered at stage centre, rather than [as] a leader from the point of view of political and empirical prudence." That is, the universalist, postpartisan sensibility, so central to Obama's self-definition as a leader, seems particularly ill-suited in an arena of markedly competing interests. As even his loyal supporters suggest, this stance often results in serious political miscalculation, and an underestimation of any partisan obstruction. And worse yet, in the face of opposition, or even in its anticipation, we find him withdrawing and/or doing *volte-faces*, leaving the "bloody details" for his followers to sort out, or clean up.

A particularly telling, and not atypical example, was a major reversal of policy, early in Obama's presidency, which set the stage for this pattern. It concerned the release of photographs of suspected terrorists being abused in US custody. Immediately following his announced intention to do so, an explosive wave of criticism erupted from the military, the CIA, and the opposition party. In consequence, within the White House itself, a passionate debate developed between those of his national security advisors, who lobbied him to reverse himself, and those who, in effect, used Obama's own earlier stance that releasing the photos was consistent with taking the "high road" (the road, they argued, that was sensitive to American values and traditions, as well as to the rule of law). Obama initially reaffirmed his wish to release the photographs, but if anything, the storm of criticism intensified, leading to several further rounds of debate within his staff (see Calebrisi & Weissskopf, 2009, for a detailed account of this episode). A short while later Obama reversed himself again, and turned to a device he often uses to transcend political divisions: a major speech. This tactic is precisely what Dowd was referring to when she wrote the following: "...then, when you were deflated and exasperated and time was running out, [he] ensorcelled you again with some sparkly fairy dust." In a word, an elegant Obama speech was "fairy dust". One of his other common tactics for avoiding conflict is to place himself above the fray. Perhaps, the most dramatic public example is putting his major domestic policy initiative—healthcare reform—almost entirely in the hands of his congressional followers. The outcome, thus far, appears to be the worst sort of excessively compromised "policy by committee", and even, as such, it has thus far been rejected *en masse* by the opposition party. (As I write this (December 4, 2009) the outcome, both its final form and fate are still unsettled. I should also note, by the time this paper is published, the pattern of Obama's leadership I have described may be entirely dated.

Obama's leadership: A psychoanalytic narrative

Introduction: At the outset, I would like to emphasize once again that I will not be addressing Obama's personality *per se*, but rather attempting a narrower appraisal of the deep psychological capacities that I believe form the basis of his leadership. Much has been written about leadership capacity, but I wish to approach it from a distinctly psychoanalytic perspective—especially, as I have said, with reference to a particular constellation of core emotional competencies and values that I believe can best be understood in connection with M. Klein's theory of *developmental positions*. I begin, however, with the metaphor of *holding the centre* as an orienting, conceptual container for the major elements that comprise my focus.

Holding the centre: The source of this phrase refers to a line in the first stanza of an extraordinary poem by Yeats, *The Second Coming*, which was written in 1919 in the aftermath of the First World War. It is this line which both provides the starting point for my thesis about leadership capacities, and as importantly, their critical emotional and moral context.

> Turning and turning in the widening gyre
> The Falcon cannot hear the Falconer;
> Things fall apart; the centre cannot hold;
> Mere anarchy is loosed upon the world,
> The blood dimmed tide is loosed, and everywhere
> The ceremony of innocence is drowned;
> The best lack all conviction, while the worst are full of
> passionate intensity.

But what is this *centre* that is alluded to and who is responsible for holding it? A provisional answer is contained in what is directly suggested. Namely, that *holding the centre* is the basis of the "moral order". This leads to my first assertion—namely, the responsibility for *holding* it is a core function, if not *the* core function of enlightened and mature leadership. The last line of the stanza leads to my second proposition—specifically, that Klein's *developmental positions*, *P/S* and *D*, best capture those early psychological achievements and vulnerabilities, from which these respective states of mind and their associated constellation of behaviours spring. In their mature forms, they support enlightened and effective leadership, and in their debased forms, as in Yeats' poem, they result in leadership that *lacks all conviction*, or alternatively, is *full of passionate intensity*. In the context of current American politics, you will recognize, I am sure, that the conventional narrative, centring on the former (moral relativism, political correctness, dysfunctional inclusiveness, etc.), refers to the putative excesses of the Democratic Party , and the latter, to those of the Republican Party.

As examples of each, witness on the one hand the case of Joe Lieberman, a Democrat, who despite supporting the Republican candidate for president, has been allowed to retain all the privileges of party membership, including the chairmanship of several major congressional committees. And on the other, such excesses are exemplified by the extreme, inflammatory, debased rhetoric of the Sarah Palins, Rush Limbaughs, and Glen Becks, to name but a few of the more influential. A direct. historically unprecedented example was a Republican congressman shouting "liar" at Obama, during a recent presidential address.

The focus of this section, therefore, is to elaborate this notion and apply it to constructing a picture of Obama's leadership. I hope it goes without saying, that the capacities I discuss, while necessary for appraising the nature and quality of leadership, are by no means sufficient. Leadership also requires, among other characteristics, drive, perseverance, creativity, vision, and technical competence, as well as other important capacities, depending on the context in which it is exercised.

The metaphor of *holding the centre*—and it is of course a metaphor—has wide applicability. Translated somewhat generally and concretely, the meaning of *holding the centre* has a fundamental connection to the capacity of the leader to hold onto the task, to create and manage appropriate boundaries, and to keep in mind that in doing so, the *centre must* manifest the qualities of a moral order, and not merely a functional requisite for performance. In this sense, I am not simply talking about the challenges of *holding the centre* in the political or organizational realm of managing the pulls of competing groups or stakeholders, but rather the psychic and emotional challenges of holding *the-centre-in-the-mind*, conceived as integrity, on which the moral order and performance rests.

In trying to provide a shape for what I have suggested above, I apply the metaphor of *holding-the-centre* specifically to how Obama's *postpartisan dream* represents his vision of the *centre*, and the dilemmas he struggles with to hold it. I begin by suggesting, in part at least, that the *centre* for Obama is, in fact, a *meta-centre*, rather than a *centre* displaying some of the attributes described above. In other words, it is more an abstraction than a location in the political and social landscape. As such, it is a *centre* above the *centre*, and this internal conception, I argue, is a major source of Obama's leadership difficulties. From this vantage point, one may view Obama's postpartisan dream as an idealized, static state of mind, coming up against the realities of shifting political tides (the state of *realpolitik* at any given moment), the result of which is the sort of political miscalculation, and awkward turnabouts, noted above.

• Depressive position(D) variations:
sophisticated (sD) and dysfunctional (dD)
It is at this juncture that I specifically begin to consider Obama's leadership viewed through the lens of Klein's theory of *developmental positions*. For those not conversant with Klein's theory of *developmental positions*, a brief overview may be useful: she postulates that development during the very earliest months and years provides the basis of character development, which will endure throughout life. Specifically, she views early development as being comprised of two distinct but overlapping developmental *positions*, called respectively the *paranoid-schizoid* (1946) and the *depressive positions* (1935, 1940). These positions may be thought of as phases of early development. In essence, Klein conceptualizes them as configurations of psychological attributes, each organized around a distinct constellation of anxieties, object relations, and defences. Further, depending on the level of integration, one can observe, at all times, elements of oscillation between the two *positions*.

First, I begin with the suggestion that the ability to *hold the centre* can quite readily be viewed as a *depressive position* achievement. In Klein's elaboration, successfully negotiating the challenges of the *depressive position* result in a robust, cohesive configuration of values, dispositions, and attitudes, including the capacities for: *integration vs. splitting; reconciliation and making reparation; openhandedness and general amnesty for those who have done harm; tolerating ambivalence and uncertainty; realistic gratitude to those who have helped along the way; and, a desire to contribute to social and institutional development and reproduction.*

Let us pause for a moment over *tolerating ambivalence and uncertainty.* This is an especially critical capacity, most often understood in

Bion's (1970) conception of *negative capability*—namely, the capacity to function in states of uncertainty, through the creation and maintenance of a "reflective space". The concept is attributed to the poet John Keats who, in a letter to his brother, loosely paraphrased, wrote: "Negative Capability means a man is capable of being in uncertainties, mysteries, and doubts, without any irritable reaching after fact and reason." Bion notes that an incapacity to maintain this state of mind often leads to premature action as a defence against the anxiety that uncertainty engenders. It should be noted, however, that Bion developed this concept in connection with the psychoanalytic situation where the temporal demands are minimal. By comparison, there are enormous pressures—particularly on leaders—to act, and to act as if they are certain.

It is in light of this psychological picture, that we may ask: how does Obama's leadership measure up?

In framing an answer, two points are worth making:

1. It is commonplace wisdom that all virtues, practised *in extremis*, become vices.
2. It is both insufficient and unnecessarily abstract to discuss any form of psychological organization non-contextually. Therefore, when opining about a presumptive form of psychological organization with regard to leadership, on the most fundamental level the question is whether or not it is manifested behaviourally in a manner that facilitates or impedes task performance.

With regard to these points, I suggest that Obama's leadership can be characterized schematically as an oscillation between what I notate as a *sophisticated* form of the *depressive position* (*sD*), and a *dysfunctional* form (*dD*). That is to say, as the popular narrative suggests, it alternates between a morally aware, sophisticated deployment of the values, dispositions, attitudes, and capacities outlined above (*sD*), and an extreme version of these that are counter to his goals and leadership aspirations (*dD*). And it is quite clear, as the previously cited quotes suggest, how the contours of the *dD* pole of Obama'a leadership can be described:

• excessive values integration for its own sake, over partisan accomplishment

- in the face of crisis, crippled by excessive caution
- too deliberative and dispassionate
- too cool and detached
- insufficiently aggressive
- insufficiently sensitive to danger and the role of destructive opposition
- far too passive for the sake of unrequited bipartisanship
- believes that accommodating one's enemies will ultimately result in a bipartisan consensus.

In describing the *depressive position (sD)* I am borrowing the qualifier *sophisticated* from Bion (1961), in connection with his *basic* assumptions *(bas)*, and applying it analogously to *D* and *P/S* states of mind, mobilized in the service of work *(W)*. As I have suggested elsewhere (Gould, 1997), there are direct correspondences between Klein's *developmental positions* and Bion's *basic assumptions*, which refer respectively to individual and group level processes. I also note, in this context, that *sophisticated* corresponds to functional, and in clinical terms, dysfunctional would be the equivalent of regressed.

I emphasize that the core of the emergent popular narrative is consensually defined by these descriptors. As such, the dominant view is what Obama is not!, and underscores the disappointment of even his most ardent supporters. I also would note that the clearly implied focus here is not simply that he is experienced as a general disappointment in light of the above complaints, but more specifically, that he has refused to pursue and prosecute the "enemy" (i.e., the opposition party, both currently and with regard to its legacy). In this sense, he has deprived his followers of the emotional satisfaction of seeking retribution for suffering through the past eight years of destructive policies. I put "enemy" in inverted commas advisedly, since another way of articulating an increasing tension between Obama and his political followers, is that emotionally and functionally, he seems not to recognize in a visceral sense, as I have suggested above, the opposition party, especially its right wing, as the enemy. I emphasize again that potentially this is a quite serious issue with regard to what it augers for his leadership: does he avoid confrontation for tactical or strategic reasons, or alternatively, is he incapable of mobilizing sufficient aggression, even when it is necessary to do so, no matter how unpalatable? This chapter is yet to be written, but will depend on an answer to this question.

For now, as a general matter and as a link to the next section, as I have suggested, the dominant states of mind that inform Obama's leadership, from a Kleinian perspective, can be hypothesized as oscillating between the *dysfunctional* aspects of the *depressive position (dD)*, and the positive virtues and dispositions of its *sophisticated* mode *(sD)*, with the consequences of excessive *dD* best captured by Yeats' chilling phrase: *The best lack all conviction... .*

• Paranoid/schizoid(P/S) variations:
sophisticated (sP/S) and dysfunctional (dP/S)
Everything I said in the preceding section about the spectrum of *depressive position* variations, applies equally to *paranoid/schizoid* variations. That is to say, these variations range from the sophisticated *(sP/S)*, to the dysfunction *(dP/S)* with regard to task performance. Before proceeding though, I cannot emphasize too strongly, that in the context of task performance, *P/S* values and dispositions are no less important than their *D position* counterparts. I stress this point for two reasons:

1. It is far easier to notice the manifest sins of commission, than those of omission, so that all evidence to the contrary, Yeats' dire prophecy, *[that] the best lack all conviction*, seems less "evil" than *the worst being full of passionate intensity.*
2. The above point is also reprised conceptually as well, and forms the basis of some disagreement I have with a central point made in much of the published organizational case material that utilizes a *developmental positions* framework. Namely, a majority of these cases reflect a bias—implicitly and explicitly—that views the movement from the *paranoid/schizoid* to the *depressive position* as the major goal of consultation efforts (see, for example, Obholzer & Roberts, 1994). While I believe this to be true as far as it goes, I do not believe it goes far enough as an adequate account of change. What it both leaves out and underestimates is any view of *paranoid/schizoid* behaviours and states of mind as developing, becoming more sophisticated, and being in their mature form, a requisite for task performance, in contrast to viewing them, *de facto*, as

destructive. This perspective is directly implied in the popular narrative regarding Obama's leadership as being idealized and incomplete, and/or somewhat simplistic and potentially problematic—that is, when his post- or bipartisan sensibility is felt to be applied wholesale and indiscriminately (*dD*). Recall, in this connection, Bromwich's (ibid.) comment—"The conceit of accommodating one's enemies inch by inch to attain bipartisan consensus seems with Obama almost a delusion in the literal sense: a fixed, false belief." Dowd (2009b) clearly concurs, and raises the question of Obama's loyalties—"Obama can often (seem) to be more interested in wooing opponents than tending to those who put themselves on the line for him."

The general point is this: the critical role of the *paranoid/schizoid (P/S) position*, in its *sophisticated* form of values and dispositions (*sP/S*), is one of the two interdependent vertices of effective leadership. Its core elements are:

• The capacity to mobilize and deploy passion and conviction
• The capacity to mobilize and deploy anger and aggression
• The capacity for healthy suspicion (functional paranoia)
• The ability to act realistically (as distinct from idealistically)
• To have an action orientation, along with a reflective one, when required
• To actively display a loyal commitment to one's followers in the face of criticism and opposition
• And perhaps most important of all, to have a considerable capacity for holding powerful points of view and convictions in the face of resistance and rejection, and/or in the absence of sufficient data—that is, the capacity to act in the face of uncertainty.

In light of these, I suggest that Obama's leadership can be further elaborated schematically, not simply as an oscillation between $sD \Leftrightarrow dD \Leftrightarrow \Leftrightarrow \Leftrightarrow ///// \Leftrightarrow \Leftrightarrow \Leftrightarrow sP/S \Leftrightarrow dP/S$, notated to indicate that almost no oscillation occurs between the *D* and *P/S positions*, neither in their *sophisticated*, nor *dysfunctional* (regressed) forms!

From this perspective, I note with emphasis, that while the core capacity of the *depressive position* is *integration*, the core locus of psychic action in the *paranoid/schizoid position* is *splitting*. And as the popular narrative suggests in this connection, Obama appears to have little to no ability to mobilize and deploy the values, dispositions, attitudes, and capacities associated with the *sophisticated P/S position (sP/S)*. That is, he appears to have, at the very best, a quite limited capacity for *splitting and aggression*, which can be viewed as the reverse of his powerful *depressive position* predilections, with their locus of action on *integration and reparation*. To make this point in an obvious way, if Obama is the apotheosis of *depressive position man*, Bush is the apotheosis of *paranoid/schizoid man*. The parallels between the complaints and disappointments expressed in popular narrative, and the psychoanalytic transliteration of how Obama leads, are now plain to see. To wit, the desire, increasingly voiced among his followers, to have Obama be *"More Rocky"* and *"Less Spocky"*, or *more like Bush*, or, as Joe Klein (December, 2009) comments with open concern in relation to Obama's carefully reasoned decision to send 30,000 more troops to Afghanistan— "There's no such thing as a no-drama war!"

Conclusions

To conclude, it should be emphasized that my interest in an appraisal of Obama's leadership provides a starting point for developing a more general consideration of leadership capacities. My central working hypothesis is that the ability to mobilize and integrate *paranoid/schizoid* capacities in a *sophisticated* way, along with those of the *depressive position*, are an essential requisite for mature, enlightened, and effective leadership, and perhaps, even especially so, in the political arena. In a similar vein, A.K. Rice commented (in a personal conversation, circa 1969) that he believed effective leaders were those who had the capacity to mobilize a range of *valencies* and states of mind when the task required them. What he was alluding to, in the language of Bion's (1961) conceptualization, is that everyone has a *basic assumption* hierarchy of *valencies*, which include, among others, one's preferred or habitual defensive orientations in the face of stress and danger (e.g., *fight/flight, dependency*, and *pairing*). In this connection, the emotional challenge for leaders is the capacity to mobilize appropriate "countervalent" behaviours, and oscillate between them when required by the task, rather than regressing to familiar, defensive, anti-task modes of coping.

I note, with regard to this critical leadership capacity and its development over time, a brilliant paper by Britton (1998, ch. 6) in which he posits an elaborated conception of how oscillations between the *developmental positions* may be viewed. Liberally quoted, the central features are:

- a movement from the depressive to paranoid-schizoid position, as well as the other way around, is seen as a part of a normal process of development.
- ...the movement through each position in turn is part of a continuous, lifelong cyclical development and limits the word "regression" to descriptions of a retreat to pathological organization in either position
- ...in the post depressive position, Ps(n+1) (the equivalent of my *sophisticated P/S position (sP/F)*), which means the further maturing and development of the paranoid/schizoid position, the crisis is the relinquishment of cognitive and moral confidence for that of action in the face of incoherence and uncertainty
- The only alternative to continuous development is regression; in a world of flux an attempt to stand still produces a retreat. Yesterday's depressive position becomes tomorrow's defensive organization
- And finally ... if these ideas are put into mythic terms the mature paranoid/schizoid position—Ps(n+1)—is the wilderness and the mature depressive position—D(n+1) (the equivalent of my *sophisticated D position (sD)*)—is the promised land; but given the stresses, anxiety danger and lack of security in crossing the desert, regression inevitably occurs to the familiar, or as yet undeveloped depressive position: the promised land has become the reality of Israel and another struggle has begun.

To make Britton's abstractions somewhat more concrete, and translate them into organizational leadership, let me provide a few brief examples of what they would look like in their mature forms. The ability:

- to move from indiscriminate splitting, to functional, task oriented differentiation

- to move from the impulse to draw and maintain boundaries that exclude, to those that further the aims of the enterprise
- to move away from operating on the basis of paranoid delusions, to more nuanced healthy suspicion, and realistic sensitivity to danger and threat.
- to move from vacillation and obsessional second-guessing, to acting decisively in the face of ambivalence and uncertainty.
- to move from adhering to rigid strategies, to forming provisional ones that require constant testing against reality.

To pull the above threads together, I hypothesize an ideal state of mind which links task requirements and the moral order, and which requires the respective *developmental positions* to continually enrich and inform each other. In its ideal, but never fully attained form, this capacity, from the perspective of (*sD*), translates psychically into an ability to contain the experiences of incoherence and uncertainty, rather than retreat into pathological *paranoid/schizoid* organizations, dominated by splitting, moral certainty, ideological rigidity, acting out, and retaliation. But to one of my major points, the converse proposition is equally valid. Namely, that operating from *depressive position* states of mind and their corresponding values, without the robust integration of those associated with the *sophisticated paranoid/schizoid position*, often leads to its own forms of serious, individual, organizational, and social pathologies. On the individual level, these are manifested clinically in excessive guilt; depression; gratuitous reparation; a terror of destructive aggression; an exaggerated need for inclusion; and the need to be loved. On the institutional or social level, they are often displayed in leadership that is indiscriminately inclusive of both people and ideas; an inability to draw and manage boundaries; and altogether, an inability to lead change and create better adaptations, if doing so requires managing aggression, conflict, and hatred; and, a mode of operating that all too often, inappropriately depends on consensus.

Probably the major contemporary political example of the latter portrait is our former president, William Jefferson Clinton, who despite many quite positive qualities was accused—and I believe rightly so—of all of these characteristics. Similarly, the enactment of extreme *dysfunctional paranoid/schizoid* processes can also be broadly described. The all too common, familiar forms of overt malignant leadership, are exemplified by obvious candidates, such as the Stalins, Hitlers, Husseins, and Milosevics of the world, with policies like the "final solution" and "ethnic cleansing" being the extreme of violent, sadistic, and destructive splitting. In such cases it is easy, on the face it, to literally see what it means to destroy the moral order because the *centre* is a centre in name only. That is, it is a centre that *controls*—not *holds*. As such, it perpetuates and stimulates anxiety and hatred, rather than containing it, resulting in violence, dehumanization, and destructiveness that others enact on its behalf. But I cannot emphasize too strongly, that psychically corrupted *depressive position (dD)* leadership is married to sadistic, psychopathic *paranoid/schizoid (dP/S)* leadership. This malignant state of affairs is, in essence, a collusively constructed, mutual creation, which results in an inevitable and destructive outcome. As Yeats' would have it, with the emphasis slightly shifted, *when the best lack all conviction, the intensity of the worst remains unchecked*!

Summary

Rather than summarizing in the conventional sense, I would like to emphasize one major point, and to raise two questions. The major point is this. Despite Klein's unfortunate use of pathological language to describe her developmental positions, she and her followers have always stressed that they are a normal aspect of individual development. The essential human dilemma though, as I have come to understand it, is that the paranoid/schizoid and depressive positions are psychically in continuous tension, and represent two poles of the human condition. The paranoid/schizoid position provides the deep developmental basis of passion and action, and the depressive position the basis of reflection and moral concerns. The tension arc between these is the ever-present preoccupations of leadership, which give rise to common, ubiquitous dilemmas, and irreconcilable conflicts and contradictions; between reflection and action; between the right and the expedient; and ultimately between both an individual's ego ideals and integrity on the one hand, and the institutional requirement for responsible task-oriented action on the other. Put a bit differently, even the most rational, task-oriented actions may challenge or corrode a leader's ego ideals and a sense of decency; and alternatively, a leader's ego ideals may undermine the institutional will to take necessary, and often painful action in the service of the task. Very much like Krantz's (2006) notion of a leader's "betrayal" of one's followers in the service of adaptation, there is an internal parallel—namely, the "betrayal" of oneself (i.e., one's ego ideals) in the service of the task. It is in this sense, that the aphorism, the "loneliness of leadership,", is primarily an existential loneliness, and a chronic source of pain and anguish, experienced by enlightened and mature leaders.

The theme of an enlightened leader having to act "against his grain" and betray his ideals and cherished beliefs, is almost ubiquitous in narratives of heroic leadership. We see, for example, Cincinnatus reluctantly leaving his farm and being named dictator in 458 BC in order to defend Rome against the Aequi and the Volscians; or as above, the tribulations of King Arthur, having to pick up the sword he vowed to bury forever, in a (failed) attempt to restore the lost idyll of Camelot; or, Cromwell disbanding the Parliament he fought to create at a terrible price, in order to save England from ruin!

I end with two obvious questions, and the hope that what I have presented provides one set of lenses for their consideration:

1. Does the picture I have drawn add anything of value to an understanding of leadership in general, or specifically to an understanding and appraisal of Obama's leadership?
2. In light of the issues and implied concerns I have raised, and considering the challenges—personal and political—that I concluded with, a question that may be asked is this:

What does the Obama's leadership, thus far, augur for the future?

References

Anonymous (2009). *New York Times* [op-ed]. September 14.

Bion, W.R. (1961). *Experiences in Groups*. New York: Basic.

Bion, W.R. (1970). *Attention and Interpretation*. London: Tavistock.

Britton, R. (1998). *Belief and Imagination* (ch. 6). London: New Library of Psychoanalysis.

Bromwich, D. (2009). Obama's delusion. *London Review of Books*, October 22.

Calebrisi, M. & Weissskopf, M. (2009). The fall of Greg Craig, *Time Magazine*, November: 35–38.

Dowd, M. (2009a). More Rocky, Less Spocky, *New York Times*, September 9.

Dowd, M. (2009b). Thanks for the Memories, *New York Times*, November 25.

Freud, S. (1914). On Narcissism, *S.E., 14*: 67–103. London: Hogarth.

Gould, L.J. (1999). A political visionary in mid-life: notes on leadership and the life cycle. In: R. French & R. Vince (Eds.), *Group Relations, Management and Organization*. Oxford: Oxford University Press.

Gould, L.J. (1997). Correspondences between Bion's basic assumption theory and Klein's developmental positions: an outline. *Free Associations, 7*(1), No. 41: 15–30.

Klein, J. (2009). Afghanistan: Can Obama sell America on this war? *Time Magazine*, December 14.

Klein, M. (1935). A contribution to the psychogenesis of manic depressive states. *International Journal of Psychoanalysis, 16*: 145–174.

Klein, M. (1940). Mourning and its relation to manic depressive states. *International Journal of Psychoanalysis, 21*: 125–153.

Klein, M. (1946). Notes on some schizoid mechanisms. *International Journal of Psychoanalysis*, Vol. 27(3).

Krantz, J. (2006). Leadership, betrayal and adaptation. *Human Relations, 59*(2): 221–240.

Wikipedia: http://en.wikipedia.org/wiki/Spock.

Yeats, W.B. (1919). *The Second Coming*. In: W. Harmon (Ed.), *The Classic Hundred Poems*. New York: Columbia University Press, 1998.

Images of leadership

Susan Long

Introduction

Leadership is one of the most widely explored roles in social science. The role holds a certain fascination, perhaps because it is often sought but not always achieved; but most likely because leadership and authority draw on both aggressive and sexual phantasy; on power and passion. The idea of a leader evokes a mixture of emotions and attitudes. On the one hand is the presence of authority, power, heroism, and celebrity: the image of a commanding, attractive, perhaps even fierce god-like figure. On the other hand are ideas of service, loyalty to a task or cause, and care of followers: the image of the dependable, good shepherd or loving parent. Further, there is the image of the lonely philosopher leader who has a vision for the future not yet fully comprehended by others.

This is not the place for a review of leadership theories taken from social science. Theoretical reviews abound as do reviews of the often made arguments about whether leaders are born or made; or whether leadership is the result of personality traits or the environmental context; or whether indeed leadership is situational, dependent on the right mix of person, time, and task. In this vein, it seems that the most sophisticated current theorizing sees leadership distributed throughout a community or organization: leadership exercised at all levels and in many different ways in many organizational systems, including task, socio-emotional, political, economic, management, technical, and socio-technical. This line of thinking about leadership is primarily in terms of leadership as a function, whether or not one is constitutionally predisposed or whether one learns to lead on the job or in a management education programme. It is one of many roles in a group, taken up by many people. I would add that leadership occurs between roles; between leaders and followers and exists in the relation and the associated relationship between the role holders.

I suggest, however, that as well as the above, the notion of leadership is imbued with a symbolic history that reaches back through all of human history. The images of leadership that emerge in our consciousness reflect that history and are linked to deeply unconscious processes stemming from our human biology, our nature as social animals and our psychological strivings. So I will argue for a multiple basis of leadership. It is:

- a group task function that holds power if not always legal authority
- a role relation between leader and follower in relation to their tasks
- an associated relationship between leader and follower—in the mind, and
- a symbolic expression of timeless human strivings and desires.

Sometimes a designated leader may fulfil the task function but not the symbolic expression. Sometimes they may embody and enact the symbolism but are not an authorized leader in the sense of being chosen consciously by the establishment. On occasion, they may be the designated leader, the functional leader and the symbolic leader all at once: a popular charismatic leader who gives hope, Obama or Mandela, for instance.

Being a leader is experienced in many ways, both by the role holder and those who interact with him or her. Here it will be argued that the images of the role reflect the surface of the symbolic, often unconscious heritage of our deeply social being. There are powerful images that become part of the role idea about a leader and are formed in relation to the institution-in-the-mind or the institution-in-experience (and its history) of which the leadership is a part. This chapter will outline some images of leadership discussed by psycho-analytic writers and then link these to a discussion of leadership as a role within social systems from a socio-analytic perspective.

Images of leadership

Psychoanalytic writers have described leadership in many ways. I can only refer to a few. However, I will choose from the many images, those that represent the central theme of identification of the leader with the purpose of the group and of the group members with the leader. I will spend some time on Freud's views because not only within them are the seeds of later psychoanalytic ideas (and he did stress the idea of identification), but the myths and images that he uses are still relevant to the way people take up and work with leadership today. I base my discussion on the psychoanalytic assumption that beneath the surface of the rational arguments put forward about why one leads in this or that way, or why one leads or follows at all, lays a more primitive heritage—both personal and social.

Leadership, narcissism and aggression

Freud's myth of the primal horde with its tyrannical, despotic father/leader who monopolized sexual relations with the females and cast out any male competitors provides a powerful image of leadership. He says:

> In 1912 I took up a conjecture of Darwin's to the effect that the primitive form of human society was that of a horde ruled over despotically by a powerful male. I attempted to show that the fortunes of this horde have left indestructible traces upon the history of human descent (1921, p. 154).

Freud recognizes the myth as a hypothesis: "a 'just so story' as it was amusingly called by a not so unkind English critic" he says, "but I think it is creditable to such a hypothesis if it proves able to bring coherence and understanding into more and more new regions" (Freud, 1921, p. 154). In this way it serves as a metaphor.

The primal horde myth is based on ideas proposed by anthropologists of Freud's time. Its accuracy as to human history is not as important as its fidelity to a kind of primitive mentality found in regressed groups, described by Freud following studies of Le Bon, McDougall and Trotter on irrational crowd behaviour. In such groups, individual discretion is absent and a thought-full pause between intent and behaviour is lost. I am reminded here of the frenzied buying or selling that occurs sometimes in stock markets following the initiatory actions of some of the larger players. It is as if the market—a mindless collection—has no real leader, only endless followers that act this way or that way according to a mass system dynamic. Similarly, the mass adoption of technologies like mobile phones and "texting" cannot be fully understood by marketing methods that promote leaders who use them; it is more like a Mexican wave whose momentum is triggered rather than led. The regression involved is a re-enactment of the primitive horde members. In the myth, there is a leader who remains the only true individual who thinks, decides, acts and holds sway over the emotions of the crowd. But he is less what we might think of as a leader, and more a tyrannous controller of the emotions that spontaneously erupt in the mass.

Such leadership, argues Freud, is achieved through the leader's holding himself apart from libidinal ties.

> Consistency leads us to assume that his ego had few libidinal ties; he loved no-one but himself, or other people only insofar as they served his needs ... even today the members of a group stand in need of the illusion that they are equally and justly loved by their leader; but the leader himself need love no one else, he may be of a masterful nature, absolutely narcissistic, self-confident and independent. (Freud, 1921, p. 156)

The picture is bleak. But is it so different from the image portrayed of the independent corporate CEO of the 21st century? Take the following for example. In his investigation of the crash of HIH the huge Australian insurer, Justice Owens describes the HIH organizational culture as one of poor management and governance. Central to the picture was the attitude and behaviour of the leadership which was alleged as being arrogant, patriarchal and which gathered together a band of unthinking "yes men". Owens says that there was:

> a blind faith in a leadership that was ill-equipped for the task. There was insufficient ability and independence of mind in and associated with the organization to see what had to be done, had to be stopped, or had to be avoided. Risks were not properly identified and managed, unpleasant information was hidden, filtered, or sanitised, and there was a lack of sceptical questioning or analysis when and where it mattered. (Owens, 2003, p. 3)

Several similar stories can be drawn from the corporate world (see for example, Barry, 2003). It seems the image of the narcissistic, self-confident, and independent leader that Freud saw as a throw-back to the primal horde father is still alive and well and drawing support from big players in the financial sector not simply from small investors. Too often corporate leadership is regarded as a symbol of unrestrained greed (Czander, 2009) (see Scene 6 in this volume).

The primal horde is archetypal, to use Jung's phrase, rather than a singular truly historical event although it plays itself out time and again through history. It can be enacted easily in modern organizational life. Short-lived in any one organization, the primal leader moves through the jungles of multi-national corporations, picking up fruits as s/he goes, sometimes being driven out by a pack of "sons", sometimes roaming himself to better pickings. I write s/he but it is still mostly he. This is not to deny those corporate leaders who are thoughtful, empathic, and generous in their role. They have to work against the dynamics of the horde in the establishment of an ethical and civilized organization.

An important aspect of the primal horde myth or metaphor is the murder of the leader by the frustrated and angry brothers. Freud draws clearly the picture of how such an imagined event led to an inner psychology for the brothers through the process of anger, ambivalence, murderousness, grief, remorse, and identification. Interestingly, the brothers work through their remorse by their identification, each with a different part of the leader, so that his original leadership becomes shared, dare I say distributed, through their now truly social organization. As mentioned earlier, members of the primal horde have no real individual psychology, only a mass psychology reminiscent of a stampede of cattle. This means they do not have a truly social group of linked individuals. They form a mass or crowd. They murder in a frenzied thoughtless way, out of frustration and anger, caught up in the madness of the moment. Only following the murder and their remorse do the mythical "brothers" have a true group with a distribution of the leader's powers among the group members. In the myth, the original leader is narcissistic, greedy, proud, and vengeful, although also loved. The brothers, through their aggression, steal the leadership but rather than continuing the pure narcissism of the prior chief, they develop a social organization with differentiated roles.

The myth is enacted and re-enacted sometimes with a dominant leader—who can be supportive and more than benign to those who obey—sometimes with a democratic group of brothers. So what is so new? We still have autocracies and oligarchies and we still have democracies and socialists. We still debate whether or not hierarchy or small autonomous yet broadly democratic groups are best in management (see, for example, the debate between Jaques and Amado in *Human Relations*). In terms of the task, the answer might well be ... "it depends"—on the context, the particular decision, the particular task, the timing, and so on.

Later psychoanalytic writers and commentators follow Freud in examining the formation of democracy through the overthrow of tyranny (Brown, 1959; Slater, 1966), emphasizing the nature of brotherhood (and perhaps sisterhood) as a social form quite different to the hierarchy of chief and subordinate roles. The image of leadership in this democratic form is different, whatever the reality in any actual democracy. It is an image of the leader bound to others through a common destiny, a common task, a common action or common love and devotion. This brings forward the idea of identification as a primary group tie with the leader as first among equals.

Leadership, love and sexuality

How do we love our leaders? There is certainly deep emotion felt for symbolic, popular leaders, hence the displays of grief in the UK when Princess Diana died and Michael Jackson more recently (see also Scene 7 in this volume). Freud believed that love is the basic tie that holds group members together. But it is not always directly expressed as love. In psychoanalysis, love is transformed and has many expressions. Fundamentally, love is rooted in polymorphous sexuality and however transformed or disguised, it will show itself as such, even if in small ways. Freud said that love and work were both important with the most important word being "and".

What are these transformations of sexuality and how do they relate to leadership? Freud (1921) distinguishes the restricted or inhibited libidinal nature of organized group life as opposed to the uninhibited nature of the unorganized crowd or mob. (I use the word mob here in its Anglo-Saxon meaning of rowdy collective. In doing so, I note that the indigenous people of Australia use the term in another way, indicating a friendly community, i.e. "our mob"). Inhibited libidinal ties may be expressed as non-sexualized, tender love or as identification, depending on the dynamics involved.

Whereas libidinal love says "I want you", identificatory love says "I want to be like you". This distinction allows the resolution of the Oedipal conflict as the boy chooses to be like father, strengthening his earliest identifications with him and allowing him to repress his wishes to "have mother". Lacan draws heavily on this distinction in his theories about the developing alienation of the ego through multiple identifications. He regards identification almost as absolutely distinct from libidinal love. In this chapter, however, I argue for their links and regard identification as another form of libido, distinct from tender love and uninhibited sexuality.

Freud argues that group members are tied to each other primarily through a form of identification where each holds and internalizes the leading group value or idea in common with other members. The leader represents this leading value. Thus we can say, as Freud suggests, that members incorporate the leader as their ideal and identify with one another in light of this. Additionally tender love or friendship may also be a factor in group cohesion, often growing as a result of the identifications. Group members, then, are held together first and foremost through their common identifications and second through their friendship and loyalty ties: both transformed forms of basic polymorphous sexual desire. Or using another frame, they are transformations of the need for closeness with others.

The glue of group life is a common task or destiny and common basic assumptions are at the basis of group emotional ties (Bion, 1961). Each of these basic assumptions is linked to a different image of the leader. For example, the basic assumption dependency leader is dependable, does the thinking, has the vision, does the problem solving, and takes care of the members if they remain compliant and dependent. The basic assumption fight/flight leader is strong, decisive, and determined, fights for the group cause, and defends the members or leads the flight. He or she requires unquestioning loyalty and obedience to orders. The basic assumption pairing leader provides the promise of hope for the future through a close pairing with a member or the group as a whole. The work group leader stays with the task, but has a predisposition or valency for one or other of the basic assumptions.

Here, my interest is with the emotional ties between group members and their leaders and their basis in inhibited sexuality. It should be clear that this is not the same as repressed or denied sexuality, but a transformation of libidinal ties. Although identification and tender love are distinct from uninhibited sexual impulses in their nature and consequences, the implicit sexuality is evident in such behaviours as:

- adoration, or its opposite, vilification of leaders
- members' jealous vying for the attention and favour of the leader and, most importantly
- the sexual attraction inherent in the leader's authority.

In the state-of-mind of the primal horde, a mindless basic assumption type of group psychology exists where the brothers are forced into inhibited sexuality and tender feelings towards one another because the chief monopolizes the women. This analysis ignores an uninhibited homosexuality among the brothers, but the idea of homosexuality in the crowd is not antithetical to the main argument. The brothers want both power and sex.

Freud's analysis of groups sees members as basically linked in an erotic tie to a leader who unconsciously represents the primal father who persecutes them and is feared, but is later transformed (by an illusory reaction formation, or after his death and deification) into a father who loves and cares for them. In psychoanalysis the family myth holds a privileged position. Although the mother holds a central role for the pre-Oedipal infant, the father's role is present in the family structure even if only as an internal object for the mother. But is there a pre-family form of organization?

In his description of the primal horde myth, Freud often refers to the leader or chief as much as the father. This suggests that the primal horde is pre-family or at a more primitive level than the family myth where Oedipus plays a role. I wonder about market dynamics in this regard; if they follow the horde mentality rather than the family myth mentality? Listed company managers are influenced significantly by the stock market and if this does operate according to horde dynamics then the influence is occurring psychically outside the Oedipal context with its recognition of the incest taboo. Without the incest taboo all generational boundaries dissolve and with this, the recognition of inheritance becomes problematic. Market crashes might represent an analogue of such a situation. What is the taboo here that is being broken? The sub-prime mortgage crisis in the USA, for example, dissolved a boundary between real and imagined assets. Investors inherited a wraith.

The primal horde myth is, however, aligned with Freud's thinking on the rivalry between fathers and sons exemplified in the Oedipal story that formed the major analogy for his theory of psycho-sexual development. But the Oedipal myth is within a special form of group—the family, not the horde.

The central aspect of Sophocles' story that was seized on by Freud was that of desire for the mother and murderous aggression towards the father. The sexual drive must indeed be strong to cause such anxieties and warrant such risks as taken by Oedipus in his journey toward kingship.

The Oedipus story is, of course, far more extensive than that part drawn on by Freud. But, the aspect of the myth he uses, i.e. the image of Oedipus' parricidal triumph and subsequent leadership is not the same as that of the several raging, unthinking brothers as those described in the primal horde, but an image of the clever, resourceful leader. True, he is driven by his fate which he both attempts to avoid and then denies—as with any true perverse character; and through this fate kills his father and marries his mother. Also it is true he killed the king on the road in arrogant anger. He does have something in him of the psychology of the brothers. But distinctively he is able to solve the riddle of the Sphinx and save Thebes from its terrible plagues and it is this deed that wins him Jocasta and importantly his leadership of the great city. In this myth, Freud has found a personalized individual form of the primal horde myth. Oedipus, driven as an individual by the same emotions displayed by the crowd, is nonetheless not unthinking. Clever, resourceful, but mostly in denial, quick to anger, even quick to turn on himself as when, no longer able to deny his deeds, he blinds himself. Perhaps, like other tragic figures such as Shakespeare's Othello, Lear, and even Hamlet, Oedipus is primarily gripped by pride.

The symbolism of the myth told in Sophocles' plays tells us that despite the painful and difficult achievement beyond the "Oedipal" situation, the riddle of leadership is still unsolved. It continues within the rule of Creon and the fate of Antigone. Christopher Bollas (2008) interprets the myth in terms of the human search for meaning. He draws attention to the unending questions posed— infinite questions about the nature of human emotions and destiny. The answer to the riddle of the Sphinx is just the beginning of other questions about meaning and the nature of things. Pride comes with achievement—some small part of the riddle is solved. But pride without humility is dangerous in leadership.

The image of the proud leader

Pride is at the basis of another image of leadership. It is clear that collective pride acts as social glue. Many group and organizational leaders attempt to heighten collective pride in their work, their people, and in their accomplishments. Advertisements often stress the pride that company members have in their products and services. This enhances a belief in the quality of the product, but also through identification, the consumer can feel pride in the new acquisition.

Beneath this pride lurks the possibility of its opposite—shame. Excessive pride is often a defence against the experience of shame. And shame is a very public emotion. To feel shame is to see the self through the eyes of a disapproving other. Pride, to the point of arrogance, then, is a cover up. (The work of Adler is important here. He developed the notion of the superiority complex as a defence against feelings of inferiority.) Good to feel proud of a job well done, but as they say, pride comes before a fall and the fall may occur because pride led to arrogant blindness. (See the case of LTCM in *The Perverse Organization and its Deadly Sins* (Long, 2008).

Also, shame is a real possibility in a cohesive group where each member's vulnerabilities become evident. Pride with and in the leader can help defend against the feared shame. But if group cohesion is based on defensive pride, then the fear of shame may become debilitating and curtail creativity.

The proud leader image has several variations. He or she may be proud in the sense of recognizing the accomplishments of the organization. This shows the leader as reflecting glory for the group. Images of sportsmen and women claiming their medals at the Olympics or business leaders winning awards for their companies come to mind. When this captures patriotism in political leadership or its equivalent in organizations—the culture of IBM for many years for instance—the leader may become quite idealized, just as Oedipus was idealized. However, should the leader become overly proud about his or her own accomplishments with less recognition of the group, then the image is one of arrogance. Ken Lay and the leadership of Enron are a case in point (see also Scene 4 in this volume). Another image is one of pride in a more heroic sense. That is, the proud leader who has lost the battle but still holds his head high for the group, perhaps even dies for the group and its values. Oedipus, Othello, and Lear each have elements of these variations. It is their recognition of the group and its values that is the basis of their idealization and their arrogant, blind pride that is their tragedy.

Sometimes the image of the proud leader is highly sexualized in overtly phallic ways. While power in itself is often regarded as sexually attractive, the image of the proud, clever yet sometimes quick to anger leader (this shows masculinity; his macho style; his testosterone) provides a strongly phallic image. Similarly, the image of the proud and narcissistic femme fatale provides a female equivalent. Like the Sirens, she leads men to their destruction.

The idea of a proud leader, or an aggressive, or envious or greedy leader, or, indeed a leader with strong emotional characteristics of any kind takes us now to an exploration of what the leader expresses for the group. An image is, in any case, a representation of something and in psychoanalysis the image stands for some, often unconscious, inner individual or group process.

Leadership and group defences

Leaders are regarded as the people who "show the way". In simple terms they take up the front position, which may mean taking a lead in thinking about the future for the group. But in taking a psycho-analytic perspective, we have seen that identification and love play a strong part in the dynamics between leaders and followers.

In 1942, a German psychiatrist, Fritz Redl published an excellent paper on different types of leaders and how they interact with the libidinal and aggressive urges of their group members. His examples are about teachers and adolescent male students. Perhaps that is why his paper is rarely alluded to in the systems psychodynamic literature working with organizations. Nonetheless, I have been recommending it to management students for many years because of its relevance to their work.

Redl uses the term "central person" rather than leader and this designates the role as operating at the centre of identificatory dynamics:

> the person around whom group formative processes take place: the "crystalisation point" of the whole affair ... the one through emotional relationship to whom the group formative processes are evoked in potential group members. (Redl, 1942, p. 576)

Sometimes the central person is the designated leader, such as Redl's images of "the patriarchical sovereign", "the leader" and the "tyrant". These are central persons who have some of the qualities alluded to previously, who through authority and sometimes personal power hold control, whether by force or love. But often the central person is a member of the potential group, not yet actualized but ready to come into being, such as—"the seducer", "the hero", "the good influence" or "the bad example". These kinds of central roles speak for themselves. They act as attractors for, or symbolize, those latent group processes that represent collective urges and desires. The central person is a stimulus or conduit for their expression: the ring leaders.

Redl offers ten images of central persons. Identification of members with the central person is described (i) as being on the basis of love or fear (for example, love of a benign father figure or fear of a despotic one), (ii) as the object of libidinal desires or aggressive drives, or (iii) as a support to the ego in the service of ego defences (the good influence), or as an initiatory act in by-passing defences to allow drive satisfaction (the seducer).

Here Redl pre-dates the more developed work of Jaques (1955) and Menzies Lyth (1971). (The work of Jaques and Menzies-Lyth is so frequently described in the literature that it would be redundant to repeat it here. Their work has stimulated a whole genre of theorizing—social defence theory—that I discuss elsewhere (Long, 2006).) In the theories of social defences against anxiety that follow their contributions, the institution and its leaders are seen to provide unconscious support for individual defences against the anxieties arising in the course of undertaking tasks in a workplace. Redl also pre-dates the work of Bennis and Shepard (1956) in relation to the way an "unconflicted member" may act as the stimulus for new phases of group formation. Bennis and Shepard suggest that groups move from initially dealing with the dynamics of authority towards the dynamics of intimacy. In this journey, members pass through several phases, including a kind of short more "civilized" or symbolic version of the primal horde myth as they move from dependency on the leader to an overthrow of the leader, at least the leader-in-the-mind.

The "central person" way of thinking about leaders brings with it the idea of leadership being a role not so much in charge of the group as a role that plays out something for the group. The scapegoat figure is akin to this. In Girard's (1977, 1986) views of the scapegoat phenomenon, the underlying group dynamic is one of revenge and counter revenge in a seemingly endless procession that is only stopped by the formation of an (unconsciously) selected scapegoat. The scapegoat is vilified and punished in order for the feuding or warring parties to cease their mutual hostilities. A kind of justice is seen to be done: a righting of wrongs, through a commonly agreed victim who carries the blame. Although this is a primitive way of settling disputes—a dynamic employed prior to modern societies who use the institution of the law with its many agreements and regulations—it is present in many groups at an informal level: rough justice, if you like, used to prevent the escalation of aggression and anger spilling into chaos. The newer recruit in the armed services or the new child in school, in fact many of the victims of bullying, are often scapegoats in this sense. Rather than simply individual victims, they are unconsciously selected by the system to serve the purpose of maintaining the current order. (See Long (2008, ch. 7) where the case of a bullied army recruit is discussed in light of the military training culture.)

Why then might a scapegoat be considered a leader? In some primitive societies, leaders were sacrificed. Even if their lives were not taken, they were held in a captive state; "protected". The image of the leader as a scapegoat is present where the leader is able to take on the sins or trials or difficulties of the group and in a sense "right the wrongs" through his or her self-sacrifice. The sacrifice of Christ is one such powerful image: the ultimate scapegoat who turned this role on its head, transcending in imagery from victim to triumphant leader, thus helping the group to "escape" the overwhelming feuding (see Rene Girard, *The Scapegoat*, 1986).

Nowadays the sacrifice of the leader who works constantly for the group, its values, and mission such that he or she sacrifices family, health, and other self-interest in the name of the company or perhaps an organizational cause, provides a similar image. Financial and status rewards may provide some impetus for this behaviour, or perhaps a compensation for such sacrifice. But often identification with the company task is explanation in itself, especially in not-for-profit welfare type organizations. Hospitals are also examples where medical leaders may work ceaselessly for extended periods of time in the name of the task; or research institutes, or churches and missions.

The image of the martyr is scattered throughout religious history and is echoed in the leadership of organizations with a "cause", even though at times the martyr may be less a victim than an embodiment of vengeance. For example, I have found in my research and consultancy to hospitals that leading medical and other staff members will sometimes work extensive hours to the detriment of their family life and other interests in the name of a cause—say fighting cancer or saving the lives of children. At times they may act like martyrs as victims of the "system" that relentlessly demands they fill a limitless need with limited resources. In this role they are often resigned and resentful. Yet, at the same time they represent fight leaders in the cause—a "war" on illness that includes a "war" on authorities and politicians who refuse to see the problems in health care provision.

In this role they become angry, sometimes politically active and represent the underdog in a fight with "uncaring" authority. This can be constructive while the extreme case of a vengeful martyr that is most often destructive may be found at the basis of terrorism.

Perverse leadership

Perverse dynamics occur in groups and organizations when a pervasive denial of important aspects of reality occurs alongside a narcissistic group culture with an instrumental attitude towards interpersonal and role relations (Long, 2008). Such denial may be evidenced in the group or organizational leadership turning a blind eye to corrupt processes or the stubborn denial of risk despite what from an outside perspective can be seen as strong indications of risk. In talking of perverse leadership, I am not saying that the leaders are perverse people in the clinical individual sense. I indicate that they are instrumental in helping to produce a perverse culture. In such a culture, tasks and roles become corrupted (Chapman & Long, 2008) and digress from their originally intended purposes. The process of gradual corruption in the perverse culture may not be consciously apprehended but may increasingly pervade the culture, bringing with it more denial.

Examples of perverse leadership can be found in many corporate stories where dominating leaders, through pride, greed, arrogance, lack of due diligence, and/or a failure to listen to others fail to stay in touch with the realities surrounding their decisions—sometimes to the extent of following a failing strategic or economic course in the mistaken belief that they can pull out of the problems they have led the organization into. It is often at the point of no return, when reality can no longer be denied, that the corporate cover-up stories begin. Too often such leadership has corrupted the use of authority.

Leadership and authority

What is the nature of authority? Authority has the quality of holding and commanding. It makes you stop in your tracks. It makes you listen and heed. When you hesitate, it seems sure. When you don't know, it does. Sometimes it is desirable to be in the presence of authority, its certainty, and its favour. Within the establishment it can protect you. At other times it is best to be removed from its omnipotence and its omniscience. It has the right to question, interrogate, even detain and incarcerate you. You might disagree, you might feel angered by its surety, its dismissal of your contrary thoughts and it might stir rebellion within you. But when you stand in its presence, you feel its requirement that you submit—whether out of love or fear. It inspires awe: a kind of mystical power, derived from the gods.

There is good and bad authority. Good authority works on your behalf as a member of society and enables you to develop creatively. Bad authority is really the abuse of authority. Its power is taken over and used for personal gain at the expense of others. This is perverse. There is authority delegated downwards from higher up the hierarchy and authority endorsed from the masses, upwards. There is hierarchical or vertical authority, and horizontal authority, between peers. There is the authority of the parents, of the group, of the organization, as well as the authority of the state. Authority belongs to the role or office. And yet, there is personal authority.

Sometimes we refer to personal authority as that characteristic held "naturally": a quality popularly known as "presence" or charisma. This betrays the nature of authority as an internal quality that may be gained through long experience, such as the gaining of authority through knowledge and expertise, but may also be inherent in some people. Such inherent authority felt to be in "natural" leaders, when officially sanctioned brings together the strands of personal and group based authority. It is not surprising that such leaders draw strong identifications.

Personal authority seems a contradiction. In general authorization means that the person, in their authorized role, acts on behalf of the group, not simply on behalf of themselves. Such a role can make decisions—within agreed limits—for the group. But personal authority may come as the result of gaining reputation within one's profession or trade or any walk of life. Here authority is conferred by the group but then taken up personally and is not simply the result of the role or office held. Past presidents, retired professors or former athletes most often retain their personal authority gained while in office well beyond the active role-holding period.

So, it seems that leadership authority, although conferred and sanctioned by the group and therefore presumably legally able to be taken back, is experienced as an internalized power that often "sticks" to the previously authorized leader. Although leaders may be dismissed, come to the end of their terms, or are deposed, this "stickiness" may account for difficulties in ensuring continuing authority often found in organizational succession planning. Psycho-analysis tends to talk about this "stickiness" in terms of transference. Authorized leaders are loved or hated because they unconsciously draw the love and hatred felt for many if not all previous authority figures in their followers' lives. Such burdens are not easily shifted.

Leadership and authority go together like the proverbial love and marriage or hand in glove. Authority is sanctioned power and a for-mal leader is sanctioned to use the power that comes with the office. Good leadership knows the strengths and limits of that power and is able to use it in the service of the group's work. The question of who or what does the "sanctioning" is interesting here. Historically, within a religious tradition, all authority originally derived from God or from the highest being: a sanctified authority. For the Tudor and Stuart kings of England, it was divine right, that is, authority from God that informed their leadership. The image of the leader in this instance is that of a sanctified leader who can do no wrong. The pope seems to lead with such an authority within the Catholic Church, despite more recent questioning.

Within the Tavistock tradition of group relations (Fraher, 2004; Gould, Stapley & Stein, 2004; Aram et al., 2008) the answer to the question of "what confers the sanctioning" sees that authority comes from the task which has its own structures, dynamics, and demands. This is a sort of socio-technically derived authority: a power sanctioned by the nature of the task and supposedly given to those best able to undertake the task: the authorized experts. How-ever, the tasks to be undertaken in a group, organization, or society are derived from agreements within the groups themselves, within the broader social system, or from powerful players. The general understanding of authority derived here is as a legitimate political force. These two different forms of authority clash when, for exam-ple, a whistle-blowing employee questions the authority of a socially sanctioned leader.

Sometimes leadership emerges in the moment, and the sanction-ing process occurs unconsciously or instantaneously as the group responds to the moment. Perhaps this is a moment of crisis or when facing a difficult problem, or in flight or anxiety. Examples abound in situations such as natural disasters—during the recent bush fires in Australia, or during the Asian tsunami. Someone might gather others together to respond. Another example is during escalating violence in a psychiatric ward. One nurse may quickly move in to handle the situation through using physical restraint. The other nurses quickly take up followership in the situation, aiding in the restraint and de-escalating a dangerous situation. The first nurse leads the way and others follow his or her cues, knowing that a disorganized response will increase the potential dangers. The authority here comes from persuasive and pervasive unconscious group forces and assumptions. Such informal leadership might be transitory—while the danger is high—or may last for a long time, growing into a more formal leadership during disaster recovery times, for instance.

The symbolic leader

The leader who somehow captures the desires of the group, or ameliorates members' anxieties, or brings them hope, is likely to satisfy a deeply symbolic function. This leader fulfils the requirements for Redl's central person. But more! The symbolic leader is also able to signify the task of the group. As Freud described, she or he stands for the task and its underlying purpose and values. Most importantly, the symbolic leader brings meaning *to* the group and holds meaning *for* the group.

Examples of the symbolic leader range from state leaders, to popular figures in the media, to local leaders in groups and teams. The symbolic leader symbolizes the reasons members come together—sometimes symbolizing unconscious as well as conscious reasons.

The creation or discovery of meaning in life is a central human quest (Frankl, 1946, 1984; Bollas, 2009). But it is a difficult and sometimes dispirited quest because much of life appears meaningless. Greed, anger, and cruelty alongside generosity, empathy, and kindness appear as deeply human traits. The rise and fall of fortunes often seems as much accidental as planned. Social and economic forces appear chaotic despite our theories of their determination. Indeed chaos theory seems one of the most plausible for large-scale systems. However, psychoanalysis argues that we create our own meanings unconsciously and personal analysis works hard to discover these.

Socio-analysis looks to the unconscious infinite (Bion, in Lopez-Corvo, 2003; Lawrence, 1998) to discover social meaning in the web of unconscious connections that link us. In comparison with the world wide web (www) of cyberspace, we can call this the unconscious web (ucsw) that links us in social connection. It is evidenced in communities where the same idea springs up from sources that have not previously been in conscious connection: for instance, new scientific ideas, or in dreams. If we consider that associative thinking is at the basis of this web, then we can understand that social meaning may be discovered through considering the chains of associations that develop in groups, organizations, and communities. These chains of meaning, or chains of signifiers (Lacan, 1977) may be found in social history, discourse, and actions. Sometimes the meaning is only discovered at the end of the chain, as at the end of a series of events when we look back and finally understand the meaning of something that happened long ago. Sometimes it is discovered in the midst of a chain of thoughts, so that further implications can be unfolded, such as when a scientific hypothesis predicts an event. Or while, having seen the start of a fall, we watch frozen, knowing, as time slows down and the inevitable occurs.

Symbolic leaders each form an important signifier in the chain of meaning that is created and discovered socially. They hold the chain of meaning together. I wrote earlier about the images of the leader emergent from the Oedipal myth. In Sophocles' story, there is the image of Laius the father who, in fear of his own destiny, sacrificed his son. But destiny (his meaning) was not to be denied and he was murdered by Oedipus, his son returned. The old leader, who had to be sacrificed in order for the new leader to emerge, was sacrificed in an unconscious, unthinking, and seemingly unsanctioned manner. (Bollas (2009)argues that the murder was unconsciously sanctioned or why would the city of Thebes offer the hand of Jocaster to the solver of the riddle? The murder was implied in the offer.) Next in line appeared the image of Oedipus, the clever, yet "blind" leader: the son who was to become father himself to Antigone, the daughter who defied authority in her attempts to honour and forgive her brother. Each image is an imaginary leader derived from "the-name-of-the-father" (the name of authority itself), which is a signifier or meaning that holds the family myth or family chain of meaning together (Lacan, 1977). Such authority, essentially religious, can be upheld—even to the extent of dictatorship, or mediated and softened or transgressed (Reiff, in Manning, 2003). The various images of power and leadership and the struggles of the characters in the Oedipal myth can all be seen as attempting to find meaning in the face of the power of the gods and fate (the unconscious).

A group or organization can be seen as a system of inter-linked roles and tasks tied to a purpose. The purpose gives the tasks and associated roles their meaning. The roles and tasks are an unfolding of the implicit/ implicative meaning in the purpose (Bohm, 1980). They are an enactment of its meaning. Of course, they can be corrupted or perverse, in which case they betray the purpose in a double sense in that they betray the spoken conscious purpose but also betray (portray) the real purpose behind the corruption or unconscious perversion. Such has been the case in many of the corporate disasters that have been seen in recent years (Long, 2008). Nonetheless, if the tasks and roles are an unfolding of purpose and meaning, they can be regarded as a chain of meaning for the purpose of the group or organization. The symbolic leader is an important link in that chain. S/he represents the very purpose in a nutshell.

The current purpose of an organization comes from a combination of its history and its current context. If we see that leaders are unconsciously selected to represent the organizational purpose—the leaders that we deserve (Mant, 1985)—whether that be the avowed or hidden purpose, then those leaders have in their own role biographies (Long, 2006) the traces of this purpose, as does the history of how the role has been enacted in the past (Chapman & Long, 2008). The current leader will take up his or her role at the point where biography meets organizational history. But beyond the particular purpose of the group, its more general social purpose in (i) holding members together, (ii) defending them against anxieties and depression, (iii) providing a vehicle for the expression of sexuality, love, envy, and hostility and (iv) providing meaning, is represented through the image of the leader and the leadership relation between leaders and followers.

Conclusion

This chapter could not hope to examine all the multitude of images that have arisen from socio-analytic and psychoanalytic theories.

I have focused on the images put forward by Freud, Bion, Redl, and Girard and linked these to ideas from Lacan, Bollas, Lawrence, and the group relations tradition. These and other powerful images, I suggest, unconsciously infiltrate the way that leadership is experienced in the psychological space among and between leaders and followers. If the images arise from the deeply symbolic meaning that leadership has in representing the group purpose and enables members to find concrete ways to identify with that representation for good or evil, then we may expect current images of leadership to represent our attempts to work with the turbulence experienced in our times. Although this turbulence includes facing such challenges as global climate change, global economic instability, and further rapid technological innovation, in its midst we yearn for a sense of meaning and stability. The rise of fundamentalist leaders may be one dangerous outcome of such collective yearning (see James Krantz "The Evolution of Basic Assumptions in Twenty-First Century Organizations", 2009). We need leaders able to face the hard tasks required of them in both facing turbulence and representing our hopes for a better, more sustainable future.

References

Aram, E., Baxter, B. & Nutkevitch, A. (Eds.) (2008). *Adaptation and Innovation: Theory, Design and Role Taking in Group Relations Conferences and their Applications, Volume 11*. London: Karnac.

Barry, P. (2003). *Rich Kids*. North Sydney, Australia: Bantam.

Bion, W.R. (1961). *Experiences in Groups*. London: Tavistock.

Bohm, D. (1980). *Wholeness and the Implicate Order*. London: Routledge.

Bollas, C. (2009). *The Infinite Question*. Hove, England: Routledge.

Brown, N.O. (1959). *Life Against Death: The Psychoanalytic Meaning of History*. Middletown, CT: Wesleyan University Press.

Chapman, J. & Long, S. (2008). Role contamination: toxic leadership. *Organisations and People*, 15(3): 40–48.

Czander, W. (2009). Personal communication.

Fraher, A. (2004). *A History of Group Study and Psychodynamic Organisations*. London: Free Association.

Frankyl, V.E. (1984). *Man's Search for Meaning*. New York: Washington Square Press.

Freud, S. (1921). *Group Psychology and the Analysis of the Ego. S.E., 19*. London: Hogarth, 1949.

Girard, R. (1977). *Violence and the Sacred*. Baltimore, MD: John Hopkins University Press.

Girard, R. (1986). *The Scapegoat*. Baltimore, MD: John Hopkins University Press.

Gould, L., Stapley, L. & Stein, M. (Eds.) (2004). Experiential learning in organizations: Applications of the Tavistock group relations approach. London: Karnac.

Krantz, J. (2009). The evolution of basic assumptions in twenty-first century organizations. *Socio-Analysis*, 11.

Lacan, J. (1977). *Ecrits*. London: Tavistock.

Lawrence, W.G. (Ed.) (1998). *Social Dreaming @ Work*. London: Karnac.

Long, S. (2008). *The Perverse Organisation and its Deadly Sins*. London: Karnac.

Long, S. (2006). Organisational defences against anxiety: What has happened since the 1955 Jaques paper? *International Journal of Applied Psychoanalytic Studies*, 3(4): 279–295.

Long, S. (2009). Sad, mad or bad: what new approaches should we take to the study of organisational states-of-mind? In: B. Sievers (Ed.), *Psychoanalytic Studies of Organizations: Contributions from the International Society for the Psychoanalytic Study of Organizations (ISPSO) 1983–2008*. London: Karnac.

Lopez-Corvo, R.E. (2003). *The Dictionary of the Work of W.R. Bion*. London: Karnac.

Manning, P. (2003). Phillip Reiff's moral vision of sociology. *Journal of Classical Sociology*, 3(3): 235–246.

Mant, A. (1985). *Leaders We Deserve*. London: Blackwell.

Owens, N. (2003). *The Failure of HIH Insurance*. Report of the HIH Royal Commission. Canberra: Commonwealth of Australia.

Redl, F. (1942). Group emotion and leadership. *Psychiatry*, 5: 573–596.

Slater, P. (1966). *Microcosm: Structural, Psychological and Religious Evolution in Groups*. New York: John Wiley and Sons.

The Epilogue

Lionel Stapley

The players have left the stage but the drama continues, not least, in the minds of the readers. What sense will they make of the various contributions as a whole and where does it take us in terms of understanding the future? In this final chapter I am going to view the occurrences from a global societal perspective which will, it is hoped, add a new dimension to the chapters already included. At the end of his chapter, Wesley Carr introduces us to the societal perspective when he says "the individual is a creature of a group, the group of the individual" (Miller & Rice, 1967, p. 17). This sentence by two doyens of the understanding of groups, Eric Miller and Ken Rice, is almost now a gnomic mantra. But the group is a group so long as it remains firm in a context. When we enlarge that context, e.g., from "group" to "society", the dynamics obviously change. But they do not become any the less explorable or instructive.

In 1985 Olya Khaleelee and Eric Miller published a paper "Society as an Intelligible Field of Study". In brief, this paper sought to show that society was but a (very) large group and that the same theoretical understanding used in group relations learning—where both small and large group dynamics were the subject of study in temporary institutions—could also be applied to the study of society. Working from this theoretical base, our primary focus in groups (including society) needs to be "the group-as-a-whole" and this also includes what individuals or sub-groups may do. Roles that are taken up by group members could be seen as a function of "the group-as-a-whole" and the behaviour of a person in a group might have more to do with the group than with the person's individuality.

As members of a society we are still part of a group, and the same theoretical and practical findings associated with group relations learning can be applied to society. There is much evidence to suggest that as in smaller groups so also in societal groups, various individuals and groups are motivated to act on behalf of their society. Thus we may see trades unions mobilized to lead the fight against perceived social injustice at work. A group of entertainers may be mobilized to lead the fight against perceived injustice and starvation in a foreign country. A group of anti-war protesters may be mobilized to fight against the perceived wrongness of war and aggression. In order to understand the dynamics occurring around these events we need to take our analysis further. In all these and similar situations we need to ask what the societal sub-group is doing *on behalf of society as a whole*. We need to ask what is the underlying anxiety experienced by members of society that they are reacting to.

Studying societies from a *group-as-a-whole perspective* leads us to add to Khaleelee's and Miller's thinking to include the notion of societal culture. We can say that culture develops out of the interrelatedness of the members of a society and the societal holding environment. The external and internal worlds of members of societies are in continual interaction: what goes on in the minds of members of societies is partly reactive to what happens around them, but is also very much proactive. The ideas and ways of thinking of members of societies influence the way they act upon their surroundings to bring about change in them. In this way we can develop the understanding that culture is *in the individual* and that *the individual is in the culture*. The constant interaction between the individual and culture is fundamental to any study of culture, or for that matter, personality, as they are indivisibly linked (see Stapley, 2006a).

Societal culture, as well as organizational culture can be seen as something that a society "*is*", as opposed to a notion that culture is something that exists as a separate entity: something that an organization *"has"*. This is an important point because viewing culture as something that a society "is" leads us to the notion that culture is within all of us who are members of a particular society. *We* ultimately comprise society and societal culture and, in effect, *we* are societal culture. The link between the individual and culture leads us to the notion that the purpose of culture (as was the link between mother and child), is to provide for consistency, continuity, and confirmation of the individual members of a society. Thus culture, like mother with the child, is an important aspect of our lives.

In recent years there has been so much unprecedented and imperceptible change that most existing methodologies have proven inadequate in providing us with explanations and understanding of current dynamics in society. Indeed, as was referred to in some of the National Reports from other countries in 2006 "the intellectuals" have disappeared from the public scene, they are not contributing their social commentary, and perhaps they appear as helpless as the rest of us. However, a unique practical application based on the theory and practice of group relations learning, as described above, has been developed by OPUS over the past 30 years. It is this methodology and other experiential learning groups that OPUS brings to this important area of research which makes possible the exploration of societal dynamics as an identifiable field of study.

The methodology, referred to as OPUS Listening Posts enables us to explore societies as societies and to expose and explore beneath the surface experiences in societies so that we can analyse and develop hypotheses that may account for what we do not understand. The aim of Listening Posts is to enable participants as individual citizens to reflect on their own relatedness to society and to try to develop an understanding of what is happening in society at any given moment. Listening Posts provide an opportunity for participants to share their preoccupations in relation to the various societal roles they may have. The participants are also collectively invited to try to identify the underlying dynamics, both conscious and unconscious, that may be predominant at the time.

Since 2004, OPUS has organized an Annual International Listening Post Project that involves up to 36 countries in all continents across the world. The project results in all National Reports being forwarded to OPUS in a similar format, where they are researched and analysed by OPUS staff, in order to produce a Global Report. It is these Global Reports that will largely be used to provide the following global societal perspective.

Before this is done, a brief historical perspective may provide a helpful context for what follows. The Industrial Revolution (1789–1848) was a period in history that is regarded as the great divide between the past and the present. As is currently happening, it transformed the whole world and took the form of European expansion and domination of the world. It is said to have been the true beginning of modern times. A measure of the powerful impact of the Industrial Revolution was that communism was created largely as a reaction against it. This was the "new way of life" that continued until the effects of globalization were experienced across the world. A measure of the powerful effects of globalization and a major result of its impact has been the way it has brought about the end of communism: this to be seen as part of the end of the way of life as we knew it. A considerable result of the end of the Cold War was to remove the established and well-known scenario that we were able to use for the splitting between good and evil and the projections upon the "other" of the stranger/enemy inside ourselves. So, from the outset of globalization, we had to face the discomfort of taking back our projections and owning them.

The overwhelming, dominating influence on the world we live in over the past 25 or more years has been, and continues to be, globalization. It will therefore be helpful to reflect on globalization as a background to understanding societal dynamics. We can say with some degree of confidence that starting in about 1985 a dramatic and growing change started to roll out across the globe and that this was largely, though perhaps not exclusively, driven by the implementation and availability of the world wide web (www). However it was not just the change in technology, but the fact that the new technology has brought into being a new way of living. Globalization was originally driven by economic need but has developed way beyond that to begin the process of creating in societies throughout the world a new way of life. Currently we cannot predict what that new way of life is likely to be; at the same time we are experiencing the "death of a known way of life". We are living through a period of our history which can be viewed as *a great divide between past and present.*

Although frequently referred to, the true extent of globalization is seldom fully appreciated. A summary of the characteristics of globalization by various authors provides the following view:

- Globalization looks at the whole world as being nationless and borderless
- Goods, capital, and people have to be moving freely
- The global enterprise is less place-bound and less tied to the traditions of a single nation
- The break with national traditions is a result of geographic separation that occurs when a firm operates largely outside national borders
- Boundary is permeable or transcendent
- There is a high rate of change, a growing number and diversity of participants and rising complexity and uncertainty.

These are the principal features of globalization with the stated aims that goods, capital, and people are to move freely in a nation-less and borderless world. Behind the notion of globalization was the belief that trade would lead to growth, to international relations, to democracy, to almost *anything*. It was as if trade had become the engine of the world, a panacea for all problems. It was an attempt to simultaneously reshape economic, political and social landscapes (see Stapley, 2006b).

However, those principles of globalization were also steamrolling and trampling the needs of members of societies across the world and destroying the continuity, consistency and confirmation of their world provided, in large part, by their societal cultures. If the roles and possessions by which we gain our continuity, consistency, and confirmation are experienced as being chaotic, then it is likely that we will also lose our ability to predict and to act appropriately. If our perception of our world begins to crumble, our view of ourselves inextricably linked to our view of the world will begin to crumble too.

The main finding of the 2004 International Project was that members of societies were experiencing *"death of a way of life"*. This was not so much in the nature of a sudden death such as a heart attack but a sort of creeping death like a cancer spreading through a body. Save, of course, that this has been a psychological death of "a way of life". Since then, there has been a progressive spreading and deepening of this death through various facets of our societies. These include the considerable technological changes, but also through much more important changes that include religious and moral, social—which includes immigration and the movement of peoples across national boundaries, political, and philosophical, and more recently, through the financial crisis, an economic death which should also be considered as part of the continuing process (Stapley & Rickman, 2009).

On war and conflict

The first International Listening Post Project in 2004, organized in mainly Western countries, began to open our eyes to the nature of changes occurring throughout the world as a result of the effects of globalization. Analysis showed that "the reported experience regarding the nature of social change is such that one can only conclude that it is in the nature of a 'revolution'. The depth and quality of change that causes members of society to refer to feelings of de-Christianization, dehumanization, and a loss of known values, 'an unravelling of the social threads that have held us together', can only be regarded as 'the death of a way of life'" (Stapley & Collie, 2004). Subsequent analyses have left us in little doubt that the experience was, and is, much the same in other societies, including Muslim societies.

The background to war and conflict in recent years has essentially been the conflict between Western societies and Muslim societies: two societies with very different cultures. It is vital, therefore, that we understand that we should see the conflict from the binocular position of the two societies. As a starting point it may be important to view this conflict as an inter-group experience. From a group relations perspective we can see the way that competition can be highly toxic as, for example, each society competes to be the dominant world religion. Both parties can also be seen to use the "other" to establish and strengthen their own identities. For example, when Muslims regard actions such as the war in Iraq as an act of "the great Satan"; or when the West sees Iraq as part of "an evil empire", each party uses the "other" to deny their own unbearable thoughts and feelings so as to be able to say "we are not like that".

However, it is when we begin to analyse the situation from the perspective of a society as a whole that we begin to gain a different understanding of Islamic terrorists. Set against a background of an invasion by the West of Iraq and subsequent attempts to impose a democracy on that society, it is not difficult to envisage that Muslim societies experience this as a serious threat to their own way of life, particularly bearing in mind that this was occurring at a time when the impact of globalization was being experienced around the world as "death of a way of life". Seen in this light, it may be taken as near inevitable that the same degree of threat was also felt through-out Muslim society and that various groups are mobilized to be the "fight leaders" on behalf of that society. Thus we could see al-Qaeda as being mobilized by Muslim society to act on its behalf. As those who work in group relations events will appreciate these are very powerful dynamics which act over and above individual dynamics.

It may also shift our focus from viewing the conflict as one regard-ing a group of evil terrorists to an understanding that the heart of the conflict lies in a cultural clash between Western and Muslim soci-eties. Doubtless it suits the purpose of politicians to say they are dealing with an identified group such as al-Qaeda but there is con-siderable evidence to show that those concerned feel they are doing something on behalf of Muslim societies. When the conflict is seen in this light it opens the opportunity to adopt a somewhat different approach to bringing about a resolution to this conflict and the kind of leadership that is now required.

On the financial crisis and the disappearing containers

Seen in the context of the stated aims of globalization, i.e., "that goods, capital, and people should be moving freely in a nation-less and bor-derless world" it becomes clear that the so-called "credit crunch" was simply a continuation of the effects of globalization. "The free movement of people" for economic purposes had resulted in massive immigration across Western national boundaries without any real attempt to control them at a national level. While actively encourag-ing such economic migration, politicians first sought to portray them as asylum seekers. It was only when it became clear that they were indeed economic migrants that politicians sought to assure members of their societies that immigration was good for their national econo-mies. In the meanwhile, societies struggled to come to terms with the changing nature of their national culture. In a similar manner, "the free movement of capital" for economic benefits resulted in the transfer of toxic debts across national boundaries, seemingly ignoring any national controls or safeguards that existed. At the same time, politicians sought to assure us that this was a wonderful era when the past evils of "boom and bust" had finally been conquered and that this blissful state would continue without end.

It would appear that governments across the globe had bought into the theoretical notion that by enabling the "free flow of goods, people, and finance in a nation-less and borderless world", we in the West would be entering a golden age. This approach would enable the West, without any form of hindrance, to take advantage of benefits available to them throughout the world, in the form of massive cheap commodities, even more so, the ready supply of cheap labour, and by ensuring that capital might be used in an unrestricted manner. By doing so the West would be able to control much of the world resources to the benefit of Western societies. Sadly, no one seemed to consider that adopting such a theory would provide a golden opportunity for crooks, thieves, and incompetent and greedy business leaders. Politicians seem to have been dazzled by the same gold that attracted the crooks and the incompetents.

Meanwhile, it would seem that no one noticed that the impact of globalization on societal culture, first reported in 2004, had now reached breaking point. Now (in 2009), the experience of the external world of members of societies throughout the world was that, with the exception of a few basic "*objects*" such as the family, the multitude of "*objects*" that members of societies had used for their positive and negative projections were no longer available to them. And so individuals and institutions that were essential "*objects*" for providing containment for members of societies were no longer regarded as being in existence for this purpose. This was now a world seen as being in total collapse, a death of the world as we know it, and this experience was provoking apocalyptic and annihilative feelings.

On leadership and the illusion of containment

As early as 2005 the Global Report commented on the all encompassing nature of change that had left individuals, and those responsible for the management, leadership, and administration of political, economic, and social institutions in a state of bewilderment. The report stated: "They are seemingly unable to make sense of this 'new way of life'. So far-reaching is the change that in many instances individuals and groups simply have no previous knowledge as points of reference, and therefore no language, to express their experiences. It is as if they are on a journey without a map or language to guide them." Or as the Italian Listening Post suggested: "The metaphor of being on a journey at sea was put forward to describe the experience of having left the security of a well known port and being in the middle of the ocean, not yet at the new destination that, incidentally, we do not know."

A reported result was that "members of societies engage in splitting by creating good and bad objects as vehicles for their projections. Known and familiar objects in the shape of *young* and *old*, *male* and *female* are more likely to be used for positive projections; and the unknown other in the shape of *immigrants, fundamentalist* and *'different' others* are more likely to be used as repositories for negative projections." With the benefit of this hindsight and seen from a global societal perspective, one which is experienced as "death of a way of life", it may be helpful to see the incredible emotions expressed by members of society as a result of the death of Princess Diana as displacement of the emotions surrounding, but not identifiable with death of a way of life. While not to the same degree of intensity, but still widespread, was the displacement of emotions surrounding the death of Pope John Paul in 2005.

There is every reason to believe that those responsible for the management, leadership, and administration of political, economic, and social institutions have been, like other members of society, in a state of bewilderment. This has largely contributed to their lack of ability to take the required actions in relation to a number of major occurrences over the past decade or so. In the 2005 Global Report it was hypothesized that: "Because of the intense anxiety arising out of the 'loss of a way of life' and attempts to make sense of and adapt to a 'new way of life', those responsible for the management, leadership and administration of political, economic and social institutions throughout the world find it impossible to know with any certainty what is going on; there is no 'right' response when faced with such complexity. At the same time, politicians and policy makers are forced to act, as people put projections of incompetence into them, thereby rendering themselves infantilized and impotent."

Leaders, who take on the projected expectations of omnipotence and omniscience in the paranoid schizoid position, fail to go through the proper process of honest consultation, instead taking the path of power by stealth. They also devise a proliferation of catch-all measures of accountability as a defence against the risk associated with uncertainty. A result is that the controls not only diminish risk but also lock out creative potential: the capacity for thought and deliberation, the tolerance of difference and ability to use exploration in the face of change. This is seen as an abuse of authority by government appointed regulators and inspectors, who ignore the formal authority of the managers they are regulating or inspecting. This results in a distrust of current leaders.

By 2009 members of society were viewing their societies as some sort of doom laden and unbearable world and were possessed of a desperate need to retain some vestige of hope. The report stated: "It seems clear that there is a basic human need to experience any sort of situation as providing hope. This extends to the notion of seeing hope even in the very act of destruction: crisis as ruin—crisis as rebirth. At this time, the exceptional presence of Barack Obama provides a major catalyst for such hope. In some instances this is blind faith, an illusion or a phantasy. It is idealization to a massive degree; as if Obama is a sort of Superman who will soar through the skies to save the world from this madness. However, at another level, and in all cases, hope is qualified by a massive doubt that it will not be fulfilled. The experience of members of societies at this time is one of hope laced with fear."

There can be little doubt that Obama was, and is, subject to massive idealization and regarded as a repository of hope for the world. That he has not become the omnipotent, omniscient leader that others would make of him says a great deal about the man that he is. His ability to resist such massive projections also enables him to take up a leadership role that seeks to develop a relationship where both the West and Muslims can see each other as complete human beings who are capable of both goodness and badness. Such leadership has provided an opportunity for learning where both sides can work together across the boundary to develop a new understanding that takes account of the need for a pluralistic world community.

To achieve this will require that both parties develop a binocular view based on an in-depth understanding of the "other". In entering into a relationship it means that neither side has to lose their self concept. Indeed, the nature of the relationship is a mutual recognition of sameness and difference that results in binocular vision. And this will require leadership on both sides that is based on an ability to interpret the traditional values of the society in such a way that it includes the "other", without utterly reconstructing the "other" and denying their true "otherness" (see Stapley 2006b).

Concluding remarks

As Jim Krantz said in the Prologue,

> "Psychoanalytic thought contains the insight that we participate, often unknowingly, in creating our misfortune. Clinging to the myth of rationality, and thus enforcing denial of the unconscious, irrational strata of human life, sets the stage for the often catastrophic events considered in this play and in countless other situations as well."

While Mario Perini helpfully argues against psychoanalytic thinking becoming idealized, there is something gratifying in the fact that the editors and authors have had the courage to express their views on these important aspects of our contemporary world. No one should be under any illusions that this book will have an instant impact on our world and on world leaders. Acceptability of psychoanalytic thinking has been a long and arduous road as is reflected in the experiences of William McDougall, who when writing in 1908 stated:

> "It is, then, a remarkable fact that psychology ... has not been generally and practically recognised as the essential common foundation on which all the social sciences—ethics, economics, political science, philosophy of history, sociology, and cultural anthropology—must be built up."

In many respects, those comments might well have been written today, in 2010. To McDougall's 100-year-old lament, I would add the case for going beyond psychology to the understanding of psychoanalytic psychology as first developed by Freud, also over 100 years ago. This especially applies to unconscious processes concerned with making sense of our world and those that we use as defences against pain and anxiety. These "beneath the surface" processes will affect us whether we are ignorant of them or consciously choose to deny the existence of such phenomena. They will still be ever-present whether we like it or not and will be having a constant impact on the dynamics of societies, institutions, organizations, and other groups of which we are members. Seen in this context and, as Mario Perini stated, "a psychoanalytic approach might make conflict more readable, more sustainable and somewhat more manageable".

How far, then, must we go before we can say that we have developed a new way of life? Everything points to the possibility that current global dynamics will continue to intensify and deepen in the foreseeable future, or to be more accurate, *unforeseeable future*! Given that there are few signs that individuals or those responsible for the management, leadership, and administration of political, economic, and social institutions currently have the ability to adopt the required reflective approach that will help to make sense of this, still developing "new way of life", there is not much hope of serious understanding. It would seem, then, that global dynamics will continue to be dominated by defences against anxiety. These words were part of the 2006 Global Report, since when matters have become even more complex.

However, a significant change has been the election of President Obama which may offer us cause for cautious optimism. It would seem that in Obama we have a leader who is capable of being reflective and providing sound and thoughtful leadership through this difficult time. However, if we were to take as our guide the only previous experience that comes anywhere near to shedding light on the current situation—the Industrial Revolution—my guess is that we have probably another 25 years to go until we truly experience *a new way of life*.

To describe where we are currently and what the future holds for us it seems highly appropriate to quote another famous leader, Winston Churchill:

"This is not the end, it is not even the beginning of the end, but it is perhaps the end of the beginning."

The drama continues… .

References

Khaleelee, O. & Miller, E. (1985). Society as an intelligible field of study. In: M. Pines (Ed.), *Bion and Group Psychotherapy* (pp. 247–254). London: Routledge & Kegan Paul.

McDougall, W. (1908). *An Introduction to Social Psychology*. London: Methuen.

Stapley, L. (2006a). *Individuals, Groups and Organisations Beneath the Surface*. London: Karnac.

Stapley, L. (2006b). *Globalisation and Terrorism: Death of a Way of Life*. London: Karnac.

Stapley, L. & Collie, A. (2004). Global Dynamics at the Dawn of 2004. *Organisational & Social Dynamics, 4*(1).

Stapley, L. & Collie, A. (2005). Global Dynamics at the Dawn of 2005. *Organisational & Social Dynamics, 5*(1).

Stapley, L. & Cave, C. (2006). Global Dynamics at the Dawn of 2006. *Organisational & Social Dynamics, 6*(1).

Stapley, L. & Cave, C. (2007). Global Dynamics at the Dawn of 2007. *Organisational & Social Dynamics, 7*(1).

Stapley, L. & Rickman, C. (2008). Global Dynamics at the Dawn of 2008. *Organisational & Social Dynamics, 8*(1).

Stapley, L. & Rickman, C. (2009). Global Dynamics at the Dawn of 2009. *Organisational & Social Dynamics, 9*(1).

INDEX